THE 40- to 60-

A GUIDE FOR MEN—
AND THE WOMEN IN THEIR LIVES—
TO SEE THEM THROUGH THE CRISES
OF THE MALE MIDDLE YEARS

YEAR-OLD MALE

Michael E. McGill, Ph.D.

SIMON AND SCHUSTER • NEW YORK

COPYRIGHT © 1980 BY MICHAEL E. MCGILL
ALL RIGHTS RESERVED
INCLUDING THE RIGHT OF REPRODUCTION
IN WHOLE OR IN PART IN ANY FORM
PUBLISHED BY SIMON AND SCHUSTER
A DIVISION OF GULF & WESTERN CORPORATION
SIMON & SCHUSTER BUILDING
ROCKEFELLER CENTER
1230 AVENUE OF THE AMERICAS
NEW YORK, NEW YORK 10020

SIMON AND SCHUSTER AND COLOPHON ARE TRADEMARKS OF
SIMON & SCHUSTER

DESIGNED BY EVE METZ
MANUFACTURED IN THE UNITED STATES OF AMERICA

4   5   6   7   8   9   10

LIBRARY OF CONGRESS CATALOGING IN PUBLICATION DATA

MCGILL, MICHAEL E
    THE 40- TO 60-YEAR-OLD MALE.

    1.   CLIMACTERIC, MALE.   I.   TITLE.
RC884.M28   616.6   79-25840
ISBN 0-671-25133-3

To Mom, Dad and Tim
To Janet, Jimmy and Adam

In loving relationships there is joy in all of a man's ages—beginning, middle and those yet to come.

Contents

PREFACE

THIS BOOK REALLY BEGAN in response to a research article I wrote some time ago when I first became interested in the phenomenon of male mid-life crisis—its frequency, causes and effects. The article struck a resonant chord. The research was reported widely in the popular press, there was a flurry of media exposure—radio and television. Most impressive to me, however, were the hundreds of letters I received and the scores of people who sought me out, middle-aged men, their wives, children, mistresses, employers. The letters and personal contacts had two recurrent themes. One, people wanted to tell their own stories; comforted by the existence of a theory to explain what had happened, they found in their own lives ample illustrations. Their second purpose in coming forward was to ask for help, "What can I/we/he do?" I determined at that time it was important to share with a broader, popular audience what was known about the causes and consequences of the male mid-life crisis and what could be discovered about how to deal with crises. The original survey research was expanded to include hundreds of interviews with people involved in one form or another with the male mid-life crisis. From these, case studies were constructed and this book started to emerge.

The above reads as though I was the single driving force behind this book. In fact, however, I feel as though I was merely the agent of a number of forces which actually made this book possible and I would like to acknowledge some of those many contributors here.

I am most indebted to the hundreds of men and women who have shared with me their opinions, feelings and life events with an openness and honesty that is all too rare today. Knowing that the only possible reward was the chance that their story might help others, countless people opened their hearts, minds and lives to me during the course of this study. I have altered names, occupations and locales in telling their stories here to protect their privacy. They may well recognize themselves in these pages. I hope with these few words of acknowledgment they will recognize how indebted I am to them for their participation.

The decision to write this book for a general audience as opposed to an academic treatise was a difficult decision. It represents a personal and professional departure for me. I was supported in this decision and throughout the preparation of the book by the advice and counsel of friends and colleagues without whom the project might never have been undertaken. Frank Kirmss, a good friend, provided much of the initial inspiration and support for this book—it quite probably would not have happened without Frank. Tom Barry, Gene Byrne, Jim Rothe and Mike Wooton are friends and respected colleagues whose encouragement of this project was important to me.

Throughout the preparation of this book I have been blessed with some excellent hands-on help. Christa Juergens was my research assistant during the project and was instrumental in designing ways to best present the material. Lee Godwin, Gail Roberts and Jane Yoder all typed parts of the manuscript in its various stages. I am indebted to each of them for their skill, sensitivity and good humor.

Peter Schwed, my editor, has helped me to present my ideas more clearly and convincingly than I ever thought possible. Throughout the publication process he has shown a degree of care and concern for the project that will forever serve for me as a model of how these matters should be handled.

Helped as I was by all of these people, I alone am responsible for what appears here.

Finally, I want to acknowledge a group of people whose imprint is on every page, providing as they have caring, sharing relationships which have supported me in my work and been of special significance in this book. My family, of course, to whom this book is dedicated; my good friends Pat and Al Miller, Linda and Hal Williams; my extended family, Doris and Stan Sofas. Though it may not be possible to see their contribution in these pages, I hope they know how much I feel their contributions.

MICHAEL E. McGILL

Dallas, Texas, 1979

"The tragedy of life is what dies within a man while he still lives."

ALBERT SCHWEITZER

". . . a more fundamental malaise, that latitude in middle-life of alternate doldrums and uncertain winds when one realizes that hopes deferred are no longer realizable, that ports not visited will now never be seen, that this journey and others before it may have been a mistake, that one has no longer even confidence in charts and compass."

P. D. JAMES

1

Middle Age: The Modern Male Madness

"ON THAT LEDGE in Atlanta, about twenty-four floors up, that's when I knew I was middle-aged and about to see to it that I'd never grow one day older—middle-aged and going mad."

Larry Renspar, forty-five, is describing the time he first became aware of the phenomenon which has dramatically altered his life over the last two years—"middle age."

"I don't remember when or how it started. I say that because while I remember very clearly when I became aware of it and how I became aware of it, the awareness came only after I had been into it for a long time. It was something that had been happening to me for a long time and something that I was only recently being made aware of. Oh, yes, I remember when I became aware of it. Very clearly.

"I was in Atlanta at one of the big new hotels there, attending a company convention of some sort. I remember I had a room on about the, I don't know, the twenty-third or twenty-fourth floor—up pretty high, and I had been going at it with some girl there—her name was Suzie or Sally, one of those 'ie' sounding names that *girls* seem to have, never women—every time you say it, it reminds you of how much younger they are than you. As I recall, it was a good thing she was young. She needed all of that youthful exuberance for sex, as well as a hell of a lot of expertise to get me to the point where I could do anything, and even then I probably wasn't too terrific. I had literally spent myself, done all that I could with this girl, and as she was lying there in the bed sleeping, I stepped out onto the balcony to recuperate and have a cigarette. I remember so clearly. I stood there on the balcony smoking a cigarette, looking down, and I thought, 'Jesus, how many times have I done this? How many meetings, girls at the meetings, hotel rooms and balconies have there been?' I was feeling guilty and depressed—guilty at what I had done and depressed that I hadn't been better at it. They were feelings I had many times in the same situation, which I had also had many times. I thought, of course, of Mary and the kids as I usually do in those moments and I thought, 'How many more will there be? Is there ever any difference? Will there ever *be* any difference?' I finished my cigarette and flipped the butt over the edge and kinda watched it fall, twisting and turning, slowly drifting down. The flight of that cigarette was so hypnotic that I lost my thoughts and myself in its descent. I wanted to jump and try to catch it. I mean I could actually feel my body move. I flexed and started to lift myself onto the ledge so I could jump over and try and catch the cigarette butt and I thought about how I would feel falling, you know, would I spin around, would the air rush up, how fast would I fall, and how hard would I hit. What it would be like lying down there—dead. I thought about all of that and I wanted to do it. It took the most intense concentration of will that I can ever recall in my life not to get up on the ledge, but to stay with my feet on the balcony. I wanted to jump so badly. Why? It wasn't the girl, because there had been other girls; it certainly wasn't anything that was going wrong at the meetings, the whole purpose for those meetings was for me to meet with the franchisees of the tune-up service I'm president of—things are going better than ever there —making money hand over fist. Mary and the kids—I was pretty happy there, too—well, maybe not happy, but I was certainly contented. I mean we had all of the things we seemed to want. Sure, maybe the same spark wasn't there between me and Mary that had been twenty-three years ago, but it was pretty good still. And yet I wanted to jump. I really wanted to end it all. I don't know how long I was out on that balcony—it could have been five or ten minutes or it could have been an hour. Finally, I heard the girl's voice calling out to me, 'Hey, what are you doing out there?' I looked back from the edge and saw her on the bed there, sort of playing with herself and she said, 'Why don't you come do something for me?' I moved away from the ledge into the room and toward her. It was as though I was drugged, every step a strain on mind and muscle. I fell into her arms and began to cry. I hadn't cried since I was a boy, but there I was, naked in bed with a girl half my age crying my eyes out as she cradled me and cooed at me like a mother. I'm sure she had no idea what was going on. I recovered in time—made some explanation to get her out of there. But that moment on the balcony haunted me. That balcony really started me thinking about where I had been, where I was, where I was going. For the remainder of the convention it consumed me. I was so haunted by it that I thought of little else for the next two or three weeks. It must have seemed very strange to everyone else. I know that I appeared preoccupied to Mary and the kids. I didn't have much attention for my business partners nor the problems of the business. I didn't have much energy for my friends, in fact, I didn't see much of them. There wasn't anybody I felt that I could talk to about what had happened to me. I didn't want to talk about anything else. You always hear about how you ought to go to your doctor or your minister and discuss these problems with them. Well, hell, I've never seen a doctor who had the time or a minister who had the talent to deal with the sort of things I was thinking about and I sure as hell wasn't going to go to any 'shrink.' As for my friends, Christ, you just don't sit down after a round of golf with your buddies at the clubhouse and say, 'Hey, I've been thinking about killing myself. You want to talk about that?' As for Mary, she would just have gotten upset and not been much help. I felt like there was no place or person I could go to. No one to talk to. Nobody who would understand—I felt so alone. It seemed to me like I was the only one who ever had this desire. Of course I know differently now, but at the time it seemed like I was all by myself out there on that balcony . . . wanting to jump, wanting to be at the bottom.

"So, alone with my thoughts over the period of the next two or three months, I began to kind of review where I was, to take stock of me. I had a marriage that I wanted to keep. Sure there were those occasional girls, but those were one-night things and they meant nothing other than the challenge of trying to get somebody in bed. I had a business that was very successful—but so successful that I really didn't have any work to do. See, right out of college I got this idea for this series of tune-up garages, you know, major tune-ups on American cars at cheaper prices and better service than you can get either at a dealership or at your local gas station. I opened a tune-up shop and did most of the work on the cars myself. As business increased, after a while I got some people in to help. We did good work for people and got a good reputation and I was able to get some money and start another one and then another one and now there are twenty-six of them, mostly in the Southwest. They are doing real well. But outside of an occasional meeting with the bankers and the sorts of meetings you have to have with the management people, I don't do a whole lot anymore. The business is at the place where it pretty much runs itself. To tell you the truth, it's not much fun.

"As I thought about it, it seemed like if I didn't do something real fast, right then, I was going to have more of the same for a lot of years to come. I mean more of the same sort of marriage, more of the same sorts of relationships with my friends, more one-night girls, more of the same job. I decided more of the same is not really more—it's less, *much* less. So what I did was, I quit.

"I sold the business and I bought the ownership of this additive products company. I wanted to stay in the automotive line because that's what I know best and I thought that if I have this product and I was responsible for getting it produced and selling it and making it go, I would be able to add back the challenge, the spark that had been missing for the last years. That was two years ago, and the last two years have been so tough, it seems like four. We have used up about every bit of savings that we had. I've long since sold out my remaining ownership in the tune-up business. I've taken a second mortgage on the house and with all that, we're not making it at all, not even close. The financial strain has been tremendous and that's put a strain on everything else. Mary and I are continually at each other—she's even talking about taking a job. It seems like I have bit off a little more than I can chew and this damn challenge I've created is about to swallow me.

"I know now from books, people on the TV talk shows and the magazine articles that Mary is always putting out for me that I had and I am having one of these male changes—'mid-life crisis' they call it. I know, too, that it's happened to lots of other men. But to tell you the truth, reading all that stuff doesn't make it any easier. I don't see anybody who has really been able to understand what happened to me and to be able to give me anything that'll help me and help Mary. More and more lately I've been thinking about that balcony. To tell you the truth, I've been staying away from high places. I'm more than a little fearful because the way things are now and where I am right now, I just can't guarantee you that if I was out on that balcony this time I wouldn't go ahead and jump."

"How did this happen to me? I'm not sure how it happened, but I can tell you what happened. Maybe in the 'what' you can pick up some of the how and the why. I'm fifty-three years old and I lived forty-seven of those fifty-three years in Cedar Rapids. For the last year I've been here in 'the big city.' While I was in Cedar Rapids I worked my whole career for this electronics firm. We started out pretty small and I did a little bit of everything. Then we got bought up by a little bigger outfit and then they got bought up by a little bigger outfit and now I work

for one of the giants of the industry. I'm in marketing, not sales
—marketing. I don't go out and try to get people to sign on the
dotted line—I'm afraid I wouldn't be very good at that. What I
do is to try to see to it that our products are packaged in ways
that make the consumer believe they will meet his needs. Now
I'm not talking about your little computers that, you know, get
sold to the household consumer. No, I deal mostly in the government side of things. I put together packages that make these
big government contracts feel like we've met their specifica-
tions. Well anyhow, I'm married. Jane and I have three grown
kids. We just passed our twenty-fifth wedding anniversary about
a year and a half ago, but as you'll see, that's not as important
as it might sound.

"When this whole thing started, I had been asked to go over
to the Far East for ten weeks to work with the people of one of
the armies over there to try to convince them that what we had
built for them was really what they had ordered. It was a marketing job, but I don't want to make it sound more important
than it really was. There was this team that went over and I was
just more or less there in an advisory capacity to the team. In
fact, most of the time it looked like I was just going to be sitting
around. It would mean ten weeks away from the family if they
stayed in Cedar Rapids; although two of the kids are already
gone out of the house, the one that's left is in college there,
living at home. Anyhow, the good part of it was that Jane and I
were coming up on our twenty-fifth anniversary and figured we
could celebrate in Hawaii on the way back. You see, I was going
to stop in Hawaii for about a week on the way over to work with
our Far East representatives before we arrived over there, and
I figured I could take a couple of weeks' vacation on the way
back and stop again and we could celebrate our twenty-fifth on
Waikiki Beach. So that was our plan. Jane was joining me at the
back end of the trip. I went on to Honolulu and gosh, this part's
kinda hard to talk about; you know you see on the TV and in
the magazines about the changes that are going on with young
people, especially the young women—the girls' changing atti-

tudes toward sex, and well, everything. You see and you read all of that, but gosh, until you're right there with it, it doesn't make much of an impact. I guess life in Cedar Rapids is a little more sheltered than I thought it was. Lord, I have never seen anything like I saw on Waikiki Beach! You'd be out walking the main street of town or having a drink at the bar and these young things, half-dressed—I swear none of them wore bras, their breasts were just hanging out all over—it didn't seem to bother them at all and the swimsuits they had were nothing more than a handkerchief and a couple of pieces of string—and didn't cover a thing. I tell you when I first saw all that, foolish as it sounds, I kinda turned my head. I was embarrassed to look at them, but then I began to notice that they weren't embarrassed at all and damn if they weren't pretty nice to look at. But still, for a couple of days there I was just kinda like a man on a diet. I read the menu but I wasn't making any selections. I figured at fifty-three and a little bit of a pot belly and not a whole lot of hair left, there wasn't much for me to do more than look.

"Some of the younger guys on the team that went over were quite a bit more aggressive. They had the time of their lives. It seemed like they were with a different girl every night. As it turned out, we had to stay there three days longer than we thought, so a week turned into ten days. I guess it was on about the fourth or fifth day, one of the young guys there took me on a pedicab ride. They've got these little bicycles that are like rickshaws. Young girls and guys pedal them around, costs you a couple of bucks a head—it's a damn expensive way to get around town but it's kind of fun. You sit back in the seat and they pedal this big tricycle up front and you see everything and move along at a nice leisurely pace. Well, this pedicab driver was just about the prettiest little girl you've ever seen—in a little string bikini and just beautiful and this fellow I was with, he was quite a talker and convinced her to go out with us that night to dinner.

"I think it's really hard for somebody else to understand how it was then between me and Jenny, how things happened so fast and all. But she was just so good to me. You wouldn't have thought there was any difference in our ages at all. From the very first she was just real attentive to me and she kind of hung on to my arm everywhere we went and I could really protect her and take care of her and well, one thing led to another and we ended up in my hotel room that night and she showed me things in bed that I just never knew existed. I gotta say here that sex with Jane never really was all that good and in recent years, it has been pretty bad. It wasn't that she didn't want it, but she treated it more like a duty. Half the time she'd be talking about something else while we were doing it. Well, with Jenny it just wasn't anything like that. It was as though the sole purpose of her body was to make mine feel good and she could just do unbelievable things with her body. We didn't get out of that hotel room for the next day and a half and I felt younger than I've ever felt before. I felt better about myself and better about the world and I wanted to keep that good feeling going as long as I could, so I took her on over to the Far East with me and we spent the next eight weeks just having a grand time. As I said, my part of the work assignment wasn't all that demanding so we had a lot of time to travel around and see the sights and a lot of time to, to just fuck. It's funny, Jane used to never like that word and Jenny uses it all the time and it just really sounds good to me. That right there shows you the kind of change I've made. Well, it is good.

"The only bad time I had was there at the end of the trip when I was supposed to meet Jane in Waikiki for our twenty-fifth anniversary celebration and I told Jenny that I was going to meet Jane and we were going to celebrate but I'd try to get out to see her some every day and that when Jane went back, I was going to find a way to stay over a little bit and I'd take Jenny back to the mainland with me, and that's just what I did. Yeah, that's just what I did. Jane and I had a fine little celebration and we had dinner out on the town and a good time. I was able to sneak away a little bit every day and be with Jenny and then I told Jane how I wasn't able to go back to the mainland with her right away because we had a little business left to tie up there in Honolulu and so she went back alone. Part of what I was doing during the time in the Orient, and especially when we got back to Honolulu, was arranging a transfer from Cedar Rapids down to a plant in the South. When the transfer came through, Jenny and I went down there. I didn't even go back to Cedar Rapids to get my things. I wrote a letter to Jane and I told her the whole thing—that I had fallen in love with Jenny and I had brought her back with me and we were going to live down South and that I wouldn't be coming back to Cedar Rapids. I know it sounds strange, but I do love Jane and I care for her and I don't want to hurt her, but I just can't tear myself away from Jenny. Maybe it's just her youth—maybe it's just the sex, but I know I can't walk away from her. I can't go back. I feel like with Jenny I'm catching up for all of the things I lost those years I spent in Cedar Rapids and those years I spent with Jane—that I'm re-capturing some of my youth and rediscovering what it is to be young and alive. I can't give that up. As much as I don't want to hurt Jane, I can't pay the price I would have to pay to go back there. Sure, I've seen those movies where this same sort of thing has happened and the man is always made to look like a fool, being with a younger girl, trying to keep up with her, but I don't feel like a fool. I feel good. I feel like somebody wants me. Somebody wants my body and somebody wants to make me happy and I'm gonna do it—so sure I may be going through some sort of mid-life change, mid-life crisis, and maybe even-tually I'll feel like a fool, but right now it feels like the best thing I've ever done. Whenever I get torn, confused, about where I ought to be and who I ought to be with, I just see that girl and she just opens her body to me and I forget about all of those questions and concerns. I stay right with her and that's where I'm gonna stay—mid-life, old life—all the time.''

As recently as fifteen years ago, personal revelations such as those made by the men above were found only in the case files of clinical psychologists and psychiatrists. While it may have been the subject of guarded gossip, such behavior was certainly not the topic of casual conversation nor to be found in the popular magazines and newsstand literature. Many men and women suspected that such things occurred and some had firsthand knowledge, but no one spoke openly of such "goings on." First evidence of the extent of these events and concern over them emerged about ten years ago in women's magazines. True confession stories and later the more general women's press ran the commentary of the wives of these men as they retold the tales of their attempts to cope with the changes in their lives brought about by the sudden and dramatic changes in the behavior of their men. Such soap opera, "poor me" storytelling was a staple of the women's magazine literature, but seldom were these tales related to one another in other than the anguish experienced by the wives. Most often, what happened to one man was treated as a unique experience, unrelated to what happened to other men, even though what happened to the wives may have been universal. In the last five years, the men have begun to speak out. Noticeable first in medical and academic journals and then in popular magazines—both men's and women's over the last five years—first-person accounts of these mid-life behavior changes became commonplace. Today, attention to the peculiar behavior of middle-aged men is all around us. Indeed the phenomenon of major behavior changes by men in their middle years has spawned its own literature, with countless magazine articles, research reports and books, both popular and scientific, devoted to the subject of how and why men change as they age. There can scarcely be an adult male or female who has not been forewarned of the stages of a man's life and of the evil that lurks beyond age forty.

So pervasive is the popular attention to this topic that the critical observer has to ask "why?" Why this spate of current interest in middle-aged men and their behavior? Have not there always been middle-aged men and have not they always been changing? Why is it now a crisis? Why are we now so concerned? Is this phenomenon real or is it artificial? Do *real,* everyday men experience a mid-life crisis or is this a fabrication of academics and authors? More than one skeptic wife has commented, "My husband didn't think anything about a mid-life crisis until he read that he was supposed to have one and then he went out and did." Somewhat more analytically, one researcher on aging has commented, "It seems that people are now in the process of inventing the male menopause. Society invents roles. We had no problems with adolescence until society invented adolescence. Then we had them. We are a society that creates problems with many expectations, saying many will fit into this mold. So it goes for the male menopause. We give the man all of the phases he is supposed to fit into, the last fling, the obsession of reality, all of that, and he fits into these roles as he expects people to find them appropriate."

It may be that we are reading more about mid-life changes on the part of men because such changes make "good press." It may even be that many of these changes are spawned by the press. One would be hard-pressed to prove or disprove the notion that there are some middle-aged men who have a crisis only because they have been led to believe that they should have one. But there are other explanations for the current attention to the behavior of middle-aged men that are even more plausible. One of the most notable changes in our society over the last fifteen years has been the trend toward open discussion of issues previously regarded as personal and private. All around us now we see and hear open acknowledgment of behaviors and beliefs that were previously held as taboo. A former First Lady stepped out to speak of her own alcoholism. Entertainers openly discuss their own mental illness or drug abuse. Local politicians speak of their homosexuality and seek the gay vote. While men may agree or disagree that these specific issues are legitimate topics of public attention, the message underlying all of these expressions of openness cannot have been lost upon men in our society. The message is that there is an increased legitimacy to acknowledging one's own beliefs, attitudes and behaviors and, beyond acknowledgment, to analyze the cause and effect of those same beliefs, attitudes and behaviors for himself as well as for others. This "coming out," this new legitimation of open discussion of personal concerns may be at the root of current discussions of male mid-life changes. It may be that men have always experienced such changes in mid-life and it has only now become legitimate to talk of them openly, hence the current attention.

Another explanation of the great attention given to men's problems at this time is that this attention is a direct spin-off of women's newfound and newly expressed freedoms. Women in the seventies have worked hard to insure that their personal concerns, be they career, familial, health or marital, have been seen and heard by men. As women have become more vocal and visible in expressing their own developmental concerns and developmental issues, they have brought these issues into focus for men and have led the way for them to do similarly. It may be that in speaking of the beliefs and behaviors that are problem-matical in their own lives, middle-aged men are merely follow-ing the focus and form of the example set by their wives and mistresses.

Whatever the reason for the current attention to the problems of middle-aged men, one cannot deny that problems do exist. The argument that male mid-life changes are a fabrication of authors and academics seems, in the face of the evidence, not only fallacious but frivolous as well. Such arguments not only deny the data regarding the number of male mid-life changes, but turn attention away from the critical issues which involve those changes: (1) an acknowledgment that such changes do occur; (2) an analytical discussion of why those changes occur; (3) an understanding of some of the effects of those changes for middle-aged men, and women related to those men, and (4) a discussion of what can be done about male mid-life behavior changes.

This, of course, is not the first time these issues have been raised. In one form or another, in bits and pieces, these issues have been the substance of the mid-life literature. Despite the

widespread attention to these issues, there has been little resolution to date. The flood of information that has inundated the
media and popular press has led more often to confusion than to
comprehension. The man who experiences mid-life change or
the woman who lives with and loves such a man has been given
little help in understanding and dealing with the behaviors they
experience. There are many reasons why this wealth of communication has not contributed to improved comprehension.
There has, from the outset, been the problem of the language of
the male mid-life change itself. These behavior changes that are
seen in middle-aged men have variously been written about as
"the male menopause," "the male metapause," "the male climacteric," "the male senescence," "the mid-life transition,"
and "mid-life crisis." One middle-aged man experiencing what
is often called "the change" has commented, "I know I'm not
in menopause because I'm not a woman. I don't know what
metapause is. Climacteric sounds like something the weather-
man might do. Senescence sounds too old. I'm not in transit and
there doesn't seem to be a crisis, nothing that dramatic. I've
just got these problems. None of those words help."

It's true that none of those words are right, nor do they help.
Indeed, the language of the mid-life crisis may hinder not only
the helping process but the necessary prior step of seeking help.

The "mid life transition" comes closer as an acceptable label
for male mid-life. Simple, without medical or scientific jargon or
mysticism, transition implies a passage from one condition or
stage to another. Herein lies the major drawback in the use of
this label—the implication of stages. Mid-life transition is most
often used by those who subscribe to the notion of predictable
stages in adult life, hence the transition from one stage to another in mid-life. There is considerable debate over the existence of predictable developmental stages in adult life and use
of the "transition" label may be read as support of this theory
where none is intended. Moreover, middle-aged men report that
transition implies a sense of direction, from one specific place
to another, when one of the dominant experiences of mid-life is

often the *absence* of any direction or sense of direction. It seems likely that "mid-life transition" will continue to be used by proponents of predictable stages in adult life, but probably only by those proponents.

The most widely used and accepted referent for what happens to men in mid-life is the "mid-life crisis." The use of the term crisis here refers to "personality crisis"—a rapid or substantial change in personality, usually both rapid and substantial. Male mid-life crisis literally means changes in a man's personality in mid-life, changes which are substantive and occur rapidly, giving a dramatic and even traumatic character to the changes. Mid-life crisis is a simple, accurate description of the condition without prejudicial attention to one cause over another. For these reasons, "mid-life crisis" is emerging as the primary referent for what occurs to men in their middle years. The major drawback to such a label has to do with the word "crisis." Many middle-aged men feel crisis is too strong a word to describe what occurs to them, it implies catastrophe where confusion is more the case, disaster where there is only disturbance. Yet even these detractors affirm that what is at issue is a change in personality and consequent changes in behavior and to the extent that the language of crisis conveys this sense of change, it is appropriate. It has the added advantage of acting as an alert, raising concern to a level consistent with the consequences of the changes. Throughout this book the language of "mid-life crisis" will be used except where discussion of a specific theory requires use of a different label, particular to that theory.

If the only deterrent to an improved understanding of the causes and consequences of the mid-life crisis was the absence of clear and consistent language, there would be little need for yet another book on the subject. If such were the case, time and effort would be better spent developing a comprehensive glossary so that the interested reader might translate the message of the myriad articles and books about middle-aged men and their crises. But of course language is not the only deterrent to finding meaning in what is currently available to middle-aged men and those who are concerned about their crises. There are other more fundamental shortcomings which suggest that even when the messages are deciphered, they may lack real meaning. Specifically, existing treatments of the male mid-life crisis suffer from one or more of the following shortcomings: (1) the absence of a comprehensive theory and data base, explaining the causes and offering empirical evidence; (2) the absence of a full discussion of consequences, not only for the middle-aged man in crisis but for those affected by his crisis—his wife, children, employer, lover; (3) the absence of a balanced treatment of consequences—an emphasis on the sensational and the negative to the exclusion of the normal and the positive; and (4) the absence of constructive plans for avoiding crisis and for coping with crisis, plans for all concerned. A brief examination of each of these shortcomings will help to place the present work in perspective.

To date, explanations of the causes of the male mid-life crisis have come from two sources, conclusions drawn from anecdotes reported by middle-aged men or elements lifted from broader life-span development theories. The result has been a great deal of posturing with very little proof. Each theorist pumping up his or her own views while picking apart the views of others (see Chapter 2). In large measure, the confusion and conflict over the causes of mid-life crisis exist because heretofore there has not been a major empirical investigation of middle-aged men. There have, of course, been excellent major researches into full life development and some of these studies have revealed interesting data about middle-aged men. However, these studies have not focused exclusively on middle-aged men. This book is based on the results of a four-year major research effort to focus exclusively on middle-aged men and their crises. The theory purported here is supported by sound empirical evidence. In the course of this study over 2,500 people were contacted about the problems of middle-aged men. Five hundred men and women responded to the comprehensive

Mid-Life Identity and Events questionnaire (see Appendix). An additional 200 were interviewed about their own involvement with mid-life crisis and hundreds more wrote of their own cases and concerns. The reader is given the opportunity to compare his or her own experience to the experiences of those who participated in the research (see Appendix). This personal involvement further enhances understanding of the relevant theories and data and helps the reader to draw his own conclusions about the causes of crises.

The male mid-life crisis seldom affects only the middle-aged male. Changes in the man's personality bring about attendant changes in the way he views his world and consequent changes in the way he behaves toward his world and the people in it— wife, children, lover, employer, employees. Current literature tends to focus on only the man or his wife, telling their story of the change and its consequences. Rarely do we hear from the entire cast in these mid-life dramas. As a consequence, our understanding of the causes and consequences of mid-life crisis is limited by the characters we hear. These shortcomings can be overcome by seeking out the views of all involved whenever that is possible. To understand why Larry was on that ledge and what happened as a result for Larry and Mary as a couple and as individuals, we need to hear from Mary as well.

"Larry came back from a business trip to Atlanta. He had only been gone a few days, three or four, but he came back such a different man than when he left. I didn't know what had happened there and I still don't know exactly what happened, but he hasn't been the same ever since. Right after that trip, he became quiet, preoccupied, his mind always seemed to be somewhere else. I tried to get him to talk about it, but he wouldn't. He just kept saying it was something he had to work out for himself and not to worry. I tried to get him to see our doctor or our minister and he said it wasn't anything they could help with. With that moodiness, that quiet, he was so far from us. He was here in the same house but it was as if he just roomed here, like he was a stranger to all of us. That went on for four long months and all that time I agonized, not knowing what was going on. Then Larry came home one day and announced that he was selling the business, getting out and starting something new. He didn't seem very excited about it, like I remember him being when he started the garages. I can remember the joy, the excitement that he had when he started the garage business, his desire to get to work every day, a real delight in the problems of putting the business together. I didn't see any of that same spirit as he went into this new business. It was just sort of a quiet determination that said 'This is what I have to do and so this is what I'm going to do.' I didn't try to stop him. I've always let him make the financial and business decisions on his own. He's given me a very good life with his work and I had no reason to believe it would be otherwise so I supported him and said I thought it would be a good idea. I feel even if I had disagreed, he would have gone ahead. But it was so wrong. I know now that he went through and is still going through the male menopause or whatever they call it. After achieving all of that success he just threw it all away—his job was boring and the challenge wasn't there so he quit. Now he's working trying to sell this new product and I don't really know whether the product is no good or whether it's his attitude that keeps him from being a success at it, but he just can't get off the ground. We've used up most of our savings to put into the business and taken out another mortgage on the house. We're just about ruined financially. I don't know how much longer we can hold it together. Larry still doesn't know what he wants to do now and doesn't know what he wants to do for the future. I try to talk about it, but he doesn't know what's left in life for him and I don't know where we can go for help or what I can do to help him. I always thought we communicated very well. In the past, the problems we've had together, we've always been able to talk them out, but not this one. We're just at a loss to know what to do. The kids and I are probably a millstone around his neck and he would fare better being on his own without the responsibilities of a family, but I know that he considers home and family his only refuge and doesn't want to lose us. I've got barnacle qualities and I'm here to stay, but this continual depression of his sometimes pulls me down and it pulls the kids down. How long can this go on? I've always thought that life was great and worth the effort, but Larry doesn't feel that way any longer and I don't know, the more he's like that, the more I think maybe he's right.''

Clearly Mary has been as much affected by the change in Larry as he has been himself. To ignore the effect on Mary is to deal with only a part of the consequences of a mid-life crisis. What might be termed the spin-off consequences can be just as dramatic and traumatic as the mid-life change—sometimes even more so. Consider the comments of Jane, whose husband, Bob, left her for a younger woman after twenty-five years of marriage.

Jane puts the initial facts of the incident quite bluntly as she writes, ''My husband just left me the 28th of December. He had been working in the Far East and when he returned to the States, he brought his girl friend of a couple of months with him. My husband is fifty-three years old and in November we celebrated our twenty-fifth wedding anniversary. I spent the last week of October and the first week of November with him in Hawaii and we had what I would call a second honeymoon. I came back home and happily went about preparing his favorite foods, the house, you know, for a happy reunion in December. December 19th he phoned me and informed me he had brought a girl home from Hawaii with him and our marriage was over. I had a heart attack and have had another one since. I am seeing a psychiatrist every week, which has helped some. We have three lovely children who are also greatly disturbed over their father leaving us. My husband's behavior and logic changed so radically in such a short period of time, that he's nothing like the man I've loved all of my life and shared a marriage of twenty-five years with. I still love him but I've been hurt so deeply that any hope of reconciliation, should it be his wish, is out of the question. In addition to my two heart attacks, I've attempted suicide three times and I doubt if I'll ever be completely happy again.

"So many people have been very deeply hurt by unresponsible actions of two people. I would welcome the chance to know what my husband was going through, to try to help him find what he wanted in his life, but he felt that what he needed this girl provides. Instead of communicating his feelings to me, he preferred to deceive me by lying about our future, giving me love and tenderness, making love to me, showering me with attention and letting me believe things were better than ever between us. I spent those two heavenly weeks with him in Honolulu without a clue as to what was in store for me. Then he came back and told me that our life together was over. He also told me that during my stay with him in Hawaii, he was seeing this girl every day and telling her that I didn't suspect anything and would be returning to the States, so he could pick her up and they could come back to the States. He certainly did an award-winning act because even though I knew there was a girl, I thought and believed him that it was all over and that he loved me as deeply and completely as I loved him. Why he even told me 'this is a mystery to me.'

"He can't seem to hurt me enough. He now even sends me thank-you notes for loving him and tells me how happy he is with this new girl. They have been living in a motel since he left here in December. He tells me he wants nothing but happiness for me and the children, although in another breath he says he never liked our children. His behavior is just so strange. I can't understand. I just think he's extremely confused and ill. My husband and I grew up together and he was my first and only love and lover. I find it really hard to even think about another man in my life. I realize I have a definite problem so I'm seeing someone regularly, as do our children, to try to get some help. I've been out to dinner twice with male friends, and put on a false face of lightheartedness while underneath I worry that they will make a pass and I will go all to pieces. I wake up screaming in the night with nightmares about dying and my husband paying Hawaiians to mourn at my casket. I'm in a living hell. I consider myself fairly intelligent, educated, attractive, witty, personable, a good, loving mother, a hard worker. I'm in public relations and a lot of other good things but I just can't seem to accept the fact that the man I've loved all my life no longer loves me. I try not to let it show to those around me, but I can't imagine that I will ever get over him. Perhaps I'm as sick as he is but I'm afraid that I'm a one-man woman. I'm not looking for sympathy or understanding. I'm just trying to explain how the irresponsible actions of a confused, ill man can destroy an otherwise happy, healthy human being. The last time I talked to him on the phone he cried and said he wished he could turn back the clock. The next day I got a letter from him telling me he was so in love with his mistress that he couldn't help himself and he wished I'd find a man and run away with him.

"I wish him nothing but happiness, but I'm deeply hurt and bitter. It's very hard to try to understand how the man you've loved and lived with suddenly loves someone else enough to leave his wife and family. I still love him but this man is not the same man I was married to. When my husband left he told me he loved me and he wished he didn't have to hurt me. I just don't think you almost kill someone you love."

The story of Bob's mid-life crisis cannot be told by Bob alone. Jane's account reveals the scope of the changes wrought by Bob's decision but so, too, does the account of Jenny, the young girl who was a catalyst to all that occurred.

"I guess some people think that just because I'm young I wouldn't understand all that is going on but I know for the last year I've been involved with a fifty-three-year-old man, Bob, who has been struggling with this whole mid-life thing. I think I'm part of the struggle. He's certainly a scarred survivor of a long marriage and I'm a scarred survivor of a short marriage. We come from very different backgrounds; there's the obvious age difference, about twenty-five years. For three years I was married to a Ph.D. type, Catholic, liberal, Southern, but it didn't work. I would have voted for him, but I couldn't live with him.

He should have been a priest. His whole attitude toward sex was that it was something nice people didn't do. Bob, on the other hand, lived most of his life in Cedar Rapids working for the same company, raising children, being responsible. I think he got married when he was about twenty-eight. For the last year he has been living here with me in this motel, trying to get in touch with himself. He's done the whole bit—grew a beard and let his hair grow, wears a small pendant (he lost the one he had so I gave him a new one), jeans and an open shirt. Frankly, he may be older than me, but I think he's sexy as hell. He's got a gorgeous body.

"Anyway, I would very much like to encourage my bearded friend. I want to help him break away. He's torn between me and what I can offer (and I really think I can offer a lot more than a great body and a fantastic fuck) and his wife and the responsibilities of her and her family. I know he communicates with her all the time and she lays on all this guilt about how he's killing her and all. I know that part of him still loves her, but the best parts of him love me and as much as I want to help him, I can't believe that going back to her would be the best thing for him, so I'm going to do everything I can to keep him here with me and believe me, I can do a lot. That sounds a lot harder than I mean it. What I really mean is I think that I can help him find what is best for him, maybe change jobs, go back to school, get into something that really interests him. I think I can help him find all of that and I don't think she can. And because I care for him, I'm going to help him in every way I can."

Popular treatments of the male mid-life crisis are dispersed among so many publications that we are seldom presented with a full picture of what transpires for any one man and those involved with him. From one source we might hear the male perspective, Larry and Bob describing what occurred to them and why and what they're doing about it. Other publications are more prone to give us the wives' account—Mary and Jane, reflecting on their experiences. Elsewhere, the other woman, Jenny, writes of her perspective. Reading only one of these accounts gives the erroneous impression that there is only one individual involved and affected by the male mid-life crisis. But in actuality, mid-life crises seldom affect just one person. There is almost always a second person intimately involved and most often with children, mistresses, bosses and extended family, there are several others involved. Because these crises affect so many they can seldom be understood by hearing just one side. So often we do hear from just one party involved and in that sense, we get a distorted picture of what has happened, why it has happened and with what effect for others. We can overcome this shortcoming by seeking out and reporting the responses of all those involved with a middle-aged man in crisis.

A third shortcoming in the current "state of the art" on the male mid-life crisis has to do with the absence of a balanced treatment of the consequences of crisis. There is an overabundance of the sensational and the negative to the exclusion of the natural and the positive. It is this shortcoming which is perhaps easiest of all to fall victim to when one writes about the mid-life crisis because the fact is most reports of mid-life crisis for men turn out to be negative in tone. More often than not it seems that accounts of men making changes in mid-life, altering their beliefs and their behaviors, have negative consequences not only for themselves but for others and the consequences are catastrophic. While this is often true, it is not always the case. In reading what is written about the mid-life crisis one would be led to believe that is *always* so. It is understandable that people who are having problems developing an understanding of what they are going through are not encouraged to pursue that understanding by the accounts they read of catastrophic change. But there are positive changes which occur as a result of mid-life crisis, changes which lead to growth and development for all involved and which open minds rather than close them. These changes should be reported in proportion to their occurrence and in this book, they will be reported. The story of Webb and Katherine Rose is one such story and perhaps best told in the words of Katherine.

"I am forty-five and my husband, Webb, is fifty. We have three grown children, but then we had another child, eighteen years late. Our little girl led to a lot of soul-searching on both of our parts; in fact, we even considered abortion but we decided to go ahead and have her. I think I came out of the soul-searching a lot sooner and a lot better off than Webb did. He went into a real depression—a real wondering about what was going on —for him to have a baby at age fifty. Did he have the energy to raise her? Wasn't he getting too old for that sort of thing? How would she relate to him when she was fifteen and he was sixty-five? Those are probably all things that a father late in life goes through, but for Webb it seemed to be a lot more than that. He really began to get pretty down about it and so we decided to take the baby with us on vacation to Florida and there all hell broke loose.

"We were driving around Florida in a rented motor home. It was cold, for Florida anyway, there wasn't much to see and we were having a pretty miserable time. It seemed that the longer we were on vacation the more Webb lost his cool. He was doing crazy, foolish things, getting mad at people without any reason, he was impatient everywhere we went, didn't seem to enjoy anything. It wasn't very relaxing for any of us. It all came to a head when he had an accident with our motor home. Our little girl was thrown through the front window and out on to the pavement and could have been killed. Webb, of course, caused the accident—he had run a red light; it wasn't his first on the trip. That was the end of it for me. He was doing so many crazy, foolish things and this was just the last straw. The way I saw it, subconsciously, he really wanted to kill our little girl. I flew home with the baby and he was left alone to fix the motor home up and then he flew home also, and I think he realized that something was really wrong. He was terribly unhappy with his job, with himself and even with us so he got our youngest son to type up a résumé and mailed it off. He got a call that they wanted him to come to work clear across the country, and this is where I could have lost him. He was offered a job that was a little bit over his head, in fact, it was way over his head and would have challenged him to learn and do new things. He sat down and asked me what I thought. I give full credit to a very nice doctor. When I told him we would be moving 1,500 miles away from our grown children and all our friends and all my family, he said, 'Katherine, this is the best thing that can happen to anyone your age. You will not see this until a few years after you have gone, but this will help your young adult children to grow because they will not have you here to lean on. Also, at a very important time in your life you and Webb will turn to each other and the baby will be a source of joy to you both. Everyone should have such an opportunity.' I can't tell you how right he was. Here we are. Webb and I are learning new things together, trying out new foods, meeting interesting people and breaking out of all the ruts we had fallen into. It's a rebirth and change does happen. I know if we'd stayed home to stew with all of our problems Webb and I would have ended up divorced as so many couples our age do. Whether you call it the male menopause, or the mid-life crisis, it's just a name given for change in one's life. When the children are grown, people find themselves alone. I think it creates a need to change. What Webb and I say is leave it all behind you and explore those new things about yourself. It's just great."

Not all mid-life crises are resolved as harmoniously as the case described above. Nor *can* all mid-life crises be resolved harmoniously. Many seem never to be resolved at all. Yet there is as much to be learned from cases such as Webb and Katherine's as there is to be learned from the many more cases like Larry and Mary or Bob, Jane and Jenny. In many respects there may be more to be learned from those instances in which middle-aged men grow and develop from crisis and these cases should be presented as they occur, just as are those cases where the crisis is catastrophic.

The final shortcoming in the currently available information on the male mid-life crisis which deserves mention before embarking on an in-depth investigation of this phenomenon, is the lack of sound, constructive, action-focused advice. In light of the other shortcomings noted, this deficiency should not be surprising. In the absence of sound theory and data, complete and comprehensive records of consequences and a balanced presentation of effects, one would be surprised if there were sound action advice. Indeed, the character of help offered to middle-aged men is consistent with current treatments of the problem—superficial, spotty, full of axioms and platitudes devoid of action plans. This book was written in large part to remedy this situation.

The primary objective of this book is to help interested, concerned men and women to better understand the causes and consequences of the male mid-life crisis and through better understanding to deal more effectively with mid-life crises as they occur in their own lives and in the lives of those they love and care for. In so doing, every attempt has been made here to overcome the shortcomings so evident in current treatments of the subject. This book presents in one place the current knowledge and information about the mid-life crisis in a language that is at once understandable and enlightening. The presentation specifically avoids petty and pedantic academic arguments, yet in so doing, neither sensationalizes nor limits itself to the stories of only men or only women. The full range of mid-life changes is discussed, as is the full range of causes and the full range of effects, both positive and negative. Finally, there is an outline of a comprehensive, constructive plan for men and women to deal actively with these mid-life changes.

Chapter 2 is directed to an exploration of who is likely to experience the mid-life crisis, when and why. The various theories of the mid-life crisis are discussed in simple terms directed to readers, male and female, who have a desire to discover why men change in mid-life. Some simple diagnostic tools based upon the instruments used in the original research will help to involve the reader. A review of the relevant research sets the stage for the chapters that follow, which will detail specific events and behaviors associated with the various types of mid-life changes. The ensuing five chapters discuss each of the most prevalent causes of the mid-life crisis and the typical behavior changes associated with these causes. These chapters are: The Goal Gap, the Dream and Step Aside; Vanity and Virility; The Empty Nest; Meeting Mortality; and In Search of Adventure. In each chapter you will read of men who experienced a mid-life crisis which dramatically altered their personality and behavior. You will also read firsthand reports of the women, children, friends, employers who were affected by the changes these men underwent. These chapters give a full understanding of the many varied forms the mid-life crisis may take, the complexity of its causes, and the breadth of its effects. Chapter 8 discusses what to do if you are going through a crisis period, and what steps you can take to prevent a mid-life crisis from occurring. Clearly, many readers of this book will be men seeking answers to their own personal crises. There are no simple solutions but there are sound, constructive actions that can be taken. The supportive action that can be taken by those who find themselves involved in one form or another with a man who is undergoing a mid-life crisis, perhaps his wife, friend, or employer, is discussed in Chapter 9. These "significant others" in the middle-aged man's life can help him through his crisis in ways which are considerate and constructive. Chapter 10 provides a summary of the topics discussed, by presenting ten important questions and answers concerning the male mid-life crisis. Finally, the concluding postscript is a commentary on the role of men in modern American culture. It raises fundamental, practical questions about the expectations we have for men, how those are presented in boyhood, early adulthood and throughout life. It provokes questions of parenting and socialization which may lie at the heart of the phenomenon of male mid-life crisis in our time.

This is not just a book about middle-aged men or just a book for middle-aged men. It is a book about middle-aged men and all those who come in contact with them—wives, children, lovers, friends. It is a book about being, changing, caring and constructing: being middle-aged, changing in mid-life, caring for those who are changing and caring for those who are changed, and constructing from what appears to be confusion and catastrophe, a better, brighter second half.

2

Who Is Crisis Prone?

THERE ARE THIRTY MILLION men in America between the ages of forty and sixty. Thirty million middle-aged men. For nearly one-third of these men, their middle years will be years of turmoil, years of crisis, years of rapid and dramatic personality and behavior changes, not only for themselves but for their wives, families, friends and work associates. Not all of these men will experience change of such speed and scope that in their drama and trauma they are truly in "crisis," but ten million of these middle-aged men will change and it is their changes which receive most of our concern and attention. But what of the twenty million men who will move through their middle years with little thought of change, little threat of crisis? What can be learned from them about the nature of mid-life crisis, the causes and the effects? Why will some middle-aged men change and others not? Just *who* is crisis prone?

First, let us define who is middle-aged. Experts generally regard middle-aged as forty to sixty. This designation is quite arbitrary. In truth there is no precision to the definition of the middle years. Middle age itself is a comparatively new concept. Before 1900 when the average life expectancy of Americans was somewhat less than fifty years, old age was still thought to set in at about forty. People at that time thought of being either young or old, but they gave little thought to being middle-aged.

The psychologist Carl G. Jung was the first to give full attention to the mid-life period. Jung thought that the personality could not reach its full growth and development by age twenty. As he viewed adult development, the next opportunity for fundamental change started at about age forty, what he termed the "noon of life." Jung used the term *individuation* for the developmental process which begins at the age of forty and extends over the last half of the life cycle, the process of becoming truly an individual. Psychologists and other researchers began to give considerable attention to this mid-life developmental period in the post-World War II period and on through the fifties and sixties in tune with increased life expectancies. As noted in Chapter 1, middle age became the object of popular attention and concern in the late sixties and early seventies, with the new openness regarding issues of personal adjustment and development and new projected distributions of population by age groupings. The fast-growing age group in America today is the forty-to-sixty bracket, the post-World War II baby boom is about to become a middle-aged boom.

Before pursuing a discussion of the causes of the mid-life crisis and its effects, it is important to clarify once again what is meant by a mid-life crisis. Mid-life crisis refers to a rapid and substantial change in personality and behavior during the age period forty to sixty. It should be emphasized here that these changes are not necessarily negative or disruptive to the individual's development. They are, however, a departure from previously established personality behavior patterns. Just how many men will actually experience a mid-life crisis and undergo these personality and behavior changes is the subject of some debate. Some experts place the figure as high as 80 percent of all men. Others feel as few as ten percent of middle-aged men actually experience a crisis. The most recent research indicates that the actual figure is closer to 33 percent of middle-aged men. Of considerable more importance than the question "How many?" is the question "Who?". Who will experience a mid-life crisis? Who is crisis prone?

Researchers in adult development are greatly divided over the cause of the male mid-life crisis. Currently seven theories vie for attention as the major catalyst of male mid-life personality and behavior changes. Each theory is presented by its defenders as the primary predictor of cause and effect of male mid-life changes. These theories are discussed briefly here as a framework for the theory on which this book is based: a theory which stands as a complement rather than a competitor to the others. In subsequent chapters, separate causes of the mid-life crisis are discussed with cases demonstrating not only cause but effect for the focal male and for others involved with him.

The Goal Gap One view of the male mid-life crisis is most concerned with a man's work and career. Often termed "achievement–aspirations" and herein termed the "goal gap," the central assumption of this theory is that a man's personality is primarily determined by his work and his career. His personality and behavior are fundamentally shaped by what he does for a living. In mid-life, a man is faced with assessing his work achievements: what he *has done* in light of his career aspirations, and what he *had hoped to do*. This assessment in mid-life may be brought about by any number of normal work-related events which typically occur throughout one's career but which take on a special meaning in mid-life. A performance review, the promotion of a peer, a conflict with a superior, a work assignment mishandled. Very often such a career self-assessment leads to the realization by the middle-aged man that there is a gap between the career goals he has long sought and what he has actually attained and, in all likelihood, what he will be able to attain in the remainder of his career. The man whose single desire was to be company president finds himself at age forty-seven passed over for a younger man. The man whose desire was to be recognized for outstanding achievement in his field finds that his area of concentration is now outdated and viewed as passé. The man who sets successively higher salary goals is forced to take a pay cut, or lose his job. The awareness by the career man that he is not and probably never will be what he always aspired to be creates a goal gap which must be reconciled by the individual. The attempts at reconciliation may often take the form of personality and behavior changes. The man begins to exhibit not only work behaviors but personal behaviors entirely different from those which had once been his pattern. These new behaviors are manifestations of the mid-life crisis brought about by the goal gap.

The Dream It is "the dream" theory, more than any others, which has been subjected to rigorous research and academic articulation. The most recent exposition of this view of the male mid-life crisis is Daniel Levinson's *The Seasons of a Man's Life*. The dream in this theory represents not some nocturnal subconscious articulation but rather an idealized image of the self. The dream theorists believe that the process of maturing, the process of developing as an adult often requires a man to suppress certain parts of himself in order to meet family, career and social demands. As a man begins a family, as he takes on the responsibility of a wife and children, as he progresses in his career, as he acquires certain social roles, he must set aside and neglect for the moment elements of himself which are central to his identity. According to the dream theorists, the man must reconcile his life against this suppressed dream.

As in the achievement–aspirations hypothesis, the recollection of youthful aspirations toward a career is a major factor in dreams; however, in this perspective a mid-life crisis is just as likely to occur for the man who is living his dream as for the man who is not. Those men who confront their dreams once again in mid-life only to find them unfulfilled often undergo rapid and substantial personality and behavior changes in either the direction of dream denial or in the direction of fulfilling their youthful dreams. Such changes are a means of resolving the issue of their unfulfilled dreams. Other men who may have fulfilled their dreams in mid-life often ask, "Is this all there is?" "Was it worth all I had to give up along the way?" Responses to these questions may bring about changes in the way a man sees himself and the way he behaves; changes just as dramatic in their impact as the changes in the man who finds he is not living his dream. Whether the youthful dreams of the ideal self-image of the middle-aged man have been realized or not, their appearance in mid-life demands reconciliation. The middle-aged man must deal with his dreams, his ideals, and in so doing he is crisis prone.

Step Aside Yet another variant of the goal-gap mid-life crisis lies in the changes in the status and role in society which occur over the life-span of adults, many of which are focused on the middle years. Societies in general and communities, family and friends in the more immediate, have different expectations of different age groups. We do not expect the same things from our young people we expect from active adults, nor do we expect the same things from the elderly that we expect from active adults. For many middle-aged men changes in expectations of them as they move through their middle years can be disconcerting. As is the case in the "goal gap" and "the dream," this is particularly true in the area of reduced activity in work. As the more challenging, more arduous work assignments are given to younger men, as family and community roles are altered and indeed some lost entirely, many theorists argue that these role and status changes demand a refocusing for the middle-aged man, from outward environment-oriented ego development toward inward self-oriented ego development. The notion is that as long as roles and status positions are clearly communicated by others one can direct one's life by the behaviors that are expected of him. However, when these roles and status positions begin to change the individual must change accordingly, and indeed as role and status expectations diminish the individual must find the source of identity within himself. This requires refocusing, relying less on what others want of the man and more on what he wants from himself. This is frequently accompanied by personality and behavioral changes. The middle-aged man's role in the world changes, his view of himself and his behavior toward the world must change accordingly. This theory which is well documented in the research among the aged (sixty and over) is also widely used to explain mid-life changes. It is argued that the role and status changes which occur in mid-life are harbingers of the role and status changes which will follow a man into his late adulthood, and the adjustment that he makes in these middle years is an early manifestation of how well he will adjust in later life. As he is asked to step further and further aside from center stage he must find a new place for himself, and from his new place and perspective come new and different behaviors.

The Empty Nest Among the most common occurrences in a man's middle years are changes in the structure and activities of his family. These changes are viewed by many as the cause of the mid-life crisis. Typically, as a man moves into his fifth decade the children are leaving home or have left home for college, or perhaps for families of their own. Increasingly, wives are returning to school and their own careers. As the children and the wife move the focus of their activities away from the household, the husband/father may see them as moving away from him. Wife and children are less dependent upon him and less subject to his influence. His work and other activities are no longer the central focus, now each member of the family has his or her own activity, their own focus. The wife and children are less available as sources of recognition, value and ego support to the middle-aged man. The ups and downs of the family, its best and worst moments, no longer revolve around his own ups and downs, his own best and worst moments, but rather revolve around activities over which he has little or no control and in which he may feel little or no involvement. The established roles and ways of relating become precarious. He begins to question his own role in the family, the extent to which he is needed, perhaps even the extent to which he is desired.

The answers the middle-aged man finds to these questions raised by natural changes in the life cycle and structure of the family may involve changes in his own personality and behavior. In this way the normal changes in familial relationships that coincide with the middle years of the husband's/father's life can cause changes in the man's personality and behavior. The empty nest has long been viewed as a phenomenon of concern to women in their middle and later years. It is now viewed by many to be of equal importance and concern to middle-aged men.

Meeting Mortality There is another natural course of events in the middle-aged years which is viewed by many as the cause of the mid-life crisis. These events have to do with leading a man to acknowledge his own mortality. In a man's middle years he frequently is faced with the declining health and perhaps death of his parents. His own health may be in decline and by mid-life many men have even experienced major illnesses, bleeding ulcers, heart attacks or the like. Almost certainly he knows someone, close friend or work associate his own age, whose health has taken a sudden reverse and perhaps died. Even the more mundane reminders of one's diminished life expectancy such as an insurance physical or a minor illness which lingers on, all raise for a man the reality and inevitability of his own death. It is not uncommon for men in mid-life to think less in terms of what they have done or what there is yet to do, but more in terms of how little time there is left to do anything.

The realization that he will not be able to accomplish all he had wanted to because there simply isn't time can move a man to reorder his life's priorities. As priorities are reordered, his personality and behavior may change accordingly. Thus, once again events common to the middle years of any man are seen as precipitating a mid-life crisis. The attendant changes often take the form of efforts by the middle-aged man to take full advantage of what he perceives to be the little time left. Just as often, the man in crisis may alter his behavior not to take full advantage of the time left but to resign himself to the inevitable, to withdraw from life, to give in, to acknowledge that there is little time left, so why fight it. In either case, the investment in living to the fullest or the withdrawal from living are potential manifestations of the realization of life's very real and very near limits for the man who is middle-aged.

Vanity and Virility There are, of course, inevitable physiological changes that occur as men age. Most men between the ages of forty and sixty begin to notice small changes in their own body and its performance; changes in skin, hair, psyche, general body tone, come more rapidly after forty. A game of tennis or handball with opponents once conquered are first played much closer, then conceded. Sexual performance is perhaps the most disconcerting change as desire often diminishes and ability gradually declines. Many men in mid-life find they have little drive for active sexuality and some experience diminished ability, specifically difficulty in achieving or maintaining erection. All of these changes are symptomatic of the gradual physiological changes that occur in mid-life. They are manifestations of the natural aging process which affects all men. Medically speaking, these changes are associated with decreasing levels of testosterone and reduced gonadal functioning, both of which are inevitable with increased age. To the middle-aged man experiencing these changes in his body, clinical explanations are small comfort for what he sees as threats to his vitality and virility. Threatened as he is by these changes he may experience compensatory changes in his personality and his behavior, hence the mid-life crisis. There are those who feel that these physiological changes are the primary sources of mid-life personality and behavior changes.

In Search of Adventure Many mid-life theorists draw heavily upon Erik Erikson's notion of the adult life cycle. Central to the latter stages of adult development, according to Erikson, is the desire for personal growth. This desire is fundamental to the human character, so fundamental that the absence of a sense of growth, the perception of stagnation or a prolonged status quo will lead an individual to attempt to regenerate himself, to re-create a sense of growth and vitality. These views are widely held by many theorists of adult development and used to explain changes in middle-aged men. For many men in their middle years, the stability and security they have worked so long and hard to achieve in family, work and community, is perceived not as safe but rather as stagnating. Routines at home and office become ruts. Life lacks challenges and there is little promise of future opportunities for growth—no vitality, no vision. In order to get something started again, to regain a sense of adventure, a sense of challenge, to create a climate for growth, many of these men radically alter their behavior. From this perspective all male mid-life changes are viewed as a quest for growth, a quest for challenge, a quest for personal development. Whether or not the changes in fact lead to these goals is less important than that this quest underlies the motivation for change.

Much of the current attention to the male mid-life crisis is directed toward determining which of these theories has the answer. Which explains the male mid-life crisis? Which above all others will help to identify why the crisis occurs, what occurs, and even to identify who is crisis prone? There are sound arguments to be made in favor of each cause as *the* cause of the mid-life crisis and there are ample spokespersons as well. Disputes, debates and defenses aside, reason dictates that *there is probably no one theory that is sufficient to explain every mid-life crisis.* Common sense suggests that the empty-nest hypothesis does not explain the personality and behavior changes of a forty-five-year-old bachelor, yet bachelors are just as prone to the mid-life crisis as are married men. Similarly, achievement–aspirations—the goal gap—does not adequately account for the mid-life crisis of the man whose career accomplishments have far exceeded his ambitions, the man for whom there is no goal gap. Just as the evidence suggests that no one theory explains all cases, the same evidence, the hundreds of first-person reports collected on the causes and effects of the mid-life crisis, conveys quite clearly that each theory is an explanation for some men. How to resolve this apparent dilemma? None explains all yet all explain some. Is there an identifiable cause for mid-life crisis? Yes. A common thread runs throughout these many explanations of the mid-life crisis. A thread from which can be woven a theory that embraces these many explanations and at the same time points the direction to a cause and a context for predicting who will experience a mid-life crisis and perhaps even when. That common thread is the assumption of each theory that *a man's mid-life crisis is caused by threats to his identity*. For example, the "empty nest" describes the crisis as occurring when a man whose sense of identity is rooted in his family role and responsibilities finds that identity threatened by changes as that role and responsibility changes. For the man who defines himself in terms of his youthful appearance and abilities, changes in his physiology and diminished capacity are likely to occasion a crisis. Thus each of the popular explanations of the male mid-life crisis is rooted in threats to a man's identity. Where they differ is that each crisis sees a man's identity concentrated in a different set of personality and behavior patterns —primarily work, family, physical, or dreamlike in substance. The most logical and consistent view is that the mid-life crisis is caused by threats to a man's identity which occur in his middle years.

It is important to be as specific as possible about what the notion of identity implies. A man's identity consists of those aspects of his personality which have to do with the way in which he defines himself; those aspects which have to do with what he means to himself and to others. The role of identity and behavior is such that most people seek to affirm their identities through their behavior. We attempt to behave in ways that will make us seem to be who we think we are. So, for example, when a man's identity is rooted in his family roles, for that man, his principal means of defining himself and his place in the world is through the role he has as a member of the family—husband, father, son. Each of the seven popular theories of the mid-life crisis claims a different source of identity for the middle-aged man and yet each of them sees the threats to that identity that occur at mid-life as *the* cause of mid-life personality and behavior changes.

The position taken here is that a mid-life crisis is likely to occur when and because a man feels his identity threatened by the events of mid-life. Since men root their identity in different elements of self, it follows that the mid-life crises of different men will be rooted in different causes. There will be no one specific threat which explains all mid-life crises simply because there is no one identity that is true for all men. As identity alters from one man to another, so, too, the causes of crises in mid-life will alter from one man to another. For each man the potential cause of a mid-life crisis lies in a different source because his sense of self lies in a different source.

It follows from the above perspective that any investigation of the nature and extent of the mid-life crisis must begin by inquiring "How do middle-aged men identify themselves?" The following questionnaire illustrates one means of determining a man's perceived identity. The greater the value assigned to any statement the more that statement is central to the man's identity. Three response patterns emerged from this inquiry, strong singular identity, strong selective identity, and dispersed identity. One-third of the middle-aged male respondents (including responses about middle-aged men made by others) showed a strong preference for a single descriptor over all others combined. Approximately 50 percent of the middle-aged men distributed the majority of points to a selected two or three identity descriptors. Less than one-fifth of the men dispersed their preferences evenly over four or more identity descriptors. These choices were cross-checked against the "major concerns" list that follows (see the full questionnaire in the Appendix).

PERCEIVED IDENTITY IN MID-LIFE

Please rank the following descriptive statements according to their desirability for you at your present age. Using 100 total points, assign some quantity to the statement *you would most like to be able to make about yourself,* a lesser number to the statement you would next most like to be able to make, less to the next and so on down to the statement that is least desirable to you. Our interest is in what you would like, not necessarily what is. Remember, the sum of the values you assign should not exceed 100.

_____ I am successful. I have met my career goals. (The Goal Gap)

_____ I am growing and developing as a person. (In Search of Adventure)

_____ I am virile, masculine, attractive to women. (Vanity and Virility)

_____ I have realized my full potential, my ideal self. (The Dream)

_____ I am healthy and have a long life ahead. (Meeting Mortality)

_____ I am close to my wife and family. (Empty Nest)

_____ I am active in professional, civic and social affairs. (Step Aside)

From these responses the most prevalent sources of identity for middle-aged men are, in order of occurrence: 1. work and career, 2. long and healthy life, 3. personal growth and 4. family roles and responsibilities. The men reported that realization of "the dream" was only of moderate importance as a source of identity, and role status and physiological descriptors were rated as least important to their sense of self. However, as we mentioned earlier, a major shortcoming of current information about the mid-life crisis is the tendency to concentrate on reports from men only. This was overcome by research seeking information from others who might be involved with the men reported in the study. These others included wives, mistresses (where we could identify them), friends and employers. It is interesting to note that using the women's responses about the middle-aged men they were related to, the same list of primary sources of identity emerged, with one exception, that exception being that the women reported vitality and virility as the most important source of identity to the middle-aged men they knew.

The men in the study may have been either too vain or too imbued with the macho ethic which prohibits expressions of personal physical, sexual concerns. The reports of the women regarding the importance of sexuality to the men that they knew are credible enough to warrant significant attention to vanity and virility as a primary source of the male identity in mid-life.

The final ordering of sources of identity for middle-aged men is:

Most Prevalent: Career
                     Vanity–Virility
                     Health–Life
                     Personal Growth
                     Family
Least Prevalent: Dream–Ideal Self
                     Role Status–Active

Consistent with the theory that mid-life crises are caused by perceived threats to a man's identity subsequent questions (see questionnaire I-1 through VII-6 in the Appendix) sought information about middle-aged men's experience with events relevant to these sources of identity. For example, I-5. "Within the last two years have you: a. Been terminated? b. Promoted? c. Demoted? d. Had your responsibilities reduced? e. Changed careers?" These responses were then weighted according to the importance assigned that source of identity to get a measure of the impact, the perceived threat experienced by the middle-aged man.

From this data it is possible to say that the men who are most likely to experience a mid-life crisis are those who find their identity in a *single source*—whatever that source may be. Time and time again, these men were most threatened by the relevant events of mid-life. Curiously, there were no significant differences in education, career or income among these men whose identity was so singular.

Subsequent requests of these men and those involved with them produced detailed descriptions of the consequences of crisis for these men. From these descriptions it is possible to project a pattern of behavioral responses to the different kinds of crises middle-aged men experience—crises experienced by perhaps as many as one-third of all middle-aged men.

What of the remaining two-thirds; the twenty million middle-aged men who do not and in likelihood will not experience a crisis? What do we know of them and their relationships? There are countless cases of middle-aged men who do not experience crises. The absence of crises in the lives of these men is not a self-delusion. Looking to reports of their wives, families and friends, it is clear that these men move through their middle years without threats to their identity, without challenges to their personality, without dramatic alterations in the way they see themselves and the way they behave toward the world. What accounts for this relative calm in the middle years? Who are these men? Consistent with the theory presented here it must be argued these men do not experience crisis because they do not find their identity threatened by the events and occurrences of their middle years. Yet, common sense suggests that *every* man must face *some* of the events in mid-life which can be a catalyst to crisis. Every man faces alterations in the structure and nature of the family. Every man faces career changes. Every man must deal with his own declining virility and health. How then do some men manage to escape crisis in light of these events?

The research data demonstrates that those who are not threatened are those whose identity is not rooted in one source or even in two sources but rather they draw their sense of self, their personal definition, their direction for relationships in the world from a variety of sources. For every investment of self they made in their career they made a similar investment in their family or in an avocation or in their own health and well-being. Thus, threats to one or even two sources of identity were not seen as devastating because they could fall back on other important definitions of self, other significant measures of meaning. In this way they averted crisis in their middle years and in all probability will avert crisis throughout their lives. This is not to suggest that these men are healthier or more normal than other middle-aged men; it only means that they are less crisis prone during their middle years.

The middle-aged crisis is many headed. It can bring about personal disaster or it can be a catalyst to a significant period of personal development, an enriching and enlightening time for the man and for those around him. Knowing that it does occur and knowing *why* it occurs and *to whom* is the first step toward understanding and ultimately controlling *how* it will affect all those concerned.

In the next few chapters specific occurrences of the mid-life crisis, their causes and their effects for a number of men and their families, are explored in detail. From these explorations it is possible to develop an action plan for responding effectively to the events and experiences of mid-life—the environment of crisis.

3

The Goal Gap, the Dream and Step Aside

" 'HI, I'M BILL WALTERS. I'm with Glastex right here in town. If Glastex or I can ever do anything for you, you let me know.' That's how I used to introduce myself to people, everywhere. It didn't make any difference whether I was at the grocery, or the gas station, greeting folks Sunday at Church or up at the Lodge . . . to everybody I was Bill Walters, 'Glastex right here in town.' Why, I was so proud of working for them that sometimes I know I just said 'Hi, I'm Glastex' and people would say to me, 'I missed your name' and I'd say 'Bill Walters, Glastex,' but I knew that I'd said 'Hi, I'm Glastex' and that's the way I thought of myself. I was that company and that company was me. But all of that is gone now. I can't ever think of myself that way again, not after the way they treated me.

"I had worked for Glastex part-time in the summers while I was going to high school and then when I got out of high school they offered me a good job out there in the foundry, and to tell you the truth I didn't see any sense of going to college, it being so expensive and all, so I joined right up with them. I got married and there was a baby on the way, and that had no sooner happened than I got drafted and sent over to Korea. There I was in the service going to Korea and I just knew I'd come back with no job. All of those lucky bastards who didn't have to go would be in the good jobs and I'd be out on the street. But Glastex kept my job open for me. None of my Army buddies was treated like that by their bosses. People from the company wrote me all the time while I was overseas and when I got back that job was there and ready just for me and I stepped right back in like I hadn't been gone a day. Right then I knew that I was going to be as committed to that company as I was to my marriage. They had been faithful to me and I let them know I would always be faithful to them. So I started up the ranks. I mean I started working out there in one of the foundry crews and then I became a foreman, and then a supervisor and then a manager.

"All along the way I did everything for that company. If ever there was a need for somebody to work overtime, I worked overtime. Lots of times I didn't even bother to put in for it. If ever somebody had to be shown around the plant, well I was the one who showed him around. If somebody had to handle the United Way drive, I handled the United Way drive. I mean that company was my life and I gave my life to that company. Even without a college education I hit all those steps in the career ladder faster than anybody else ever had. I made foreman before anybody else had ever made foreman. I made supervisor before anybody else had ever made supervisor. I made manager before anybody else had ever made manager. All the way along the line I was always the youngest one in my spot.

"I never thought of doing anything but working for Glastex and it was the same with my wife, Dianne. All of her friends were wives of the people who worked at Glastex—all of our friends. It was the biggest, most important company in town and I was a part of it and I was going to keep it big and important in that town, just as big and important as it was in my life. I never, ever gave a thought to leaving, except that once. That was in oh, sixty-nine, maybe. This other company approached me and offered me a real good job—much more money and more responsibility in another town and I thought it over and I went to Mr. Samuels, he's the president, and I told him about this other job and I told him how much conflict I had, that I loved Glastex and that it was everything to me but that this other job with this other company just offered so much more money and was such a good chance that even as much as I loved Glastex I didn't know how I could pass it up. That was when Mr. Samuels made me a promise. He said, 'Bill, you've been the youngest foreman, the youngest supervisor, the youngest manager, the youngest division manager and I know that you are going to be the youngest vice-president and before too long, the youngest president of this company.'

"Mr. Samuels seemed to be offering me all of my dreams, everything I had ever wanted was to be president of Glastex. That promise was made almost ten years ago. And after that conversation with Mr. Samuels, I just rededicated myself to working harder and working better and to giving more of myself to Glastex. I had always been real goal-oriented. I made all of those spots in the company long before I was supposed to make them because I had that as a goal. After Mr. Samuels talked to me I set a goal for myself of going to night school and getting a degree. I did that here at the local college and they say I'm the fastest one that ever went through. You know how there's always those goals about making your age and income. Well, I've always done that ever since I was twenty-five years old. When I was twenty-five I made $25,000, thirty, I made $30,000, when I was forty, I made $40,000, and they say you ought not to buy a house more than two and a half times your salary, well I always had a house that was twice my salary, and that bit about six months' savings, I have always had twelve months' savings in the bank. All of those things have been goals for me and I set those goals and I've met them. When I had that conversation with Mr. Samuels, I set a goal of being vice-president within five years and president within ten years and I knew I was going to make it.

"Almost five years to the day after I set that goal Pete Dopper, he was one of the vice-presidents, he left to go with another company. I thought that was my chance. I thought sure I'd be the one they would name vice-president, but it didn't happen then. They brought in someone from outside, someone a little bit older than I was who frankly had more experience with top-level responsibilities, more of a background, more of a track record, anyhow that's what they told me and I accepted that. I rededicated myself to working harder. Mr. Samuels told me once again that I'd be the youngest vice-president they ever had and the youngest president.

"Nearly two years after that, the fellow they brought in left. That opened up another vice-presidency. In addition to that, the company was growing to where we had added a new division and that too needed a vice-president, so there we were—one and a half to two years ago, two vice-presidencies open. I thought surely my chance had come, but I didn't get either one of them. Both of them went to younger men; men who had been with the company less time than I had; men who had done less for the company; men who I never heard say, 'Hi there, I'm so and so. I'm with Glastex.'

"I recall that day so vividly I still hurt. Samuels called me at home and said, 'Tomorrow I'm going to announce the two new vice-presidents and you're not one of them.' He offered to come over and talk to me about it but I was so crushed, I was so devastated that it was all I could do to say goodbye and hang up the phone. I turned to tell my wife Dianne and the tears came to my eyes and the words caught in my throat, and I didn't have to say anything. She understood what had happened. We hardly talked at all that night. There were a couple of phone calls. Dianne told them I wasn't feeling well and had gone to bed. That's the truth. I got sick, damn sick. Sick at heart, sick at soul and sick at body. I didn't go to work for the rest of the week. I know it was hard on Dianne making excuses and begging off of some of the plans we had made with people but I know, too, that she understood how hurt I was.

"The next week, the first thing on Monday morning I had a meeting with Samuels and I just asked him 'why?' Why wasn't I chosen? I knew that whatever he had to say it wouldn't be an answer, it wouldn't be satisfactory. There was no way he could justify what they had done to me. I didn't know that what he was going to say was going to hurt so much. He said things like 'lack of potential' and 'hadn't proven that I was capable of growth' and 'the long-term investment the company would have to make in me.' He didn't say anything about the long-term investment I had made in the company or the potential that the company had realized because of me or everything I had done for them. I felt hurt and I felt cheated and I felt that I had been lied to. Here I had worked all of my life for one thing. That one thing had been more important to me than my wife, more important than my family, more important than my own health. The one thing was Glastex and here, when it really counted, they said 'thanks but no thanks.' So I quit; turned in my resignation and just quit.

"We tried to stick it out there in town. I had some vacation pay coming to me and some savings so we stayed on for about six months without me working but it just got too bad. I didn't feel like I could go anywhere. I didn't feel like I could show my face. Everytime I did go out I felt people were talking about me, saying, 'There goes Bill. He was going to be president of Glastex, but they passed him over.'

"For the last couple of years I guess I have tried a little bit of everything. I tried selling real estate; I thought I might sell insurance; to tell the truth, I'm just not much of a salesman. Now what I mostly do is watch a whole lot of TV. Dianne works and that keeps us in food and rent. If it weren't for her I don't know what we'd do. I know in my head that just because Glastex didn't want me, doesn't mean that nobody would want me. I know I'm a good, solid worker, a proven performer as they say. I know the glass business and I know what I can do. But I don't feel that anybody wants me. I don't feel that I'm worth anything. I feel like all I'm good for is watching the game shows or the soap operas. I'm washed up and I'm only fifty-two."

The events which took place in Bill Walters' life from forty-five to fifty-two are so commonplace as to be almost clichés in the lives of middle-aged men, particularly middle-aged men in managerial careers. These events epitomize what is known as the "goal gap" mid-life crisis. Quite literally, the goal gap refers to the perceived distance between the goals an individual has set for himself and the achievements he has actually realized in his life, literally a gap between what he had hoped to do and what he actually has done. In Bill's case he had hoped to be president but the highest level he could attain was division manager and there was clear evidence given to him by his superiors that he would always be a division manager, never rising higher. Thus, not only did Bill realize that he had not met his goals but he was given every reason to believe that he would never meet his goals. Unable to deal with this gap in other terms, Bill saw it only as a reflection on himself, his ability, his self-worth, his *identity*, and he withdrew from the source of that reflection, Glastex.

The goal gap is perhaps the most common of the causes of the male mid-life crisis, most common because it is spurred by two dominant dynamics in career paths: (1) the rapidly rising career expectations and (2) the mid-career crisis. The modern American work force is the most educated work force in the history of the world. One result of this education boom is that ours is the first society to have more of its workers in white collar jobs than in blue collar, labor-intensive jobs. Another result, less tangible but no less real, is the phenomenon of rising expectations. As the level of education rises the level of expectations rises, most often in a geometric progression. The more workers know, the more they expect to be able to achieve using what they know. In fact, however, career opportunities are not unlimited. There are real ceilings—ceilings which are bumped into mostly in mid-career.

The confluence of the mid-career crisis and the mid-life crisis creates considerable confusion about each. Mid-career crisis refers to issues which must be dealt with as one moves up the career ladder, and particularly with issues that occur at those plateaus in the middle of one's career. Such issues deal with specialization versus generalization, the establishment of a unique organizational identity, accepting the responsibilities of mentoring, balancing work, family and self. This means that in mid-career workers must ask themselves questions such as: "Shall I be a specialist or generalist?" "What is my unique identity in this organization?" "Should I be more active in developing subordinates?" "How do I balance time given to work and family?" Career theorists suggest that issues of this sort arise for all individuals regardless of age as they move through a career ladder. They are natural consequences of the interaction over time between an individual and his or her organization, his or her career.

When career issues arise for middle-aged men, they can often bring the situation beyond a mid-career crisis and cause a mid-life crisis, such as the case in the life of Bill Walters. The promotion of two of his peers over him raised questions as to his own organizational identity as the youngest, brightest, best. Consequently, because his organizational life—his career—was the foundation of his own personal identity, this questioning caused him to question who he was and what he was about, hence his mid-life crisis.

As a cause of the mid-life crisis the goal gap almost always deals with career goals. However, there are other significant goals which often occasion a similar crisis. Materialistic goals are a good example, the desire to own a certain kind of car, have a certain value house, to be able to live in a certain lifestyle often are the standards by which men measure their goal achievements. While these goals may be related to career and career attainment they are nonetheless somewhat apart. A man can experience some measure of career success without in fact meeting these material goals. The perception of the inability to meet those goals now and in the future can occasion the mid-life crisis just as surely as does the perceived inability to meet career goals. There are numerous examples of men who met crisis because they could not join the best club, afford to move into the best neighborhood or send their children to exclusive, expensive private schools. These goals are no less real than are career goals, nor is the failure to meet them any less devastating to the man who holds them key to his sense of self.

The nature of individual goals varies greatly from person to person, the source deeply rooted in each individual's socialization. Despite the differences in goals among individuals, responses to the mid-life crisis brought about by the perception of a goal gap are remarkably similar. The majority of men who experience a mid-life crisis caused by a "goal gap" feel a profound sense of inequity. As Bill Walters expressed it, "I felt like I had been cheated. I had been lied to. The company owed me something for all I had put in, for all I meant to them, for all they meant to me. They owed me and they didn't pay up. It just wasn't fair." The major behavioral effects of the goal gap as a cause to mid-life crisis are attempts by middle-aged men who perceive a goal gap to reconcile the inequity they experience. These behavior changes aim at reconciling the gap between what was aspired to and what was achieved, and typically take one of these forms:

• Withdraw from the arena of goal achievement and set aside the goal aspirations.
• Maintain goal aspirations, alter the arena of goal achievement.
• Reinvest in aspirations and arena of achievement.
• Change goal aspirations.
• Act against the arena of goal attainment.

Any of these responses has profound effects on the middle-aged man's behavior not only toward his work but toward his entire life and all those involved. Bill's effort at reconciliation, withdrawal, not only from the company but from work, is perhaps the most characteristic response, even though Bill was somewhat extreme. The extent of Bill's withdrawal can be seen in conversation with his wife, Dianne, about what happened to Bill.

"I've never been so frightened in my life as I was in the few days after Glastex passed Bill by. He went crazy—not crazy in a wild, violent, throwing things sort of sense—that probably would have been better. No, Bill went crazy in a quiet, too calm, remote sort of sense. The very first thing he did was to methodically go through the house and throw away anything that had anything to do with Glastex. There were bowling trophies, framed letters from company officials, pictures, souvenirs from different company meetings, places we'd gone with the company—everything went into the trash. Then he demanded that we cut ourselves off from anyone who had anything to do with the company. For us that meant just about everybody we knew. For years all of our friends had been company friends. All of our associations, our social activities, everything we did revolved around that company. Not only would he not see those people, he wouldn't let me see them. When they called, he hung up on them. I had to start going to a different market, a different laundry, nothing could be the same, nothing could have anything to do with Glastex.

"I might have been able to live with all of that, as hard as it would have been, as hard as it has been, but then there was the sitting. Sitting in front of the TV, just watching, not even really caring what was on half of the time, I think. He just sat there and he watched and that would go on for a couple of months and then he'd think that maybe he ought to try to get a job, but I don't think he ever tried any of those jobs more than three or four weeks and I know he never gave them his best effort. It was only through the good graces of some friends that we've been able to make it financially. I went back to work and now I'm really doing pretty well, but Bill, he's still sitting at home most of the time. Every now and then he'll try something else. I just can't tell you how depressing it is. It's gotten so I don't want to go home at all and every day I come a little bit closer to not going home. I don't think Bill and I will make it, not unless he starts making it for himself."

Not only were Dianne's attempts to keep Bill from withdrawing thwarted, but similar efforts by his friends and colleagues were rebuffed as well. Mr. Samuels in talking about Bill notes, "I knew how hurt Bill would be but we simply had to go with the people who had a track record that gave us reason to believe they'd have some potential, and frankly, the job was over Bill's head. In retrospect, I was probably wrong in not communicating with Bill earlier what some realistic personal goals for him would be in Glastex. He simply couldn't have made it to vice-president and certainly not to president. I know I wasn't completely honest in not telling him that but Bill was so loyal to the company, he had done so much for the company that I wanted to keep him involved, keep his interest. At the time it was just easier in those conversations to say that we had high hopes for him and that he could play an important part in the company's future than it would have been to tell him that he was performing pretty much at what we thought he could do and didn't expect much more out of him. How do you tell that to someone?

"After he resigned, I wasn't willing to accept that and I tried to call him several times. He refused to speak to me so I finally sent him letters, I think there were three of them in all. In each one I outlined a new, exciting kind of project that we at Glastex were willing to give him that would be his alone, to try and get him back in the fold, to get him involved again. He never responded to any of my letters. I even went so far as to get one of our competitors to offer Bill a job. He owed me a favor anyway and I thought this was as good a way as any to collect on it. I know that he made Bill an offer and it was a good one, but Bill turned it down. So I . . . I feel like I've done more than my share to try to compensate for any hurt he is feeling or any sense of loss, but it really wasn't my fault—we just had to go with the people who have potential."

Attempts to draw back into the organization those who have withdrawn in response to a perceived goal gap seem fated to fail. Wives, friends, employers cannot reconcile the inequity the middle-aged man feels and often their attempts to do so merely serve to remind him that he is not and cannot be what he aspired to and *everyone* knows it. An almost total withdrawal such as Bill's, from an organization, work, society, and ultimately withdrawal from himself, while extreme, is by no means unusual.

There are numerous cases reporting similar total withdrawals and the attendant symptoms of depression, restlessness, and inability to be committed to and involved in relationships of any sort. As devastating as these withdrawal symptoms are for men, they are usually just as traumatic for the women involved with those men. This problem seems to be heightened in those couples who do not share work and career concerns as a normal part of their relationship. In these instances, the wife may become particularly embittered because something she has little knowledge of or involvement in—his work—is damaging their relationship.

As one wife wrote, "I know my husband is going through this change, I know that he has had setbacks on his job and in his career, but he refuses to talk to me about them. I find this hard to cope with because his being down is pulling me down. He has no desire to do things the way we used to do. He has no pep, no energy at all. His problems at work have been cheating me out of part of my life for the last three years. I finally decided to go back to work because I'm so bored with the whole situation, bored with him. I can't let him pull me down anymore. He says he wants me to go back to work, but he gives me no support with anything I do. It seems as though he has no energy for anything, doesn't care about anything, including me. We used to bowl together all the time in a league, but he doesn't even do that anymore. We have problems raising the teenagers. He can't seem to cope with their changing moods and high energy levels. He has no interest in them, no interest in himself. He's totally bored with his life and himself. I can't communicate with him. He keeps saying we shouldn't be married because we have such differences but the differences weren't there before his problems at work, before he began to withdraw. When he withdrew from work, that's when the differences started, and now the differences are real, they're deep and I don't know if we can overcome them."

In many instances the withdrawal is not so severe, the middle-aged man merely withdraws from the organizational career or work situation which has brought about the perception of a goal gap and moves into another career arena, one which will offer better opportunities for him to meet his goals. Many men recognize the need to leave a career in which they realize their goals cannot be met, but have trouble finding another career which does offer better opportunities. One respondent wrote, ''I am forty, hold a master's degree in American History, and have been teaching high school social studies for the last twelve years. Last year I resigned my teaching, giving up tenure, a nice vacation, and a good pension plan to the dismay and surprise of my school administrators, relatives and friends, but not to myself and my wife. I would have made $28,000 this year and could have become department head if I had wanted to. I had been told many times that I was one of the better teachers in our high school, but over the years I became more and more disillusioned with the kids and the educational process and attitudes in our school district. Also, it was no longer any fun or challenge to me. I began to fear each school day. I don't know how I survived the 1976–77 school year, but I did. I finally refused to compromise my own goals anymore as it would mean giving in and becoming a slave to an incompetent and apathetic administration. I'll never again teach in a public school since I never again want to experience the depression, anxiety and utter emotional and psychological feelings that were consuming me as a teacher.

''We have no children and my wife is working so that at the moment there is no economic problem. I've taken a course at our local junior college for people wanting a career change and even was under the guidance of a career counselor, but I stopped seeing her since she was of little help. I live in a rural area and there are few colleges and other such schools within driving distance. I enjoy living here and I do not want to move. I have applied for some jobs in the area that I thought I would be interested in, but I have been turned down. At the moment I can't decide on what to do to earn a living. I must work at something which I can enjoy and which helps me meet my goals, something I can find satisfaction in, not just watch the clock. I have been tested and I appear to show interest in working with people and also the allied health field. I'm not going to become desperate and get in the same rut I was in for too many years. I'm not going to fall into a career just because it's convenient. I want something that moves me toward my goals. I would like to open an antique shop since my wife and I love such artifacts and one of my hobbies and main interests is collecting American paper memorabilia. But the area is flooded with such shops and I'm pretty sure I couldn't make a living at it. I know I'm not alone and that there are many others in my situation out there, and more than that, I know there are many others who would be in my situation if they only had the courage to give up what they are doing and to get after what they'd like to be doing. I wonder if there is an organization for people in my position, such as AA for alcoholics and Weight Watchers for overweight people. Maybe I should start one. I could call it 'Goal Getters' for people who are going to get out and get after their own goals.''

It does take courage for a man to give up in mid-life what he's been doing and to get after his goals in another career arena. Many men find it easier to live with being less than they had hoped to be than to run the risk of possibly falling short of their goals a second time. For others, the realization of a goal gap spurs them on to greater efforts at goal achievement in the same arena. Without changing their aspirations or their chosen avenue for achievement, these men respond to the goal-gap crisis of their middle years with renewed commitment, as though challenged by their own goal shortcomings. The changes in the personality and behavior of these men can be as dramatic as the changes seen in men who choose other responses to the goal gap. Art Ruber is one such man, at forty-three he and his wife, Ruth, underwent major changes as he responded to his declining performance at work. First, Art speaks of what happened.

''For as long as I can remember wanting to be something, I wanted to be a partner in an engineering firm. That's what my dad was and what I grew up around, talk of the big, important projects and visits to the sites. It was pretty impressive to a young, impressionable kid. That's what I wanted to be, all through high school and college. After I got out of college I joined up with this company because it was small but growing and seemed to offer me the best opportunity to move up. I worked my way up the ladder and I got up to what I thought was a good promotional spot where I could go into being a partner. At the same time I was enjoying other things in life. We bought a lake house and I enjoyed going out there every weekend. The kids were growing up, playing ball, and I'd coach every now and then in the evenings. Things seemed to work out fine. I was doing well at work and yet had lots of family time.

"The big flareup came over some overtime. Now it seems like kind of a small thing. The company never had a firm policy about overtime for the professional staff, the engineers. All the hourlies got paid overtime, but if you were an engineer it was just kind of assumed that when a project required you to stay late, you'd stay late and nobody said anything about it. Most of the time, I was happy to do that, but then along came this project. It wasn't just a matter of staying late a few nights. They wanted us to be there on weekends, every weekend for about four months. Well, there was just no way I was going to give up my weekends. I made a big deal about it and I told them in no uncertain terms that I had signed on for a forty-hour week and I was willing to give forty and a little more when it was demanded, but there was no way I was going to work weekends. I felt if there was that much work. they should hire some extra help.

"I know that other people felt that way but I was the only one who said anything about it. I'm sure that during the length of that project I was the only one who didn't work weekends. When it came time for the next performance review, the one that I had figured would put me in as a partner, I went in and sat down with my boss and was told that my performance was just fine. I was perfectly promotable with one exception. He had written down on my review form 'bad attitude.' When we started talking about that I found out that what they were concerned about was the fact that I didn't work on weekends. As he described it to me, that was 'absence of loyalty and commitment' on my part and that as long as there was evidence of absence of loyalty and commitment, they didn't feel that I was promotable to partner. Well, I got pretty pissed off about that and resigned on the spot. I went home and figured that I had done the right thing. Later that week, talking about it with my dad, I began to see that maybe I had done the wrong thing. Dad helped me to realize that if I believed in my goals I was going to have to behave in ways to help me reach those goals, and I did believe in my goals. It was very important to me to be a partner. I was prepared to do anything that it took to become a partner, even work weekends.

"Dad got me a job with another firm and from the day I joined that firm I worked with a dedication that I really didn't know I had in me. I put in ten- and twelve-hour days. There wasn't a weekend that went by that I didn't work at least Saturday if not Saturday and Sunday. Sure, there were sacrifices. There wasn't any more time at the lake house and there was less time at the kids' ballgames, but it all paid off. I am a partner here now and I love it. It's what I always wanted. That fight I had over overtime really brought about a crisis but that crisis brought about the best change that's ever happened to me, even though my wife doesn't think so."

Certainly Art's wife does not think so. Ruth writes bitterly about the changes in their marriage as Art acts once and for all to get his goal: "There's not a whole lot I can say now about what happened. Art got what he wanted and the kids and I lost what we wanted. We are separated now—legally, that is. The divorce will be final soon. We have been separated ever since he took that other job because he changed when he married that other job. The kids and I never saw him. We had no time together as a family, no social life. He just changed. I had never seen that side of him. I couldn't and wouldn't live with it.

Maybe being a partner was that important to him, whatever being a partner means and however important it is. All I know is that it's important for me to be married to a man who is a partner in the marriage and the family, regardless of what he is at work. Art showed me that if he's going to be a partner to his work, he's got no time to be a partner to me.''

Art Ruber's mid-life crisis led to a reaffirmation of his career goals and renewed efforts at achievement. There are those who would argue that the price of attainment was too high—he achieved what he aspired to but lost a wife and family in the process. Art Ruber's case illustrates a behavior that characterizes so many middle-aged men's response to the goal gap, behavior that is very ego-centered and without apparent consideration of others. In Art's case they were *his* goals and it was *his* decision as to what to do about them. Many middle-aged men presented with a goal gap in much the same manner as Art described reported very different responses, still selfish and ego-centered, but responses which resulted in changing their goals. As one of our respondents put it, ''I began to think perhaps, if I wasn't doing well at this, I shouldn't be doing this in the first place.''

One way of resolving the feelings of inequity brought about by the perception of a goal gap is to change goals. This response has the effect of saying ''I didn't achieve what I aspired to because I really didn't want it in the first place. Now I can go after what I really want.'' This response can represent a convenient face-saving rationalization or it can represent the conclusion drawn from a process of genuine introspection. In either case one of the most frequent behavior changes reported as a result of the goal gap was a change of goals and direction in mid-life. Jerry Leonard, former college professor, tells of his own mid-life crisis and in so doing, provides the outline of a scenario revealed by hundreds of middle-aged men.

''I loved the teaching part of being a professor but I could never get into all of that writing and publishing. It just seemed to me like it was another form of mental masturbation. All people ever did was to write about this little statistic and that little statistic just so they could have it read by people who were interested in this little statistic and that little statistic and it never really made any difference to anybody. So I didn't do much of it. I concentrated on teaching, on being a good teacher. I suppose that somehow I knew that being a good teacher was not going to be enough to get tenure. Universities just don't hand out lifetime appointments to people who can teach well. They like to have people who are going to contribute to their reputation and maybe get a research grant and all that means that you've got to publish. Because I didn't publish, when I was thirty-eight, I was told by my school that I was not tenurable. Now I wasn't at the kind of school that makes tenure a very tough decision. It was a good enough school, but its reputation was not like that of Stanford or Yale or Harvard and when you didn't get tenure where I was, well that was pretty much the bottom of the line unless you wanted to go way, way down the list. So there I was, four years of undergraduate school, three years of Ph.D., thirteen years of teaching and no tenure—no future. That's what they're really telling you when you don't get tenure. They're saying, 'You've got no future.'

"I wasn't as devastated as you might have expected. Actually, I began thinking about what I really wanted to do. It seemed to me that the goal of being a professor didn't hold a lot for me. While I loved the teaching part of it, there was too much else involved with being a successful academic that I didn't care for. I felt like I needed to seek out something that was more rewarding. I realized I needed to change my goals, so that's what I did. Now I'm a trainer with this company and we've got a large industrial and management training section and I do all of that. It has all the teaching that I need and none of the publishing requirements. I've come to find that the goals that one sets in a business environment are much more comfortable to me, much more compatible with my own behavior than the goals that are set in university environments. So these are my new goals—to be a successful business trainer and I couldn't be happier. I only wish I had found it out sooner."

Because these redirection decisions are so often made by the middle-aged man acting alone, without consultation or consideration of his wife and friends, they are usually catastrophic for these relationships. The middle-aged man takes off in a new direction, leaving others confused and upset by the suddenness and substance of the new goals. There are cases where the change in goals is recognized by all involved as positive for everyone involved. Jerry Leonard's goal-gap crisis is such a case, as his wife, Jean, writes. "The change in Jerry was so dramatic it was like living with a different man. No longer did he come home every night, sit at his desk, stare at his books, agonizing over whether or not he should write something, whether what he wrote would get published or wouldn't. He constantly felt guilty that he wasn't doing more. I know he was disappointed when they told him he would not get tenure. He was crushed, but he sprang right back. He took that defeat as an opportunity to look at his life, our life, and decide what he really wanted and he decided that being a professor was not really it. There was just too much wrapped up in being a professor that he couldn't identify with—goals that other people had that he couldn't work for, and so he began to build some goals around the things he liked doing, the parts of his job that he enjoyed and felt rewarding. He found this training job in Mobile and he just loves it and he's great at it. He's constantly getting praise from his superiors and I know he feels satisfied and enjoys his work. He can hardly wait to get there in the day and he comes home at night feeling like he's done a good day's work and can relax and be with us. When he was working toward those other goals, when he was trying to be a professor, even when he was with us he was never really there. Do you know what I mean? It was like a part of him was always somewhere else, a part of him was thinking he ought to be doing something else. Now when he's at work he's at work, and when he's with us, he's with us and it's great. If there was a mid-life crisis involved in not getting tenure, I am thankful for it. That crisis has given me a new man. He's middle-aged but he's brand-new and I love him for it."

The changing goal orientation does not come as easily to all middle-aged men as it came to Jerry. For many there is a period of drifting and wandering, not the kind of drifting and wandering that one sees in the withdrawn middle-aged man who is seeking to escape goals, but rather a drifting and wandering that is a sincere attempt to find a new source of identity, a new set of goals, a new definition of self to order his activity. This drifting, wandering, searching is frequently more frustrating than an abrupt change of direction. The frustration seems to be felt less by the middle-aged man than by those who must live with his wandering. A college-aged student wrote of her father, "It's pretty tough to tell your friends that your father is forty-seven and he spends most of the time searching for himself. He's been into one thing after another, he's had this job and that job, he's bought this business and he's bought that business and it seems like nothing satisfies him. I'm beginning to think that nothing ever will. What angers me the most is that he doesn't see anything wrong with what he's doing. He doesn't suffer any—Mom and I do all of that for him. I've been to four different schools in three years, a different one for every job that Daddy has. I can't believe how Mom's been . . . I mean, she's a saint. She's supported him, she's put up with him, she's encouraged him, she's helped him. I don't think I could do it. In fact, I know I couldn't do it because he and I have had some pretty harsh words over his searching while Mom suffers. Here I am, twenty-one years old and I have a better idea of what I want to do in the world than he does at forty-seven. Don't you think it ought to be the other way around? I keep saying to him, 'Daddy, when are you going to grow up?' and he keeps saying to me, 'I'll know what's right for me when I find it.' I'm about ready to give up on him."

Changing the goals acquired over a lifetime, changing goals which have directed a man's major life decisions for forty years or more is not easily done. It requires both the courage and patience of the middle-aged man who is attempting such a change and of those who are involved with that man and dedicated to helping him through this difficult time. It is so difficult

to change goals in mid-life that most men choose other responses to the mid-life crisis occasioned by the goal gap, frequently either withdrawal or reinvestment, rededication to
long-held goals. Many middle-aged men find it easier to give up
entirely or to get with it, to reinvest themselves in a familiar
pursuit, than to go through the tortuous process of reexamining,
realigning and altering their own goals. There is yet another
behavioral response to the goal-gap crisis, indeed the most prevalent response, that leads the middle-aged man not to give more
or to withdraw or to change but to stay involved with the organization. Most middle-aged men perceiving achievement–aspi-
ration inequities choose to maintain the career context, to stay
involved in name only and, instead of giving more, to give far,
far less.

Gary Berman, vice-president of a national restaurant chain,
speaks of one such reaction in a case he's familiar with. "I guess
we realigned Rob's district about a year and a half ago. When
we did that, we passed him over for division manager. His profit
picture had been pretty good and his restaurants were clean and
reasonably well run, but quite frankly, Robbie just can't relate
to people. Whenever we confront him with his need to change
his behavior, he tells us that he has lived this way for forty-eight
years and that there ain't no reason for him a-changing now.
Well, you can see what we're up against. Another version of
'You can't teach an old dog new tricks.' But in this case the
reason you can't teach an old dog new tricks is because the old
dog doesn't even recognize the need to learn new tricks, so we
passed him by a year and a half ago and now what are we left
with? Well, we are left with a manager who takes every opportunity to dissuade young people from making a major commitment to the company; a manager who continually flouts
company policy, ignores accepted company procedures,
disrupts every managers' meeting we have and in general does
everything possible to be a complete pain in the ass. Why don't
we get rid of him? We don't get rid of him because he runs a
damn profitable restaurant and he's a longtime leader among the
managers. It's his style more than anything else. If you're

around Rob at all you can tell how bitter he is, how angry and how he's going to push us at every opportunity. It's clear to me that he is just waiting out his retirement and he's going to do nothing to help the company while he's waiting. You see it time and time again—people who are passed by become pissed off and are going to make the company pay. I think we'd be better off just to buy him out.''

Robbie is indeed embittered and frankly admits to his position. "They screwed me good and now they can't do anything about it. They won't fire me so I'm just going to hang in there for the next fifteen years, then I'm going to take my retirement and run. In the meantime, they're going to have to go over me, around me, under me and by me, but they aren't going through me to get anything. I was cheated and now they're going to pay the price. That's all I have to say about it.''

Robbie's wife, Darlene, talks more freely about what happened and what is happening to her husband and his goals. "You have to understand that Rob came from nowhere. He started in that restaurant business bussing tables and moved up the ranks to be a manager. There was nothing more important to him than being district manager, and when he didn't get it, well he just couldn't understand it. He has always been a little harsh and a little cynical and I can see where people down at the company would feel that he doesn't get along very well with people, but he deserved that job and he would have been good at it. Now he's so bitter he takes it out on the company and on everything and everybody else. I've never seen him so critical and so uncaring. He doesn't have a good word to say about anybody or anything. He's pretty much turned off all of our friends and we have a hard time going anywhere without him getting into a fight. Just the other day at the movies he just about got into a fist fight with some man who accidentally stepped on his foot crossing the aisle. Reading the paper or watching the news only sends him into sort of a soapbox speech about everything that's wrong with the world, and somehow it all gets back to the company. He wasn't always that way. He used to be a lot of fun to be with and to be around and I wish I could get that part of him back, but now, now he just wants to strike out at everything and everybody and he's going to find some way to get back at that company.

"I even think he lashes out and strikes out at me. That's a way of getting back at the company. Oh, I understand why he does it and I'm willing to put up with it, but things sure would have been different if he'd been able to meet his goals. They weren't all that high, if only he could have met them, if only they would have let him."

Not too many middle-aged men thwarted in pursuit of their goals strike out at what they see as being the obstruction. Most seem to accept their fate passively and, though embittered, choose merely to stay in the organization, spending their time without real contribution or without real conflict until they can leave. These cases are concerning primarily because of their number. This acquiescence, this passive acceptance is the most characteristic response by middle-aged men to a perceived goal gap. There is also reason for concern here because of the sense of defeat communicated by these men. More than defeat, it is forfeiture, they have given up to the goal gap, given up on themselves. Thus, without furor or fanfare, these middle-aged men seem to forfeit the second half of their lives.

Fred Stanner tells how it is with him. "They told me when I was manager at forty-eight that I wasn't being made regional manager because they thought that was as high as I could go. As they put it, my real ability was as manager. As I saw it, the president as much as said to me, 'Fred, we don't expect anything more out of you than what you're doing now.' So, by God, they're not going to get anything more out of me. It's been five years since that happened. I'm fifty-three. Now with the new retirement laws I can be here until I'm seventy if I want and I got no place else to go so I may as well be here. They've got seventeen more years with me taking up this desk, just doing enough to get by and believe me, that's all I'm going to do is get by. I do my job but no more than that, that's for sure."

Fred's supervisor comments, "Yeah, I know what Fred's doing but I can't do anything about it. He's not the only one. In this office alone we've probably got another twenty-five or thirty managers just like him—men who moved up pretty fast, got to the limits of their abilities and that's where they are going to stay. Some of them are even pretty young—thirty-five, thirty-six years old. Most of them are over forty or, like Fred, in their fifties, and we've got a couple who are near retirement. It's not so much that they've become bitter, it's just that they all know there's no place for them to go. They've given up and they're just waiting it out. Whatever it was they wanted when they came into the company they are not going to get it now. We know that and they know that so they're willing to settle for what they can get. They've stopped working for what they wanted. What they can get is a nice cushiony job with not a hell of a lot of responsibility, no stress and pretty good pay. They are content to settle for that and so we're stuck with them. They're middle-aged, middle-career, and now all they're going to do for the rest of their career is get old.''

Middle-aged, mid-career—the combination describes the condition of management in most organizations today. Over eighty percent of the people in managerial positions in today's organizations are within the age group thirty-five to fifty-five. The average age of the chief executive officers of *Fortune*'s 500 is forty eight years old. These men and those who work for them have been raised according to the work ethic that taught them they are what they do. Moreover, that work ethic went hand in hand with the democratic ideals of our society and led them to believe that they can *do* and therefore *be* anything they desire. For all too many of them, the career-related events of mid-life have brought them to the shocking realization that they are not, nor will they ever be, what they aspired to be. Their goals will always remain that—goals, unattained, unattainable. To the extent that these men have allowed their career goals to become the primary source of their own identity, the predominant description of who they are and how they relate to the world, the realization that their goals are not and cannot be met will inevitably bring about crisis.

Case after case has illustrated that when he is forced to confront the gap between his goals and his achievements, the middle-aged man feels that something or someone has cheated him out of what was rightfully his, a title, a life-style, a living. Out of this sense of inequity he responds in ways which lead him to behaviors and attitudes dramatically different from those which characterized his life heretofore. He may, as did Bill Walters, view the judgment of his organization as a judgment of himself and withdraw from the organization, from society, and finally from himself because he cannot cope with the reality each presents. He may, in a more positive vein, withdraw only from that work context which denies him goal achievement, finding in the same career, perhaps in another organization, opportunities to meet the goals he has sought so long. He may use the occasion of a perceived goal gap to question his goals to begin with, to spend time searching, exploring new goals, new avenues of achievement and definition. He may seek to recommit himself to his original goals, to rededicate his efforts to achieve the career rewards he has sought. He may strike out against the organization or he may do nothing. He may merely accept the fact that he is not, and probably will never be, what he sought to be, and just go on.

Whatever his response to inequities he perceives, the changes this middle-aged man experiences will have dramatic impact on his wife, his children, his employer, bringing changes in their lives as well as in his own. Certainly there are other causes of the mid-life crisis beyond the goal gap, but career goals play such an important part in our society and are so central to the identity of men in our society that we must recognize it as a central cause in the entire phenomenon of the mid-life crisis.

So much of the meaning and status of a man in our society is based on career accomplishment that many men quickly learn they are no more than their business card or title. It is as though identity is defined completely by work. A man begins to accept as his own the goals that may in fact belong to others, goals of being presidents of companies, goals of earning a certain income, acquiring a certain life-style, without examining these goals to see if they are truly his, if they are descriptive of the things he is capable of or even wants most in life. Many men fall too quickly into believing that a career is an end, a goal to be sought in life rather than a means to an end, a way to achieve other life goals. In this context, the confrontation of reality, the realization that a man's achievements do not and can not meet up to his aspirations, is for most men the most traumatic experience of middle age—change seems inevitable.

The symptoms of the goal-gap mid-life crisis are many and varied. Most often there is a dramatic change in work behavior, accompanied perhaps by a dramatic change in the man's relationships with others, his wife, family and friends. A sense of aimlessness and meaninglessness may accompany the perception of a goal gap. Very often there are real physiological changes that attend these psychological changes—headaches, fatigue. These various symptoms may contain the seeds of resolution to the goal-gap mid-life crisis, but this possible resolution will center on the settlement of several issues, which deal both with the goals and the man himself. Do the goals continue to have meaning for the middle-aged man? Are they a viable source of identity and definition? If they do continue to have meaning are they realistic goals or are they out of touch with his personal capabilities and talents? Are the goals out of touch with the opportunities afforded in his present career context? If the goals are viable and realistic, what then of the perceived goal gap? Where are the shortcomings for the middle-aged man? Are the shortcomings present in his own abilities and efforts or is there an organizational context, a climate which has thwarted realization of his goals? If the goal gap is caused by his own energies and abilities he maintains some control over the situation and faces the choice of either altering those energies and abilities or giving up his goals. If the goal gap is occasioned by an organizational climate, a career context which for one reason or another does not afford him an opportunity to meet his goals, then he must face the decision of leaving that organizational context and finding another. If examination of his goals reveals them to be no longer meaningful, no longer acceptable as describers of who and what he is, then he must seek alternative sources of definition either in the establishment of new career goals or in a search which takes him beyond career goals and aspirations into alternative arenas of his identity.

For many men who consider these issues as they attempt to deal with the goal gap in their lives, resolution leads to as much personality and behavior change as the crisis itself. This is particularly true where the middle-aged man dealing with the goals and the gap discovers that the goals are not his but belong to others. Wife and family create and promote aspirations for the man. Organizations foster the belief that men can achieve whatever career heights they aspire to. In order to resolve the goal-gap crisis in these cases the middle-aged man must first resolve the relationships which create the conditions of crisis. Jack Warren, a forty-four-year-old dentist, had much to resolve.

"When I fell apart from the drinking and the depressions, therapy helped me to realize that it was because I wasn't meeting the goals that I had set for myself and it didn't seem as if I was going to, so I escaped in order to avoid trying and failing. Coming out of that depression, coming out of the alcoholism on my own, I saw that the goals weren't really mine in the first place. All I had ever wanted was a nice little practice in some quiet little town, to play golf on Wednesday afternoons and the weekend, raise the kids and live the good life. It was Opal who wanted the Mercedes, and Opal who wanted the swimming pool, and Opal who wanted the guesthouse, and Opal who wanted the country club, Opal who wanted the vacations in Hawaii and Mexico and Europe—Opal and Opal's family. They wanted it all. I didn't want any of it, but they had me convinced I needed it—I wouldn't be a real man without *all* of it. Do you know the only good screws I ever got from Opal were after I'd bought her something—the bigger the purchase the better the screw.

"I was seeing patients damn near twenty-four hours a day, hitting liquor and pills to have the energy to see them. Instead of being just a dentist I became a goddamn corporation. I had more interests than you could shake a stick at and it all fell apart when I had that malpractice suit. When I could finally acknowledge the alcoholism and the depression I could also acknowledge that the goals weren't mine in the first place, they were Opal's. It seemed to me like the only way I could resolve them at the time was to split. It was the best thing I ever did. I got away from all of the pressures on me to achieve, to be, be, be, buy, buy, buy, and I could just be what I am. I'm just a regular old dentist in this little town here and I play golf on Wednesday afternoons and on the weekends. I don't get to see the kids as much as I'd like, but I sure as hell don't miss all that pressure from Opal to achieve. The way it was going, she would have pressured me right into the family plot.''

The first crisis in Jack's life came when he realized he wasn't meeting his goals. The second crisis came when he realized the goals weren't his to begin with. The first nearly destroyed him; the second has led to a reconstruction of a sense of self and a reaffirmation of what he wants, not what others want for him. Those related to a middle-aged man who experiences a crisis as a result of the goal gap have the obligation to help that man explore the nature of his goals, the causes of the gap, and to help that exploration without burdening him with their own goals for him, their own agendas for him to actualize. It is a task much easier described than done.

It is easy to understand the mid-life crisis of men who experience a goal gap. Because it's not difficult to identify with these men, their cases evoke concern and compassion and it's easy to direct attention to constructive support of their crisis resolution. People can readily identify with their disappointment because most people have experienced some degree of rejection in their goal achievement efforts, and the dejection and momentary depression that follows such rejection. Indeed, few people ever achieve all they aspire to do, and the goal gap rather than being specific to middle-aged men may be a congenital condition for all would-be achievers in our society. So cases such as Bill, Art,

Jerry and Robbie are read with interest and sincerity. Readers recall circumstances and contexts in their own life in which they have experienced comparable disappointments and turn their attention to how these men and others might be helped.

It is more difficult to understand and harder to empathize with the mid-life crisis experienced by men who have achieved all they aspired to, and who are now disaffected. The popular press is dotted with stories of those in the entertainment industry, in sports, or in politics who have achieved the pinnacles of their career with attendant wealth and fame and (what for most of us would be) great personal satisfaction, only to find they are unhappy, dissatisfied, indeed bothered by the very fame and success they have achieved. Rather than meeting these stories with concern and caring, the natural response is to harbor some resentment against those who have achieved far beyond one's own wildest dreams, and still are not satisfied, are not happy. There is often a great deal of anger directed at those who get it all, only to throw it all away.

It is also difficult for most people to empathize with the middle-aged man who is gradually moved out of the arena of achievement. The common perception is that as a man matures, achieves, he is duty-bound to move aside to give others a chance to achieve. For many middle-aged men, the pressure to move over despite their achievements foretells the end of achievement and is something to be resisted at all costs. Both of these causes of the male mid-life crisis, the achievement which is unappreciated, and the pressure to step aside and let others achieve, can be viewed as variations on the goal gap, or as causes in and of themselves. Because these causes are so closely related to career concerns, and because they are reported by so few middle-aged men as being central to their crises, they are discussed only briefly here.

One view of the mid-life crisis explains not only the crisis of those who do not meet their goals but also those who have met their goals. This theory is commonly known as "the dream." In this perspective all men develop in early life an idealized self-image, a dream if you will, of who and what they are going to be in the world.

For many who have attempted to live out their dreams only to find in mid-life they have been denied and are likely to be denied in later life the behavior response is very much akin to the responses to the goal gap. But for most men their dream is not as clear and as measurable as their goals are and, therefore, it's more difficult to say specifically that their dreams have been denied. Indeed, the most common perception a middle-aged man has of his dreams is a sense that they have been deferred, put off, while he has gone about accomplishing other things. The real departure between the goal-gap view of mid-life and the dream perspective comes with the consideration of the crisis of the successful middle-aged man, the man who has met his goals, lived his dream. The man who has lived his dream may come to ask in mid-life "Is this all there is?" or perhaps, "Was it worth all I had to give up?"

Peter Ward at forty-eight is by any measure a successful man. In a relatively brief time, twelve years, he has amassed a net worth which would easily qualify him as a millionaire. Starting with a small production-related operation, Pete acquired other domestic and overseas operations and eventually controlled a holding company with over ten separate entities. Pete described what began to happen to him.

"As long as I can remember I wanted to be my own boss, have my own business. Even when I was working for a large company my whole idea, my dream, was to get out and do something on my own. I was constantly on the lookout for an opportunity, the break that would start me out. How it happened is not so important now, it's enough to say that I got the rights to this particular new part, started producing it and it just got bigger and better. One thing led to another. I bought some related businesses and some unrelated businesses, went through a divorce, an IRS investigation, lost some money, made some more and here I am.

"The mid-life thing began for me a couple of years ago. It

wasn't something that came up dramatically or suddenly, looking back I realize it had probably been going on for a year or more before I was even aware it was happening. I was letting it all get away. Here I had everything I had ever wanted, ever dreamed of having. Hell, I had everything *anyone* could ever dream of having and yet I was letting it drift away. It just didn't seem important, didn't demand my attention—the little things seemed to consume me. I was irritated with waiting in line, angered by crowds, had no patience for anything, no interest in anything. Especially no interest in keeping the dream going. There didn't seem to be any point—I had it but I wasn't motivated to keep it—no reason to try to get more.

"A lot of people probably think I had a flash of conscience, you know, decided my pursuit of wealth and self-reliance was superficial and too costly with the marriage and all. Well that's a lot of bullshit. To begin with, I didn't have to sacrifice that much to get where I am. As for my marriage, it was a mistake long before I started working on my dream. As for other things, other interests, there never have been any for me—no hobbies, no sports really, just that dream. Then, when I got it (I realized I had it when the IRS came after me), instead of euphoria there was an emptiness, like that Peggy Lee song, 'Is That All There Is?'

"I got so caught up in my own depression, my 'crisis,' that all I had achieved began to slip away simply because I didn't give a damn any longer. That went on for about two years. Now I'm back on top of things. I don't have any dreams anymore. I've had them and they've come true and I was left feeling 'So what?' Now I have no dreams, just problems and challenges. No dreams but no disappointments, either."

For most men their aspirations so outdistance their actual achievements that they have little reason to fear a crisis of the sort experienced by Peter Ward; most middle-aged men have little reason to identify with any of Pete's experiences. Those few middle-aged men who *do* achieve all they aspire to, who *do* find themselves living their dreams, may ask, "So what?" This is less a question about what the dream has meant in the past than a wondering about what it means now that it has been attained, what it means for the future. As one successful middle-aged man commented, "You live with a dream for so long it controls everything you do. All your decisions, about business, how you spend your time, who your friends will be, everything is considered in terms of the dream. You ask yourself, 'If I do this will it get me there sooner, will it come true faster?' Then when you've got it, all of a sudden that framework is gone once you attain your dream and it doesn't provide direction anymore. It's like it only means something to you if you don't have it."

The crisis many middle-aged men who carry out their dream experience is a crisis of meaning, a bewilderment at where direction for their lives will come from now that the dream is realized. Other men are less concerned about where they are going than they are about the cost they have paid for achieving it. For these middle-aged men the dream crisis is captured by the self-searching question, "Is it worth all I had to give up to get it?" The path to dream fulfillment in middle age is often littered with broken marriages, superficial friendships, and a singlemindedness which forces out other interests and activities. Coincident with realizing he has arrived, the middle-aged man may also come to realize just how much the trip has cost.

A prominent attorney wrote, "When you are caught up in doing it, consumed with your dream, you really aren't aware of what it's costing you, at least I wasn't. The long hours, the time away from home, the pressure—it's all just part of what you have to do to get what you want. Then when you've got it— whatever your dream is—for me it was being a partner, you sort of stand back to survey all you've accomplished and that's when you realize you've lost your wife, your kids. The price was too high, but you've paid it. You bought the dream and there's a strict 'No returns, no exchanges' policy." The cost of success, the cost of making dreams come true, is a common cause of crisis for successful middle-aged men. It occurs far more frequently than does the "So what?" reaction to dreams realized.

These interpretations of the potential crisis in dream achievement for middle-aged men complement the goal-gap discussions, providing as they do further career-related circumstances which may cause a crisis. Another perspective on middle-aged men and their careers explains an additional circumstance which can create a crisis: "step aside." A common occurrence in the careers of most successful middle-aged men is the pressure to step aside, to allow younger men the room to achieve their goals, to realize their dreams. This pressure is felt not only in the work setting but in all the arenas in which the middle-aged man is involved—church, club, community service.

"First they kick you upstairs then they start to move you toward the door, that's the way it was with me." Lee Moon talks about his career and community service without any attempt to hide the bitterness he feels. "Just when you get to the place where you have the time and know-how to make a real contribution, they shunt you off into something that doesn't take any time or know-how. Sure you get a fancy title, maybe even more money, but you don't get any more work—you don't get anything that has any meaning for you. At fifty-three I went from Vice-President running an entire division to Senior Vice-President on 'special assignment.' I was 'available to be called on company-wide,' but it was really just their plan to get me out of the way to make room for somebody else, somebody younger.

"The same thing happened in my service club after I had served my year as president (the best year our local *ever* had, ever!). They gave me a "Past President" title and never called on me again. Even when I tried to get involved with projects they said, 'Oh no, Lee, you have served your time, we wouldn't think of asking you for more.' They don't seem to understand that the work is the purpose—no matter how much you do or how successful you are, you've got to have the work. Instead they put you out to pasture, not even good for stud. If this is what retirement is like I hope to God I don't live that long. What would there be to live for without work of some kind?"

In truth, the "step aside" phenomenon seems to be active as a cause of the mid-life crisis for only those men at the upper end of middle age, fifty and older, and even then, only for a few men. As a cause of crisis it is closely tied to the retirement syndrome that has received so much attention from gerontologists. Work serves many purposes for men, beyond being a means to other ends (earnings), work defines who a man is in society, what he is capable of doing, even how he shall spend his time each day. With retirement the source of identity, competence and time structure is removed, leading predictably to depression and very often to the onset of major physical illness. For the older middle-aged man the subtle and not-so-subtle pressure to step aside is often viewed as a harbinger of what is to come—the absence of work and all that it means. For the man who has enjoyed success in his career and met his goals, forced inactivity in an arena in which he has been so active is all the more threatening. The successful man has not anticipated that he would level out in his career, and cannot imagine being asked to step aside. When that happens, crisis is often the consequence.

While few middle-aged men have crises which are brought about by "the dream" or "step aside," these causes do explain some special cases. In particular, "the dream" and "step aside" complement the goal gap by explaining the career-related crises which can affect the successful man in mid-life. These crises are just as sudden and as severe in their effects as are those goal-gap crises of less successful middle-aged men, even though the crises of success evoke less empathy. The centrality of career in the identity of middle-aged men leaves them particularly vulnerable to career-related crises just as success, failure, or simply "getting by" each carry their own threats to a man's sense of who he is and how he ought to behave in the world.

This is a goal-oriented society in which achievement is the universal measurement. There is nothing inherently wrong with setting goals, with having aspirations and with striving to achieve them. Goals serve to focus and direct one's actions and thus shape performance and progress. There is even nothing wrong with having career goals as one's primary source of identification in society, although it can carry a risk for any individual to rely on one aspect of self as definitive of his identity (a theme explored throughout this book). The major danger in setting goals and striving mightily to achieve them is when others' goals are accepted as our own, be the goals dictated by family, friends or society. There is also danger in setting goals the achievement of which lies beyond personal capabilities or the opportunities existing in an organization or career. There is danger, too, in setting goals which have immutable measures of self-worth, measures which cannot be altered with time, changed with circumstances or moderated by maturity. Such inflexibility of goals, such immodesty of aspirations, such insensitivity to self-insight can be dangerous personal practices for men or women of any age. They become particularly dangerous for men of forty to sixty because the natural progression of their careers will confront them during this time period with considerable goal achievement information, whatever their chosen line of work. To the extent that men have totally invested their sense of self in their goals, they are likely to be unable to deal with a goal gap and therefore be prone to a mid-life crisis. If these middle-aged men are further unable to resolve the critical goal-related issues associated with such a crisis, they will respond with dramatic changes in their own behavior and attitudes (particularly toward work) that may see them withdraw from work, society and self; reinvest in work to the exclusion of all other activity; reject the workplace and all that reminds them of their own work behaviors; find new avenues for goal achievement; or passively endure an evaluation of their middle years which downgrades them as unable, unachieving and unworthy, capable in their remaining years only of growing older.

4

Vanity and Virility

"HE SAYS THAT being middle-aged is no big deal, he hasn't changed any, he's as normal as ever. Well, I say he's actually made middle age into one hell of a big deal, he's changed plenty, and if he's normal, then where do I meet some *ab*normal men? Is it normal for a wife to have to make a *date* with her husband in order to get a little affection? Is it normal for a wife to make all the sexual advances, for her always to be the eager one and for her always to be rejected? He may not think he's changed but I *know* he has and I just wish he would admit it. If he did that I think he'd be on the way to changing back."

Middle-aged men seldom report concern for their own vanity and virility. Middle-aged men are most likely to say that the major cause of the mid-life crisis is career related and can be described by the goal gap, or that other causes such as the "empty nest" or "meeting mortality" play a central role in the events of their middle years. Indeed, as our study has shown, reliance solely on the reports from middle-aged men would lead to the certain conclusion that physiological changes, tangible effects of the aging process which have a primary manifestation in sexual behavior, are of little or no importance to men who are between forty and sixty. To rely solely on the reports of middle-aged men would be an error, for it is clear that the mid-life crisis affects not only the middle-aged male, but all those who relate to and with him, most especially his wife and family. These people are an important source of information about the causes of the male mid-life crisis. This is particularly true in dealing with issues of vanity and virility, as we learn from women. They are much more open, and oftentimes much more perceptive in discussing the behavior of men they know, than are the men themselves. Consider the case of Craig and Judy.

Craig is a forty-two-year-old engineer, with a large electronics conglomerate. Judy, thirty-seven, and Craig have been married for eighteen years. They have two boys who are in their early teens. Craig reports his mid-life years to be much like the rest of his life—"very normal." "I really don't notice middle age as being anything to be concerned about, but then my whole life has been very normal so there's really no reason why it should change now. I've been moderately successful at work, I've got a good wife and two growing boys, I'm in good health, things are all okay—whatever problems I have are usually fairly minor and pass quickly. No, mid-life for me is pretty much like the rest of my life."

Craig's report represents only half of a complete picture of a man in mid-life. Judy provides quite a different perspective on what is normal.

"It doesn't surprise me that Craig doesn't see any problems in himself or in our relationship. I think that's the scariest thing about this whole deal. I can tell you right now there are problems, but they're exactly the sort of problems Craig will never talk about, they're sex problems. Let me tell you, I'm so sexually frustrated I'm willing to jump into bed with the first man who makes even half a pass at me. Craig has not touched me for three months, and before that he went two months without making love to me. I think the only reason he did then was because we were at a party and he got so drunk he didn't know what he was doing. In fact, for the last two years we haven't had what anyone would call a normal sex life.

"Craig and I got married pretty young and neither one of us were very experienced sexually. I had been to bed with one other man before Craig but it had been a very brief and bad experience. I'm sure that he had not been with any other woman except me. Although we were both inexperienced, it didn't seem to affect the relations between the two of us. We had an active, healthy sex life for the first fifteen years of our marriage. It was nothing spectacular, nothing bizarre or unusual, we stuck pretty much to the standard missionary position, but it was a good healthy once or twice a week sort of sex that was satisfying to both of us. Then about two years ago things really began to change. I noticed at first that Craig seemed less demonstrative toward me; there weren't the little pats on my bottom or touching my breasts when I was wearing something sexy—he just seemed to kind of take a 'hands-off' approach. At the same time our lovemaking became much less frequent. He always seemed to have some excuse. He would stay late at the office, or come home tired, or complain that he'd had too much to drink. He always had some reason for not having sex with me when I wanted, and he never seemed to want it for himself. It wasn't that he couldn't. When I did get him into bed and get him worked up we did just fine, it was just that he never seemed to want to. For the longest time I didn't say or do anything about it. I thought it was a temporary thing and he'd soon get back to normal. But he didn't—it just got worse. Finally I brought up how frustrated I was and how I thought we ought to talk about it and maybe even see one of those sex counselors. Every time I brought it up he got so defensive and angry that it seemed by just mentioning it I was giving him an excuse for not being affectionate to me. I couldn't very well expect him to make love to me when he was so angry at me.

"For a year and a half I went through pure hell. For a while I thought it was me and that I was no longer attractive and couldn't turn him on anymore. I bought new clothes and changed my hairstyle and worked hard at exercising. I read some sex books which described things I'd never imagined doing, but when I tried them on Craig it only angered him more. I remember once trying to . . . you know, put my mouth on him while he was driving the car. I thought it would excite him but he said it was cheap and disgusting. Then I realized that it wasn't me—there were plenty of men making passes at me and I was still attractive. Maybe Craig had someone else. I went through half a year of suspecting that he had another woman and the reason he didn't have any sexual interest in me was because she was taking all of his energy. That was a pretty paranoid year—I would call him at the office all of the time and if he ever said he was staying late I would doublecheck on him. After six months of that I decided that that wasn't the case either, that there wasn't another woman. So if it wasn't me and it wasn't another woman I had to conclude that it was Craig.

"That's when I really tried so hard to talk to him about it, but whenever I brought up the subject, whenever I tried to get him into bed, he became even more defensive and withdrawn. He refused to talk about it, refused to even acknowledge that there was a problem. That's why today, when you talk to him about it and about what's going on with him, he won't admit there is a problem. But there is a terrible problem. He is afraid of sex. Why, I don't know, but he is afraid of it. You can't believe the things I've done to try to get him interested, some things I'm really ashamed of, felt ridiculous doing, but I was just so frustrated. I met him at the door in black bra and panties and that did nothing, that thing in the car and other things. That did nothing. I've flirted with other men pretty dangerously, trying to make him jealous. That did nothing. I've given up now. For my own satisfaction I masturbate, frustration led me to it and I'm not too ashamed to admit it. As for Craig's satisfaction, I've stopped caring for whether he gets it or not, or how he gets it if he does. He doesn't seem to care about my satisfaction so I don't care about his. A real 'normal' relationship, huh?

"We're still together, but when we are with other couples and I see how affectionate they are, I don't want to be with him. I don't want him to touch me anymore. I don't want to be around him. I want a man who will love me and make love to me like a man, and Craig's not that man. There's no doubt in my mind that he's going through a mid-life crisis. There is no doubt in my mind that something has happened to make him afraid and unsure, but I don't know what it is that has happened. I do know that there is nothing I can do about it. God knows I've tried and I'm not going to try any longer."

Ultimately, Craig and Judy were driven apart by their differing perspectives on reality and differing postures toward that reality. Craig, refusing to even acknowledge Judy's perception of a problem, rebuked Judy at every attempt to deal with the problem she perceived. This difference and distance in perception is a dominant pattern in the relationships of men and women who are confronted by a crisis in the form of threats to the man's vanity and virility. In case after case, reports from men of their own normalcy and lack of concern over these issues were countered by directly contradictory reports from women who know them.

A fifty-year-old physician in Dayton reported: "Of course I've noted some minor changes in my physiology but these are of little consequence and have had no noticeable effect on my behavior. They're hardly worth talking about."

His wife writes: "He went after every young girl patient and worker in his office. His reputation is considered very bad professionally. He went out and flaunted *young* girls in my face, saying us older women 'have problems,' and the young ones are throwing themselves at him every day. I almost went out of my mind with grief and heartache.

"Slowly my needs and desires were so overlooked I became mentally affected and started drinking to kill the pain in my heart. Of course, that was all he needed to leave me and to be with a twenty-year-old girl who was also married who has been working in his office (my daughter's girl friend, in fact). Now they live together way out in the country in a barn. The neighbors think the girl is his daughter. She brags to the town about sexual activities with him and admitted her affair with my husband to her husband before she left him to live with mine.

"Even before he left me, he was always flaunting openly his

desires for young girls. (Thirty years younger, *that's too much*.) They are children. It is so humiliating. I really loved him and kept hoping and praying to the end. We had sex practically every day. Then suddenly he became impotent, because, I believe, of all those young girls in his office. He has aged twenty years in the last two. He used to be tan and healthy but he is all white now, skin and hair, and he is so thin. He twitches when he sees old friends and he is with this young girl who looks seventeen years old. What happens in a situation like this? She obviously is not just his cook. Gossip is he is on dope. He has deteriorated so much and looks so disenchanted. His patients have told me he is very surly and abrupt, obviously not happy. The barn they live in has no windows. I believed he is ashamed. This young girl has sex with her ex-husband in the barn while the Doctor waits outside (according to her ex-husband). I can't believe it. How can he be so stupid to be so manipulated by this greedy young girl? Is this male menopause or egotism? I feel so used and abused that my life has been ruined."

The doctor's daughter comments with less passion but with added proof of her father's mid-life crisis. "The simple truth is my father got old and got horny. He began attacking every girl he got near—employees, patients, *my friends!* He cut Mom off physically and financially. He drove her to drink and worse. He's taken up with Marcia, who is my age, and their behavior together is disgusting. He's embarrassed and humiliated me and Mom just so he can stay young. The whole thing just makes me sick."

The avoidance of sex seen in Craig, and the attraction to sex seen in the Dayton doctor, are the two most talked about responses to the male mid-life crisis which arises out of threats to a man's vanity and virility. Of all activities between men and women, sex is the activity least talked about—that is, sex in terms of needs and satisfaction as opposed to sex as tease and flirtation. It is understandable therefore that where sexual behavior is at issue, middle-aged men and the women involved with them will have different perceptions and perspectives on the problems. This is true throughout the reports of middle-aged men, a persistent downplaying of their own concerns over vanity and virility, not just where sexual attractiveness and performance is involved, but in the generalized area of physical attractiveness and fitness as well. Yet, so compelling are the reports of women such as Judy and the doctor's wife and daughter and countless others who spoke and wrote of the behavior of middle-aged men that the concern for vanity and virility must be considered as a major cause of the mid-life crisis second only to the goal gap. (Perhaps given honest introspection by middle-aged men it would surpass the goal gap as the primary cause of crisis.)

The male mid-life crisis frequently is referred to as "the male menopause." It seems, as noted earlier, that such labeling can only serve to dissuade men and women from serious attention to the problems men confront in middle age. Male menopause is, for many men, yet another reminder that such concerns and problems are "feminine," certainly unmanly, and not the sort of thing that a strong, well-balanced man is concerned with. Moreover, to term the physiological changes that men experience as menopause is quite simply erroneous. Dr. Herbert S. Kupperman, endocrinologist at New York University Medical Center, responds to the question, "Is there a male menopause?" "No. Menopause refers to the cessation of menses. The male climacteric, however, denotes that state of a man's life when gonadal function diminishes, eventually resulting in complete cessation. It is not as specific and definitive as what we see in the female, although the onset may be precipitous—occurring over three to four months."

It is important to understand that for most men diminishing gonadal functioning is so gradual, so protracted a process that the change is imperceptible. This stage usually occurs in men between the ages of forty-eight to sixty-eight, slightly later than in the female. About 20 percent of men between forty-eight and fifty-eight experience the climacteric and about 30 to 35 percent between the ages of fifty-eight and sixty-eight. It is not as common, not as much a foregone conclusion as it is in the female. This means that most men in their late forties and fifties begin to show gradual signs of slightly diminishing androgen levels, but usually there is no such definite or profound change as the rapid estrogen decrease in menopausal women. So for the majority of middle-aged men, 65 to 80 percent, the hormonal change is hardly noticeable. Their libido, desire for sex and their fertility may be somewhat reduced but are certainly not terminated. For this majority of men sexual involution or loss of masculinity is quite gradual, so slow they in all probability are scarcely aware of any change. For some relatively small proportion of middle-aged men this natural hormonal change occurs quite rapidly, they experience a sudden decline of androgen output caused by rapid premature aging of the testicles.

The beginning signs are the loss of potentia, the man's inability to achieve erection or have an ejaculation. If he does have an erection, it's not maintained for a sufficient period of time to reach orgasm. And arousal certainly doesn't occur as frequently as it once did. Associated with this may be the same vasomotor symptoms that females experience—hot flashes—although not as severe or predominant. However, they may be severe enough to disturb sleep. He may also become less positive, less forceful, or irritable and generally difficult to live with. It may be helpful to explain here briefly how these hormonal changes in the male affect male sexual performance. The low production of testosterone and sperm in an aging testicle leads to high levels of gonadotrophins in the man's bloodstream. The pituitary keeps pouring out these hormones to stimulate production but its messages are ignored or only feebly answered by the testicles. Erection is accomplished by blood congestion of three sponge-like spaces that surround the long urinary passage in the shaft end and head of the penis. Tiny muscles constrict the veins that normally carry blood out of the penis, thus trapping the blood that the arteries are pumping into it. The spongy tissues swell, the penis increases in thickness and length and stands up stiffly. Soon after ejaculation the muscles relax, the veins expand, blood congestion in the penis is reduced and it becomes limp again. This condition is called detumescence or resolution. These muscular contractions and relaxations are not under conscious control, rather they are directed by reflexes in the autonomic nervous system. Changes in androgen levels that come with advanced age diminish testicular response to these autonomic reflexes, with the result that the man has difficulty achieving and/or sustaining an erection. This rapid decline in androgen output described above, and its accompanying sharp decline of testosterone and sperm production and resultant effects on sexual performance, is not a normal part of the aging process. It occurs in less than one-fourth of all middle-aged men. For most men then, the mid life crisis probably has little or nothing to do with hormonal changes per se. To say that most men do not experience a climacteric is not to say that men do not experience physiological changes in middle age and that these changes cannot bring about a crisis. The list of physiological changes common to middle-aged men is lengthy:

Urinary irregularities
Fluid retention and resultant swelling
Hot flashes
Heart symptoms such as pseudo angina
Peptic ulcers
Itching
Headaches
Dizziness

These changes are often associated with diseases or treated as disease by the man and his physician. There are, however, other symptoms of physiological changes in mid-life that are not treatable. Moreover, these changes are more apparent, noticeable not only to the man but to others who interact with the man —symptoms such as liver spots, baldness, gradual weight gain, fatigue, insomnia, irritability, moodiness and depression. Of particular concern to most men are noticeable changes in sexual performance which are or are not (and more than likely are not) rooted in physiological changes. Among the most common sexual changes are loss of libido, the diminished desire for sexual activity; decline or loss of potency, the ability to achieve an erection and sustain it long enough to perform a sexual act to the satisfaction of both partners; and finally, secondary impotence, the condition in which a man who has previously been able to produce an erection suffers a partial or total loss of that ability. Secondary impotence usually occurs in one of four forms—permanent loss of potency, temporary or periodic impotence, weak or short-lasting erection, and premature ejaculation.

For the vast majority of men these physiological changes are not the cause of changes in sexual interest, capacity, and/or ability. Indeed, for many men these physiological changes do not occasion a mid-life crisis at all, but rather are accepted as a natural, inevitable consequence of growing older. And yet, clearly, many men do experience changes in their sexuality and crises in their relationships with others as a result of these changes. Why? Why does the concern for vanity and virility create so many crises among middle-aged men? Why these concerns over all others? The answer lies as much in the culture as it does in the circumstances of middle-aged men. There can be little doubt that ours is a youth-oriented culture. The message is inescapable and in many ways irresistible. Even those with a minimum of exposure to the print and the electronic media are bombarded with testimony to the value of youth. To be young, athletic and attractive is to be magnetic in personal relationships, successful in business and eternally envied and desired by others. The object and the answer is to look young, act young, think young (the way to achieve this, of course, is to BUY young). It often seems that, if possible, society would legislate against ever growing old. But age comes inevitably as youth passes. For those who have invested themselves psychologically, physically, and in many instances financially in being and appearing young, the inevitability of age and the changes it brings can lead to crisis. These observations are hardly original. The youth culture has been the dominant feature of the consumer economy for nearly two decades. Entire industries have been built upon the pursuit of youth—cosmetics, clothing, cars. There has even been considerable concern expressed over the effects of this movement on those who succumb to pursuing the promise of eternal youth. For the most part, this concern has been expressed in the context of women. Today there is increasing awareness of the appeal this same pursuit has for men. One of the fastest growing industries in recent years, and a major market for the near future, is what one observer has termed the "vanity insanity" for men—male cosmetics, designer styles for men, the fitness business. This pursuit of youth is not confined to marketing consumables in the popular media but is endorsed in subtle and at times not so subtle ways by employers. Corporations and organizations of all sizes are evidencing increasing concern over the health and vitality of their executives. As often as not this concern takes the form that the young man is better than the old man, the thin man is better than the fat man, the dark-haired man is better than the gray-haired man, the athletic man is better than the sedentary man, and so on.

For the middle-aged man the message is very clear. In order to be successful at work he must be young and vital, in order to be successful in his personal relationships he must be young and attractive, in order to be anything he must be young. For many men the message is too frequent and too loud to ignore and its promise too appealing to deny. These men subscribe to the value of youth and invest themselves fully in its pursuit and maintenance—looking young, acting young, thinking young. For these men the physiological changes which accompany middle age signal the onset of what they fear most—the loss of youth. The typical middle-aged man whose identity is threatened by these affronts to his youth responds in one of three ways: (1) he takes corrective action to reduce the threat, typically changing his behavior to adopt the appearance and behavior of youth; (2) he avoids contact with the source of the threat, removes himself from those things which remind him of his age; (3) he changes his behavior in such a way to put down the threat, to attack it, to prove that he is still young, vital, virile.

The following cases illustrate these responses and reveal characteristic patterns in that the first response, corrective action, is most often seen where the predominant concern is vanity. Avoidance and attack responses are more often seen among middle-aged men who experience threats to their virility, both physiological threats and psychological threats.

Carl Foster is a forty-seven-year-old food operations executive with one of the country's major restaurant–nightclub chains. He describes himself as of average height and build, reasonably good looking and young for his age. To the eye, Carl appears to be of average height, the paunch of his middle-age spread belies his weight, and his physique is not flattered by the youthful-cut clothes he favors. His hair, thin at the sides but thick on top and of a different shade there, swoops down over his forehead in a sculptured swirl that alone indicates a hairpiece. He is a man of high energy, never sitting still, an animated conversationalist who laces his talk with the latest fad phrases. Carl is honest and forthright in discussing the transformations that he has undergone in his life over the last two years.

"I had been running the food operation side of a small family chain of restaurants in the upper Midwest. It was a quiet, regular sort of business, dependable but without much challenge. When I was first approached by CLJ's it was to run their food operation in the same region. They had been having some problems because they were growing so fast and really just didn't have in the company the kind of help they needed to meet the problems of growth. Since I knew the area and the business, and since CLJ's offered me a lot more opportunity for growth and a lot more green, it looked like a good move. Even before I moved down here I recognized some real differences in the businesses. This bar–restaurant business is faster moving, quicker paced than the family restaurant business I'd been in. The clientele is younger and so are all the people in the company. Hell, most of them started as busboys, four or five years ago, and now they shake it and make it happen. They were younger, more aggressive, moving faster—living faster than I was used to working with. I was able to scope all of that from my home region but it didn't affect me a whole lot. Up there, in the boonies, we were pretty much isolated from what was going on in the company. As things began to come together, as I began to do a pretty good job, it became evident that I was going to get a chance to go to headquarters. You have to understand that the career path in CLJ's is to hire local people in the regions, sort of test them out. Those that have potential are then brought into headquarters for a real close look-see and given the chance to move up the corporate ladder. So I knew that if the chance to go to headquarters was to come along I'd have to swing with it, otherwise I'd end up doing the same thing I had been doing, in the same sort of rut—zero gusto.

"When they offered it to me I talked it over with Helen and we decided to make the move. The girls were both leaving for college so there would be no problem of uprooting them. I don't think Helen really wanted a change but she recognized that I needed a change, so we moved down here to headquarters. Right away it became obvious that everything I had seen in the region about a younger company, a faster-paced, more aggressive company, was just the tip of the iceberg. I want to tell you that here at headquarters things *move* and the people are young enough to keep them moving so if you're not with it, you're without it. The only person in the office older than me was the president and he was only older than me by two years. I hadn't been there a week when he took me out for lunch, over a couple of cool ones, and he told me that it had been a real difficult decision at headquarters to bring me in, considering my age and all, and that there was going to be a lot of pressure on me to keep up with these younger people. They all knew I had knowledge and experience that they didn't have and that they needed, but there were some questions about whether I had the energy and the vitality—whether in fact I was young enough to keep up the pace. I later found that one of the real reasons for bringing me down was that the company was getting real paranoid about the possibility of age discrimination suits. There were investigations being brought against them and they thought they had better get some senior people in visible spots—but all of that came later.

"As if my little meet with the man wasn't enough, that first couple of weeks of work nearly blew me away. I was down here without Helen, she stayed home to sell the house and pack, so I had a chance to really get into it. I remember being amazed at how hard everyone worked *and* played. From 7:30 A.M. to 2:00 or 3:00 A.M. they were on the go! I'd never seen such a pace, let alone been part of it. I mean to tell you I was puffin' just to stay in place!

"We'd go out for drinks after work, visit one of the restaurants and end up staying there till one or two in the morning, talking to the people, meeting the customers, and everyone was so damn young. Seemed like they were more my daughter's age than mine. There I was, overweight and balding. Shoot, I wasn't even dressed like any of them. My Wisconsin white shoes and polyester suits didn't go over real big, and I could see that some of the younger people—guys and gals—were treating me like an older outsider, almost a father. It wasn't a very good feeling. At the end of that two weeks I took stock of myself and decided that I'd better do some changing.

"The first thing I did, I remember doing it that second weekend, was as we were getting settled into the new place, I went through that closet and I threw away damn near everything I owned. I mean I needed a completely new wardrobe for starters. It doesn't seem so strange to me now but I remember thinking at the time, 'Here I am with one of the fastest-growing, most successful corporations around and nobody in the office wears a tie.' Hell, they didn't even wear sport coats. So that was the first change—a new wardrobe. I went out and bought some of those slacks that don't need a belt and shirts with the colorful prints and not one single tie. I got some shoes with higher heels and a pair of real classy boots. It was a little awkward at first when I first started wearing them—I wondered what the others would say—but I felt more like I fitted in. Helen, she was trying to help—she bought me one of those gold necklaces. I still wear it.

"To be perfectly honest, the clothes didn't look as good on me as they did on everybody else. I was a little overweight and this balding head of mine didn't exactly cry out 'youth' so I decided to start jogging. In this company, everybody started the day jogging. We have a president and vice-president who run in these marathons. They've been in the Boston Marathon, and most of the others run four or five miles a day. Shit, in Wisconsin I never ran to get the paper, let alone run just for exercise, but I figured that if that was what I was going to have to do, that was what I was going to have to do, so I began running. I joined one of those running clubs that most of the other guys belong to, you know, we go down there every morning and we get a lot of business done running. As much as anything it was just being a part of the gang and showing them that I could do it just as well as they could. I could keep up with them no matter what they were going to do. Although I've got to tell you that the first month it damn near killed me. Here I was getting up at six o'clock in the morning to go run a couple of miles and staying up until midnight or one o'clock in the morning to drink with the boys. It was a hell of a pace and I had to put up with a lot of good-natured ribbing—at least I think it was good-natured.

"Then there was the biggest decision of all and that was the decision to buy this hairpiece. Of course I had been kind of eyeing them for a long time, you know, reading the ads in the back of the girlie magazines and that sort of thing, but I just never felt that I really needed a hairpiece. Hell, everybody in my family has been as bald as a billiard ball and I just always accepted it as one of those things that was bound to happen. But when you work with a bunch of people and they all have these gorgeous heads of hair, it gets to you. They take fifteen or twenty minutes to blow-dry it after they've run or played rac-

quetball and there I was wiping my bald head off with my handkerchief and I'd be ready to go. Like I said, it gets to you and
you start thinking. I had this long business trip coming up—a
swing through the West that was going to take me about three
weeks. I hadn't met any of the people out there so it seemed as
good a time as any to try out a new look, so I went down and
and I bought this 'rug' and went out on the trip. Sure I was
self-conscious as hell, you've got to put this stuff on and then
put the piece on and it's quite a shock to look in the mirror and
where you've been used to seeing skin, see a lot of hair. But
somehow when I wore it I felt younger. I felt more confident. It
seemed like I fit in more with what was going on. I had read so
many articles and everything in some of the magazines about
how it did make you look younger and feel younger, and by
God, it's true, it really did. I had those three weeks to get used
to myself and meet all those people in the West as the 'new me,'
dressing younger, looking younger, behaving younger and yeah,
even thinking younger. I even tried a little grass out there. Hell,
in Wisconsin I thought that was a sin but out there it seemed
like the natural thing to do. By the time I got back to headquarters I was a new person. I was me, the way I am now.

"I guess the total time it took for me to make the change was
three months. It's been a year now and they still haven't hired
anybody older than I am but I don't think anybody around the
office notices my age anymore. I feel like I really fit in—that I
really have recovered some of my youth, and I have to tell you
it's really helping my career. I'm doing better than ever and I
think I'm in line for a vice-presidency in this outfit."

Carl's boss, Ernie, confirms the changes in Carl and his success in the company as well. "It was a big deal for us to bring
Carl into headquarters. Here we've got a company that for the
most part is run by men and women maybe four or five years
out of grad school. It's a fast-growing company and they have
all come up fast. A lot of them started in our restaurants working
in college, moved up into the managerial ranks, showed some
promise early on and we brought them to headquarters. It's a

fast-moving, fast-living company. My people work hard and they play hard, too, and we had some real concerns about bringing in someone like Carl from such a different background and his being quite a bit older than everyone else. But he had done such a fine job for us up in the northern Midwest and he is so capable at what he does that we really felt we had to do it. To be honest, there was some concern about a possible age discrimination suit—we knew that the EEOC had been nosing around and asking some questions and we were making a concerted effort throughout the company to get some older people involved, not only in the restaurants but in the corporate structure as well. We knew that Carl would be a different entity for us and might have some adjustment problems, but frankly, we didn't imagine the sorts of adjustment problems that he would have.

"It's a little difficult to describe, but up there in Wisconsin he didn't seem out of place. He was like most of the people who are involved in the business up there, but when we brought him down here he stuck out like a sore thumb. First of all, there were those suits of his. I mean, that's just not something that we are into—the suit and tie routine. Not that there's anything wrong with it—it's just that our people prefer a little more casual style—a little more relaxed, laid-back. It's more in keeping with the whole image of the company—the image we're trying to present to the community—a restaurant and nightclub for young, affluent people. What with his age and the way he dressed and acted and all, it was clear that, from the outset, Carl didn't even begin to fit in. It was important for him to fit in with the others. I knew that no matter how expert he was, he wouldn't make an impact on the company unless he was accepted by the others. In order to be accepted I felt that Carl would have to make some changes. So I took Carl aside and talked to him a little bit about what we expected from him in the company and some of the problems he might face. I thought it was an important conversation to have and I think Carl felt it important, too. I was especially pleased at the way Carl responded to it. There was a noticeable change in him over the first three months he was with us. At first people had been kind of timid around him because he didn't seem to participate in anything. He wasn't a runner and he wasn't very athletic and he was quite a bit older than everyone and he didn't have the same interest in partying and playing. It speaks to the kind of commitment that Carl has made to us—he was willing to undergo, I think, some significant changes—changes in his whole way of thinking and approach. Now he's just another one of the gang and no one thinks about how old he is. He joined the Athletic Club, he's participating in our runs and now I feel he's really been accepted as a member of our team. We think he has a great future here and he's right—he probably will be one of our next vice-presidents.''

Often the changes brought about by a man's concern for vanity and virility are sparked by work-related events. Organizations place great value on youth and vitality and the promise of performance they portend. The middle-aged man is often threatened by youthful, energetic executives and will go to great lengths to continue to be seen as youthful himself, a ''comer.'' At a minimum, there are cosmetic changes—longer hair, a moustache, darker hair, more hair, less weight. There are almost always costume changes to accompany the cosmetic changes with the middle-aged man adopting the most youthful styles of the day (one of the least flattering of these fads for most middle-aged men was the open-to-the-navel shirt worn with heavy necklaces and pendants; it was possible to appear both faddish and foolish at the same time). Some middle-aged men change their behavior at work, play and at home. Others go beyond even this point to alter their consciousness, to *think* young. The intent of all of these changes, whatever their scope, intensity or duration, seems to be to take some corrective action to forestall the physiological changes which accompany middle age, to reduce the threat to one's vanity and virility visibly, so it can be *seen* by all that he is not losing the looks and allure that he values.

Whatever the intent of these changes and whatever their form, be they cosmetic, costume, behavioral or consciousness, it can be said that their impact extends beyond the middle-aged man himself.

There are clear and evident impacts on his relations with people at work and, perhaps more significantly, on his relations with those at home. These people may have a very different perspective on the middle-aged man's vanity. For example, while Carl and his employer report the changes in his description and demeanor as positive and rewarding, there are those at home who have a different view. One of the striking elements of Carl's description of the changes in his life is that fact there there is little reference to Helen—to the effects of his personal changes on their relationship—on their marriage. Helen reports some real concern over those effects.

"There certainly have been some changes in Carl. Anyone who knew him in Wisconsin and could see him here now could certainly see that. He doesn't even *look* like the same man. In all honesty I can't say I am pleased with the changes. I don't feel like he's the same man I married, sometimes I don't even feel as if we should be married."

Helen is a small, stout woman with a round, attractive face and soft, almost pudgy features. She described herself as an ex-farm girl and looks the part. She favors simple, loose-fitting print dresses in pastel colors. She speaks in soft, quiet tones but with conviction. For the last twenty-five years she has been Carl's wife, the mother of their two daughters and a home-maker. She professes no interest past, present or future in being anything else. She does profess to being very unhappy with the new Carl.

"I knew there would be changes in Carl's life and in our life together coming down here from Wisconsin, but I never suspected that the changes would be quite what they have been. Carl needed to get out of Wisconsin. He was bored with his work and there really wasn't any future there for him. I wasn't nearly so anxious to leave. I had been born and raised there.

Our girls grew up there and went to school there. All of my family and friends were there. It was really all I had ever known and it was enough for me, but I knew that it wasn't enough for Carl so I agreed to try the change. I had never really met that many people from Carl's new company—the times we had been together with them had been at a restaurant over dinner or something, and they tended to treat us more like strangers than like part of the group. I always thought that our daughters had more in common with the people Carl worked with than he and I did, but in Wisconsin we were pretty removed from the headquarters operation and so we didn't have to be involved with them that much. All of that changed when we moved down here.

"The first few weeks here I was just miserable. We did buy this big, beautiful house and I threw myself into decorating it and getting it fixed up the way I liked. If it hadn't been for that I think I would have packed up and gone back to Wisconsin. Carl was just never around. It seemed like he was up and away before I got up in the morning, and he wasn't home by the time I went to bed at night. He really threw himself heart and soul into this new job. But as he explained to me, it was just until we'd get settled, just until he learned the ropes and it'd be back to things as normal. Even though he said that, I knew in those early weeks it would never be 'things as normal' again for us. The change in wardrobe was just the start. I was all for Carl buying some new clothes. I always like to see him dress nice and now we had the kind of money he could afford to do it with. But the clothes he chose—he didn't buy any suits or ties—he went for these loud-colored shirts and pants without any pockets and dress jeans. The only kind of jeans we ever knew in Wisconsin were Levi's or Oshkosh and now he was buying these jeans that looked like they were out of some French fashion magazine and wearing them to work! I just couldn't get over that.

"Carl made a real effort to involve me with the people he was meeting in his business those first few weeks. We went out to dinner and to parties but I always felt so out of place—I never saw a girl who wore anything homemade or bigger than a size 8. They all had such tiny waists and such big breasts and such long hair and wore clothes that I wouldn't think of wearing. A lot of what went on at those parties I wasn't too comfortable with anyway, the music and drugs and sex stuff. I tried to get into the spirit of the whole thing. I did buy Carl that nice-looking necklace—I still can't get used to the idea of men wearing necklaces, but all of them down here do so I wanted Carl to have a nice one. I tried to buy a couple of outfits that I would feel more comfortable with at the party, but even when I was wearing them I didn't feel like they were me, and I certainly didn't want to experiment with any of those drugs or things the way Carl seemed to be ready to do. They're all just so young and I'm not. Carl isn't either, but he could keep up with them a lot better than I could, so after a while, when I felt like I was really dampening his spirits and kind of holding him back at those things, I stopped going. It was okay that he went by himself. It was important for him to do it for his business and I really was just much happier at home so that's where I stayed.

"After the clothes came the jogging. I think that's really good for him. I know it's good for his heart and his health—that may be the best change to come out of all this, but there again it's something he wanted me to do because all of the girls at the office jogged and I just can't see myself doing that. I guess I knew there was no turning back for Carl or for us when he bought that horrible toupee. It just doesn't look very natural on him. It doesn't look like him. I probably shouldn't say this, but do you know that even now I have to have him take that off before I can make love to him, before we can have sex together, otherwise, it seems like I'm with some stranger. That's really what it all comes down to. He's a stranger to me. Deep down I believe he's still the same man I fell in love with and married, but today he doesn't look the same and he doesn't act the same and I wonder if things will ever be the same again. I can't change the way he's changed. It's just not in me to try to be somebody

I'm not—to try to look and behave younger than I am. I hope and pray that in time Carl will see that it's not the best for him, either. I hope that time hurries."

There is a tone of patience throughout Helen's description of her recent life with Carl. The kind of patience that might be expected from an adult waiting for a teenager to go through a phase, a phase of looking and dressing in a way other than the parent feels the young person really is. There are many similarities to adolescence in Carl's behavior, similarities which have caused some to label the mid-life crisis 'middle-escence' and argue for the patience Helen portrays. But not everyone who has seen the changes in Carl is quite so patient with him or so understanding. His daughter Carolyn is particularly disturbed by what she has seen.

"At first I thought it was kind of cute, you know, someone Daddy's age trying to dress and look and be younger. It was all a lot of fun; I never thought it would go on as long as it has and it went from being cute to being silly and now, well now, frankly, it's just sickening. I don't know how Mom puts up with it. It's so embarrassing to be around him. Let me give you an example. Dad came down here to school for one of my sorority's father-daughter things, everyone's dad comes down and we have a nice dinner together and a program and go to a football game. It's really a lot of fun and in the past I had always looked forward to having Daddy here for it, but this year he came down here and acted more like my date than my dad. He had this gold necklace and his shirt was unbuttoned down to his navel and his hairy belly was sticking out everywhere and he was talking all this jive talk and wanted to go discoing all the time, I actually heard some of my girl friends beginning to make fun of him, calling him 'Joe Cool' and the 'Disco Daddy.' We really had it out that night. I confronted him and I said, 'Daddy, you're forty-seven years old, not twenty-seven. You're fat and you're bald and no matter how tight your jeans or how much hair you put on your head you can't change that. You're trying to be somebody you're not and it's driving all of us away, me and Sis and Mom.'

"It hurts so to realize it, but my dad is a joke. We go to these clubs—my friends and I do—and we see these old men dressed in their John Travolta suits trying to pretend like they're twenty years younger and coming up with all these lines and moves for girls half their age. We're all laughing at them behind their backs and I know that they are all laughing at my father and it just tears me apart to see it. I don't know why he can't just grow old gracefully. I don't know why he can't just accept the fact he's forty-seven and he's going to be forty-eight and forty-nine and fifty and he's going to get old. Why can't he just be a nice old man? Why does he have to be a dirty old man trying to be a dirty young man? It's so simple and so easy to see. Sure, he's had a mid-life crisis. Sure, it's hard for him working with people who are younger than he is, but the way you regain the respect of younger people is not by trying to be young like them but by showing them that you've gained something from your years . . . that you've learned something and have something to offer. Daddy is just trying so hard to fit in and he won't fit . . . you can't put a forty-seven-year-old man in a twenty-seven-year-old hole. Oh my God, that's a terrible pun, isn't it, but it's true, and that's what I worry about the most. It's not going to stop with the dress and the talk and the disco dancing, but the next thing that's going to happen, I just know, is that he's going to pick up some 'chick' who's after something—a daddy or money or who knows what, and that's just gonna kill my mom and somehow I've got to stop him from doing that."

Oftentimes those who are hardest on the vain and would-be virile middle-aged man are the very young people he is trying so hard to emulate. Sons and daughters, the latter particularly, have great difficulty accepting their father's attempts at youth. Many of the harsh conflicts between middle-aged men and their offspring are rooted in the behavior of the father, which is objected to by the offspring, rather than vice versa. In this respect Carolyn's comments about her father's mid-life changes are characteristic of the reflections of many sons and daughters to their fathers' middle years. So, too, the defense proffered by Carl is one which many middle-aged men echo.

In response to the comments from his wife and daughter, Carl notes, "I understand their concerns. I really do, I hear what they're saying and I know where they're coming from, but they really don't have anything to worry about. This younger look, it is me—the new clothes, the new 'do,' the new talk, but I don't need to go any further than this. I feel alive and vital now and trying to be younger has helped me to *be* younger. I don't have any needs for a girl in my life. I do have a need for Helen to try to rediscover some of her youth, but I don't want a younger woman. As for Carolyn, well, she's just going through one of those times when there's so much change in her life that she really needs a stabilizing force and she's having a hard time accepting the fact that there can be changes in my life, too. I'm entitled to change just as much as she is. Just because you're getting older doesn't mean that you have to just accept it, stop changing, stop trying new things. She'll come to see that as she matures, she'll come to understand what it is I'm trying to get and I think appreciate and value the fact that I am trying. I'm trying to be younger. Vanity? Sure it's vanity and I admit to it. I am vain but in that vanity I am vital and I plan on staying vital for a long time to come."

In a continued postscript, Carl did receive a promotion to vice-president. He has continued to be successful, gaining a reputation within the company for being particularly hard on those who can't keep up, those who can't match him hour for hour, at work and play. He has steadfastly argued against bringing other older executives into the corporate offices, saying on one occasion, "What this company needs are a few more hard-working boys. We've got no room for blimbos and baldies." Helen remains with Carl but admits to a growing concern that she may lose him to a younger woman. Carolyn is convinced that her father is sleeping with at least two young girls at his office and she has virtually cut off all contact with him.

For many middle-aged men who experience threats to their vanity and virility the cosmetic and costume changes such as those described above are the extent and extreme of their response. Yet whatever the reality of the male's mid-life crisis over vanity and virility, one perception of these men remains universal—the perception that they are sexually involved with younger women. Wherever the issue of the male mid-life crisis is discussed, whether in print or electronic media or in personal appearances, the response has been overwhelmingly characterized by women's concern for what makes a middle-aged man go after younger women. Wives want to know, "Is the mid-life crisis the cause of all middle-age affairs?" Just as often, mistresses wonder whether or not their liaison with the middle-aged man has any permanence. "Is he with them to stay?" "Can he really leave wife and family behind and start anew with a younger woman?" The responses of women to this particular variant of the mid-life crisis fall into one of three categories. One, those women who see changes in the sexual behavior of their men and are genuinely concerned about those changes and want to help them. Two, those women who witness changes in the sexual behavior of their men and want to be told that it is not their fault; it is nothing they have done or have not done to bring about those changes. Finally, there are those women, predominantly younger, who are having affairs with middle-aged men and want to be told whether or not it will last. These responses are disturbing for two reasons. One, it suggests that among women the conventional wisdom as to the causes and effects of the mid-life crisis centers on sexual issues. Popularly held views aside, this simply is not the case. There are many causes and effects of the mid-life crisis, only one of which is related to sexuality. The second reason for concern regarding the character of this response is that it is strikingly at odds with what men report about their own mid-life crises. Men rarely report changes in sexual behavior associated with the mid-life crisis, whereas women frequently, in fact predominantly, report this to be the major effect. What this suggests is that there are many instances of the male mid-life crisis which have their principal cause and effects in issues of vanity and virility, but there is not a willingness on the part of males to acknowledge these important issues in their lives. This seems symptomatic of the myth of machismo, the notion that to acknowledge personal, emotional problems (particularly those which may be related to sexuality) is a sure sign of weakness and even effeminate. There is much more to be said about this important aspect of the male mid-life crisis but first, here are three cases which are representative of the possible sexual effects of the crises over vanity and virility among middle-aged men.

At forty-six, Paul Ribot is one of the last men who would be singled out as a candidate for the mid-life crisis. He manages a successful chain of top-of-the-line men's shops in one of the fashion-conscious cities of the Southwest. He has full responsibility for both the merchandising and operations sides of the business and a piece of the ownership as well. Paul's job requires that he be well dressed and attractively groomed, and so his lean six-foot frame is usually accented with suits by Cardin and Yves Saint Laurent. The finely chiseled features of his face are framed by a lush hood of salt-and-pepper hair and the total look is one of success and distinction. Paul's personality, which is only hinted at by his attractive appearance, comes alive as he begins to converse, eyes twinkling, smile flashing. He seems to embrace the listener with his attention and his affability.

By his own admission, Paul's middle years have not been years of ease and effortlessness. The success he has achieved in business has been the result of hard work and dedication—the many friends who surround him have come from countless hours of personal attention, caring and commitment to them. The relationships he has developed, both business and personal relationships, have had ups and downs and have given Paul reason to be concerned in his middle years. But nothing has so troubled Paul as has his own performance as a sexual partner.

Paul's wife, Beth, is, like her husband, trim and attractive at forty-three. Beth works as a supervisor in the local social welfare office. Beth, while not as fashionably attired as Paul ("we can only afford one clotheshorse in the family"), is always seen in something tasteful which shows her girlish, athletic figure to its best advantage. After two miscarriages early in their marriage, Beth and Paul decided not to try further for children. They have contented themselves with a life full with work, recreation and good friends whom they enjoy. They have also contented themselves with what they both describe to be an active, healthy sex life. Each had a brief affair shortly after their decision not to have a family. The affairs were openly acknowledged between them, and while not affirming that there wouldn't be further such dalliances they nonetheless seemed to have found sexual contentment within their marriage for the last fourteen years. That is, until two years ago. For the last two years neither has been satisfied nor content with their sexual relationship. As Paul tells their story his concerns began as long as three years ago.

"There is no denying that sex has always been a big part of the relationship that Beth and I have. From those days we were first together in college, there was just something electric. Seems like we would just look at each other and hop into bed, just like that.

"The thing about the kids was a big disappointment, sure, and I guess for a while our sex life slacked off a little bit. Then as we got adjusted to the kind of freedom we'd have as partners without any kids, freedom to go anywhere, do anything, any time we wanted, well then it picked up again and our sex became better than ever and I guess maybe even more important than ever in our marriage. It was as though if we couldn't have kids we were going to have great sex and we did. I don't know what's normal, I never have paid attention to those studies or anything like that. I would guess we had sex four or five times a week one way or another—not always intercourse, you understand, but well, everything else. We're both into oral sex and plenty of just plain old fucking, too.

"Then about three years ago I began to notice that I just didn't want it like I always did, the desire just wasn't there. There wasn't any change in Beth. She looked just as good as she always had and she was as good in bed as she always was, it was just that I really didn't have the desire. We kept up the pace, or I kept up the pace, but more often than not it was out of a sense of duty, something I ought to do rather than something I really wanted to do. I'd think, 'I ought to make her come tonight, it's been over a week.' Before, all I had to do was look at her in a pair of shorts or a bathing suit and I got hot, just like that. Now during that time, when I looked at her nothing happened, and I felt guilty about it. I felt as though something should happen and it didn't. I wasn't interested in any other women, I mean I wasn't out chasing around, so there wasn't anybody else who was taking all my sexual energy. I just didn't have any sexual energy.

"We went on that way for I guess about a year, and I don't think that there was any noticeable difference as far as Beth was concerned. Maybe I didn't seek her out for sex quite as often, but every time she wanted it I was there and tried to just go on as usual. Then after about a year of pretending, it got to where I couldn't even pretend any longer. I couldn't perform. I mean I just couldn't get it up, and when I did get it up I couldn't keep it up long enough to satisfy Beth or myself. Talk about guilt. That's when I really got mad. We'd get into bed and Beth would do everything she knew how to do—hands, mouth, everything —and nothing would happen. There for about a year the only satisfaction I could give her was orally and I got little or no satisfaction at all. Of course it really didn't last a whole year because as soon as I realized what was happening to me I began to find all sorts of ways to avoid having sex at all. I can remember one of my favorite tricks was to fall asleep in front of the TV, kind of midway through the evening. When that didn't work, I'd stay late at the store until after Beth had gone to bed so there wouldn't be any chance of us being in bed both awake at the same time. Oh yeah, before we used to have sex a lot in the mornings—that was one of my favorite times, and we'd wake up and kinda roll into each other and celebrate the morning, but when I was going through this time when I was impotent, what I did was to get up real early in the morning and go off jogging or to a business meeting. I would try to get out of the house before she was aroused—before she got up so we wouldn't have to have that embarrassing time when we were both together in bed and something was expected of me. I guess that was just really it. I felt as though something was expected of me—I knew something was expected of me as a husband— something should have been expected of me sexually that I just couldn't deliver.

"During that stretch, that was the only time I tried another woman, actually a couple of women, both of them gals who work in my building and had a reputation of being pretty easy. Even with them I couldn't do anything, whether it was the guilt or the problem itself I don't know, but those were some pretty embarrassing moments. I mean there can only be one reason you're naked in a motel room with a strange woman and if you can't even do that, you're in pretty sorry shape. I know now that Beth was going through pure hell all that year wondering what had happened to me—what had happened to us, but to be honest, at the time I was so wrapped up in what was happening to me that I didn't think too much about what she must have been going through. I bet we went almost a whole year and didn't have sex more than six or seven times, if that. It was at the end of about a year of that period that we decided to take a vacation, go to the Caribbean and try to get it all sorted out. We both thought that a second honeymoon, a romantic spot with lots of sun and fresh air, would bring back the sex spark that was so missing in our marriage at that time. But when we got there it was even worse than ever. Here again I was in a place where I knew the purpose was to screw and I couldn't. The best thing about that trip was that despite the frustrations and the bitterness and the tears and the arguing, probably because of all that, we really began to talk about the problem and we finally decided to seek out some help. When we first got back we ran out and bought *The Joy of Sex*. We must have tried every page in that book four or five times, and for a while there was some improvement; Beth has a marvelous imagination and a real willingness to try just about anything, lotions, mechanical things, you name it, we did it. There was some improvement but there wasn't any real change. I still didn't feel much desire. I still wasn't able to perform, but Beth's patience and perseverance really carried us through. She wasn't demanding, she wasn't demeaning, she was just caring and understanding and that caring and understanding convinced me to finally go see a therapist. There we both learned that for lots of men my age there are changes in our ability to perform as a sex partner and sometimes a guy can overreact to those changes and get defensive, guarded and depressed. I'm quite certain now that's what happened to me. There were changes and I overreacted to those changes. I felt the loss of desire and the guilt associated with that projected itself into a loss of ability. Working with the therapist, taking things slowly and smoothly, we reestablished a strong, positive sexual relationship. Oh, it's nothing like it was before, don't get me wrong, but it's very good and very healthy and we both have a new understanding of the role of sex in our marriage, and I think we're stronger than ever for it.''

Beth wholeheartedly agrees with Paul's assessment that they have a new appreciation of sex in their marriage and a new strength in their marriage because of what they've been through. She tends to minimize the role of her own patience in the situation, saying, ''I love Paul and I believed that he still loved me, and though we may have had problems in bed, that's the only place we had any problems and everything else was good enough and strong enough to make me want to work out those problems, so we did.'' Beth's most revealing comments, and perhaps the comments that are most helpful to other middle-aged couples who may experience some of what Beth and Paul experienced, have to do with her feelings when Paul's impotence first became really noticeable.

''I really think my reaction was pretty much typical of how any woman might react. I couldn't understand what could be happening to this warm, loving man, this sexy man. For most of our married life I thought he never could get enough. He was always hard and ready for me. Don't get me wrong, I was perfectly happy with that, it just seemed that he was insatiable. All the time, anytime, anywhere, he just wanted it and I loved it so we did it. To all of a sudden have that turn around to where he began to find excuses for not making love to me, began to avoid any time or place where we might make love, that hurt so much. I know he thinks he was fooling me, but he didn't fool me for a minute. I knew why he went to bed so early. I knew that there couldn't be all those morning meetings. I knew he didn't have to stay up late, but as I started to tell you, I think I reacted like any other woman. I figured that it was *me,* that something about me had changed and he wasn't attracted to me anymore or I wasn't sexy for him. I tried everything. I dressed sexier. I ran around with little or nothing on and I took every opportunity to feel him up or go after him, but those only seemed to drive him further away. Of course now I understand why nothing I did worked, but at the time I didn't.

"When none of that worked I decided that it definitely *was me* so I began to test that out. I flirted with four or five men, some at work and even some friends of ours from the neighborhood. I know it sounds terrible but I really teased them along to see if I could get them excited, if I could get them turned on. I could, so much so that I did go to bed with two of them just once, but I did that because I felt so guilty about what I was doing to them, and besides, to go all that time without any real sexual attention, without feeling desired or wanted by anybody and all of a sudden to have someone really want you. Well, it felt pretty good so I went ahead. Once I felt firm in my belief that there had been no change in me, that I was still as much of a woman, as sexually attractive as I ever had been, then I really began to feel that there was something seriously wrong with Paul.

"I honestly think that for me and for other women, they have to somehow, we have to somehow come to grips with the idea that it's not us, it's not a reaction against us, against our looks and our sexuality and our attractiveness. It's the *man's* problem. Certainly we become victims of that problem but to the extent that we take it on and say 'it's my fault' we victimize ourselves. Once I came to the realization that it wasn't me but Paul, then I could throw myself wholeheartedly into helping Paul. As long as I thought that it might be me I couldn't help him. I could only be bitter that he would reject me after all we had meant to each other, or bitter that he found some other woman more attractive. When I realized that he was not rejecting me, that he was rejecting sex, that there was no other woman, that I was still attractive and sexy and desirable, then I could focus on helping him and that's when we began to make some progress. So that's my lesson for other women. You need to realize that it's a way that middle-aged men react to sex and to women and it's not you."

Many men choose to respond to the threats to their virility which come in mid-life by going to great lengths to avoid the source of the threat—avoid contact with women, avoid sex. Rather than taking corrective action, which is so easily done where the issue is vanity, a great number of middle-aged men simply try to avoid threats to their own sexuality by avoiding sex. It appears that instead of changing or seeking help, which would be an implicit admission of a problem, many men choose to avoid situations where they are confronted with the problem. This obviously places severe strain on their relationships with women, strain which can appreciably affect the way they behave toward women.

The evidence suggests that for the majority of men the threat to their virility is not rooted in major physiological changes. Rapid cessation of gonadal functioning is relatively rare among middle-aged men. However, surface physiological changes, changes in hair, weight, skin and muscle tone are common to nearly all middle-aged men as is a gradual diminishing of libido or sex drive. It seems clear that many middle-aged men overreact to these minor physiological changes and in so doing, create for themselves major psychological and sexual problems. For the most part, the women involved with these men become passive participants in the problem. Through no fault of their own they find themselves avoided and their every attempt to reconcile the problem through their own sexual advances seems only to be all the more threatening and to bring about more rejection.

At times, of course, the behavior of the woman can contribute to the cause, can initiate a crisis in virility. This is particularly true for many middle-aged men who have difficulty dealing with the liberated sexuality of today's women. Many middle-aged women who have had their political and/or sexual conscious- ness raised by the women's movement expect new behaviors from their sex partners and middle-aged men often wilt (literally and figuratively) in the face of these demands. One wife wrote:

''For most of my life as a girl and as a young woman I thought that my duty, that's right, my duty in sex was to make my man come, that was the goal—for him to get off. I don't think I'm unusual in this. I think most of us women were raised that way. I put my own satisfaction second to his and I was willing to do anything, whatever it took to satisfy him. Then through my involvement in the women's movement, first with a lot of read- ing, things like *The Hite Report* and *Female Sexual Fulfillment,* things like that and then talking with other women, sisters, I came to realize that I have every bit as much right to expect an orgasm as he does. Once I accepted that I began to demand it. I think Fred was clearly threatened by that. I stopped faking an orgasm when he came. I stopped telling him how big he was and how great it was when it wasn't. I told him right out after he was done that *I* wasn't satisfied and I didn't want him going to sleep until he had satisfied me. I know that threatened Fred. He told me as much and he began to just shrivel up, couldn't get it up. But that's not my fault. I can't be blamed for that. I gave him enough and it's only fair to expect that he should give me enough in return. I know he went looking for other women, probably younger women who wouldn't be quite so demanding of him and who might give him some sense of being virile. He just doesn't understand what a middle-aged woman needs and he's not willing to change to give it to me so I'll have to find it somewhere else.''

Darlene is particularly forthright in expressing the change in her own sexual needs and the way these changes affected her middle-aged husband. But many others, men and women alike, have commented on the changing nature of women's sexuality as a factor in the male mid-life crisis. This is a relatively recent phenomenon; heretofore it has always been assumed that it was the absence of sexual liberation in a marriage partner which drove the middle-aged man to other women. This pattern is still seen in the male mid-life crisis and is reported by men to be far more prevalent than threats posed by the sexually active wife. Moreover, this pattern seems to have more serious repercussions for the middle-aged man's relationships with other women. The response to the threat to the man's virility which is presented by the inattentive, unattractive wife is often to strike out at the threat, to affirm virility by being virile. Roy Cain is a case in point.

Roy Cain is a man like most middle-aged men, not unusually attractive, but not unattractive, not successful, but not unsuccessful, not old, but not young—a middle-aged, middle-class, middle American. Roy works at the regional headquarters of a large insurance company. He is a claims superintendent overseeing about twenty-five file clerks, most of whom are young girls with high school or junior college educations. Roy has had this position for the past eight years. At forty-six, he realizes there is really nowhere else in the company for him to go, and indeed he has little ambition to go further. The company pays well, has an excellent benefit program and provides him with a reasonable amount of status in his community. His is not really challenging work but it at least gives him a sense of competence about what he does. Roy has been married for twenty-six years, has a daughter, married and raising a family of her own. He has a son who is in college. Roy and his wife, Noreen, had settled down to a quiet life with an occasional bridge game with friends, a trip to Florida every summer and thoughts of grandchildren and retirement. Then he confronted crisis.

The first ripple on the surface was a visit by one of Roy's clericals to the Vice-President of Personnel of Roy's company. As the personnel officer later remarked, "It seemed like such a relatively small thing at the time, one of those minor indiscretions that most of us commit at one time or another in our careers. In this case it happened to offend one of the girls in Roy's section. We had had an air-conditioning failure in one section of the building and even when we got it back on it wasn't coming on too strong. To help out we requisitioned some fans and put them out there in Roy's section. The fans were blowing the papers all about and everything and what with the noise and the breeze they were creating a little bit of a problem. This one girl went into Roy's office and as she reports it [reading from file copy], 'I went to Mr. Cain and told him that I couldn't get my work done being blown on all day like that. He said, "If you blow on me all day you won't have to get any work done. I'll see to that." I walked right out of there and told a couple of the other girls. I was really upset. Just because he's my boss, doesn't mean he can talk to me like that. The other girls told me he'd said things of the same kind to them and that I should come and tell you.' [End of file copy.]

"As I said it seemed at the time a kind of minor indiscretion. Whenever you have a lot of young girls being supervised by men you're going to have some of that sort of thing go on. After a while, everybody knows it's just good-natured teasing and nothing more is said about it. In this case I guess we should have done more. There weren't any reports for about two months, then I had a visit from three girls in Roy's section. All three claimed that Roy had touched them in a sexual manner, two of them said he had caressed their bottoms as they were bent over files. The third girl said that he had placed his hand up her dress, put his other hand on her breast and said 'Guess who?' They all claimed that this was not a onetime occurrence, in fact all of the girls in his section had had something or other like that happen. They strongly asserted that no one had done anything to lead Roy on. This was quite a little bit more serious than the last incident and I decided to check into it further. The first thing I noticed was that Roy's section had had a higher than normal turnover among clericals. We didn't seem to be able to keep them in there very long. Then, too, as I talked to some of the older, respected female employees not in Roy's section, but in his same part of the building, I discovered that it was pretty common knowledge among them that Roy made advances toward the girls who worked for him. We just can't have that sort of thing going on here so I brought Roy in for a talk. He assured me that he would get squared away again, that he had been having a little trouble at home but it was all over now and we wouldn't have to worry any longer on his account. I told him that we would be watching extra carefully and that he couldn't afford to make any more mistakes in that regard. We transferred the girls out of his section and left it at that."

Roy recalls that time at the office with a real note of embarrassment, curiously enough *not* over his behavior toward the girls but because it was at the office. "That stuff at the office was really dumb but I learned a good lesson from it. I've been straight as an arrow there ever since but I'm having a hell of a good time elsewhere. As I remember it, that was when I was going through the very roughest part of this whole thing and I was into a lot of crazy stuff, not really making good decisions about where and when to do what and to whom. I've smartened up a whole lot in the year or so since that time and I'm better off for it.

"For me, it was a gradual sort of thing which picked up steam and once it got rolling there was no stopping it. I was going to live a different life. Like any other man who grew up in the thirties and forties, like just about every man in my generation, I'd been an observer of the sexual revolution, the change in young women, the change in their attitudes, the way they dress (I know for certain that three of the girls in my unit never wear *any* underwear at all, bra or panties, and I'd be willing to bet that over a dozen never wear a bra). Well, when I was growing up and courting you just didn't see that kind of thing. At first when they started to show up in my unit I pretended there wasn't any difference, like I didn't even notice them. After a while you just can't pretend any longer, it's not as though you have to seek it out—it's all around you everywhere you look. You don't have to read the girlie magazines or go to the peep shows. Why, all you have to do is go to work or walk around the neighborhood or read *Time* or *Newsweek* and watch the television shows and you see more stuff in one day than I ever saw in my whole lifetime when I was younger. Well, as I said, for the longest time I just watched and got a kick out of seeing a little ass here and a little tit there. I had my fantasies but not much more than that. I did notice after a while that sometimes when I was making love to Noreen and having a hard time with it, you know, not being able to get excited about her and everything, not that's she's not a nice-looking woman, but, well those girls, well, they're so firm and so young and sexy—they just look like they want it all the time and Noreen never ever had that look. Well, anyway, sometimes when I was making love to Noreen I'd think about those girls. That seemed to make it go a whole lot easier, and then after a while I got excited just thinking about those girls, I'd get an erection whether I was with Noreen or not, thinking about them would turn me on. Between that and Noreen, well, our sex life was really just getting bad. We'd be right in the middle, going hot and heavy, and I'd be about to shoot and she'd tell me about some special they had at the grocery store. That may sound funny but I'm not kidding you. Half of the time we were making love she'd be picking at little skin marks on my back or pulling the gray hairs out of my head —there just wasn't much of a thrill there for either of us and I just couldn't get it on with her anymore. I knew it wasn't me because I could get turned on by these girls, but still I was a little bit afraid that it *might* be it. It might be *me* and not Noreen. I decided to see what this sexual revolution was all about.

"At first, it was just all talk—you know, making some sort of off-color jokes with the girls at work. I really think they enjoyed it. I honestly do, at least none of them ever said anything about it to me. All of this time I just couldn't get it up, couldn't get turned on with Noreen, but whenever I thought about those young girls and the way they looked, that did the job for me. I got hard and I got hot. Then I guess I did carry it a little too far, especially there at work. You've probably talked to the boss and know what happened. I felt some of the girls up a little and a couple of them didn't mind it but apparently some of them did. They went to the boss and told him what was going on. By the time he called me in on it, I had already pretty much decided that wasn't the place for me to get into the action anyway. You see, by that time I'd met some other girls, not at the office, although I did meet them through one of the girls at the office. She came up to me and said that she didn't mind my attention toward her, in fact she kind of liked it. She liked the thought that she turned a man on but she preferred I wouldn't do that around the office. I asked if there wasn't someplace I could see her besides the office. She told me about a club that she and a lot of her friends went to so I started going to that club and picking up on some of her friends and, yeah, sleeping around with them. Boy, I soon realized that there was nothing wrong with me at all. All I had to do was get with one of those young girls and I could do it all night long and I usually did. Noreen and I just got further and further apart, I mean that it got to the place where there was just nothing there, nothing that made me feel like a man. It was one of those girls, Sherry, that I really hit it off with so I left Noreen and I've been with Sherry ever since. You have to understand what Sherry means to me. Here I am getting up in years and seeing everybody so young and so alive around me and I figure somebody as young and good-looking and sexy as Sherry wants to pay attention to me, then I can't be all that bad! I must have something pretty good going for me even if it is just my cock. I'm happy to have somebody want me for that and Sherry does. Here I thought I was pretty much of a dud in bed but Sherry thinks I'm a real stud. She says I'm the 'biggest and the best she's ever had.' You wouldn't believe the difference between her and Noreen in that way. In bed there's nothing like her. She scratches and bites and yells. She's a wild woman and she makes me feel like a wild man, a feeling I never had with Noreen even when I was young. Now to have that feeling when I'm middle-aged and all, well I just wouldn't go back for anything.''

Roy may have given a great deal of thought to the change in his life and the role Sherry played in his return to virility. Sherry's view of their relationship is much simpler. ''I like to screw and I like to screw Roy. It's as simple as that. Sure he's old, but he doesn't hassle me and if it makes him feel good, well so much the better. I don't see that it's hurting anybody. His wife never gave him what he wanted and he was just going to grow old and limp with her. I can give him what he wants. I can keep him hard and young. Isn't that what it's all about?''

What about Noreen? Who's to give her what she wants? What she most wants now is some relief from the bitterness and hurt that she feels over Roy's leaving. She recognizes that her own sexual inhibitions may have pushed Roy into crisis and ultimately away from her, but fears that it's now too late. Noreen writes:

''It's been exactly a year since Roy told me he didn't know what he felt for me and for me to just leave him alone. We've been married twenty-six years. When he told me this he had been under severe pressure at work for ten months, why, I don't know. As soon as it was over, he changed in personality and everything. He told me how rotten I've been and told me everything that was wrong for thirty years—even before we were married. He was justified in some cases. I did not show enough affection nor as often as I should have. I didn't think he had any reason to complain about our sex life—only that I never showed him a hug or a kiss—he did it all, but he said our sex life was nothing. I was wrong but I've changed and I love him very much. I've been in counseling for a few years, that made me first like myself—problems from childhood. He stayed here from March to this November, and then he left. He did not take his clothes with him and has not returned for them. He bought some presents for Christmas, my birthday, anniversary and 'sweethearts' day. He pays all the bills. He doesn't want any contact with me. I can only reach him at work. I don't know where he lives or stays or anything else. I don't feel yet there is another woman, and I don't think he left for that reason, although I know he needs lots of sex. He's really broken all contact with everyone including family, and our daughter and son. He does contact them finally once in a while or they contact him, but it's not the same. I've gone out and found a part-time job for five hours a day and go out with my women friends. He won't talk over this situation at all with me. I've tried and he just changes the subject, or just says he doesn't want to talk about it. He's felt this way, as I say, for a year. He used to, while he was at home, disappear for two to four days at a time. He'd just go and not show up. And he didn't want me to ask or question him at all. He'd come back with the same clothes and unshaven. He's forty-six years old and he's had a lot of pressure. From work, from our children, you name it—they've done it. I've been sick physically and I had a nervous breakdown a few years ago and he's had the pressures of bills, also. After my breakdown I've had a lot of help from counseling. What can I do for this man? I want to save our marriage—I want to be a good wife to him, and to love him with all my heart, but I just can't accept some of the sex things he wants. The next twenty years could be the best in our life, if he'd give me the chance to try and prove it to him. I've been strong this whole year and the four months he's been gone, but now I cry very much.''

Noreen is not alone in her tears or her fears. Many women of Noreen's generation, middle-aged women, have commented about their fear that in looks and behavior they are not competitive with the younger women for the attention and affection of middle-aged men. Many of them choose not to be competing for those attentions, but others ask: ''How can I keep my husband from turning to younger women?'' Their stories are among the most tragic, their attitudes among the most anguished of all mid-life crisis cases. They are so torn by the consequences that they are often blind to the causes and their own role in those causes. Carol Shirnel writes of her husband and in so doing speaks for many middle-aged women.

"Jimmy was fifty-four February 4th. He is very good looking and proud of his build. Not so proud of either his gray hair or receding hairline. He is the oldest child of three boys, and is . . . no, *was* perfect in his mother's eyes. Anything Jimmy did was perfect and she did not think he could do any wrong. Jimmy's mother was definitely the domineering factor in their family. His father died four years ago. I will be forty-nine August 1, the youngest of five children. I am not beautiful, but not homely, although I do have a fairly good figure, I guess. This was always very important to Jimmy. He hated obesity and always said he thought anyone was sick to let themselves get fat.

"We were married November 29th, 1947. We had very little money, so went through the financial problems that come with accumulating two boys, raising them, working very hard to gain what assets we have.

"Looking back, I first realized a change in Jimmy in his lack of sexual desire. His drive has never been as strong as mine, but it dropped off to practically nothing, almost overnight. At first I thought this might be due to pressures on the job. He works for the papermill in the cutting fields, supervising a crew, and is very proud that he has gone as far as he has. In February we took a vacation in Mexico, but it did nothing to relieve the situation.

"Then I thought maybe hitting his birthday may have been the problem and time would take care of it. Toward the latter part of March, a friend came in for coffee and we got to talking about this other friend who was leaving her husband and whom I had been befriending. I said I liked her and felt I should help her. She said, 'Oh, so does Jimmy.' Well, anyway, it was quite a conversation. I couldn't believe anyone would consider that Jimmy would be interested in anyone else as he has never been a chaser.

"That night I mentioned it to Jimmy and the reaction was

completely abnormal for him. You've heard the old saying 'Methinks you protesteth too much.' At that time I asked him not to take her on his crew and he let me know I wasn't about to tell him who to hire or not to hire, etcetera. Well, he did hire her on his crew the following month. We were not able to discuss her with each other without getting angry as he kept insisting there was no interest in her for him. As a matter of fact, when he filed for divorce over a year ago, he was still insisting there was nothing between them. Yet, while I was on a trip back east in January a year ago, he took her to Reno for the weekend. We have a 27-foot travel trailer and he moved this up near her house. She lived on the compound in a rented house. He spent most of his time there, after he left home.

"As soon as he took her on his crew, he started having trouble on the job. The other guys do not like her at all, and recognize her for what she is. As a matter of fact, I know of only one friend she has whom she can visit with at all. Soon after Jimmy left he took all of our money out of savings and the first thing he bought was a sports car. I understand that is typical of this thing. The rest he spent on her and her girls. She has three girls. The oldest two live with them. The youngest is twelve years old and went back to her dad. The other two are fifteen and seventeen. He recently bought them a new Mustang.

"A little over a year ago we didn't have any debts. Now Jimmy is in debt about $55,000. Five years ago he wanted to sell (and did) our home out at the ranch as he said he was too old to be paying on a mortgage. It was for $13,500 at four percent interest. He wanted to sell out there and buy a smaller house in town.

"Jimmy used to be respected and admired. While we didn't really have any close friends, we had many very good friends of all ages. His relatives and us got along very well. Now he feels they don't like him, although he goes to see them and takes her with him. He knows they don't like her.

"What can I do to get him back? How long will he want to be with someone that is so below him in every way? Will he get to the point where her youth is not enough to apparently elevate his ego, and how much do her young girls enter into it? These are some of the thoughts and questions that I ask myself a dozen times a day.

"I don't believe I mentioned that this person he is with is about five feet one and weighs about 165 pounds. She is thirty-four years old."

For every woman like Carol or Noreen, who have lost their husbands in mid-life to younger women and who openly express the anguish they feel, there are countless others who fear and suffer in silence, persevering through problems they don't understand. It is impossible to generalize in these cases. It simply cannot be said that every middle-aged man will seek to affirm his virility with a younger woman. Nor can it be said that a wife who does not adopt more aggressive, affectionate sexual behavior will drive her middle-aged husband to a younger woman. Younger women are not the threat; they are *one* response *some* middle-aged men choose when their virility is threatened, by their own changing looks and/or sexual performance (which *may* be related to the performance of their partner). Understood in this context, this particular mid-life crisis, which seems to be the single most difficult crisis for men and women to discuss and resolve constructively, may be seen as less devastating, as not necessarily destructive. Discussions of the mid-life crisis in virility which are dominated by stories such as Roy and Noreen's or Carol and Jimmy's do more to discourage mutual resolution by heightening fears and a sense of resignation. There is a need for a balanced presentation and perspective on the *many* possible threats to a middle aged man's vanity and virility and the many possible responses available to him, be it corrective action, avoidance, affirmation.

The vain male is particularly vulnerable during his middle years. His body is changing despite almost all efforts that he takes to forestall change or to alter its course. The vain male whose ego is also invested in his sense of virility, in his machismo, is particularly vulnerable. Wherever he looks in society he finds implicit if not explicit threats to his virility, challenges to his sexuality. Younger women seem to taunt him with their more openly sexual dress, attitudes and behavior. Older women, awakened to their own sexual needs by women's political and social movements, demand that he be a more responsive sex partner. All of this at a time when his own desire and abilities may be on the decline. For many middle-aged men these threats cannot go unanswered. They cannot turn to other dimensions of themselves beyond sexuality to find solace in an alternative source of identity. Challenges to their sexuality are perceived as challenges to who they are. The crisis they experience seems only answerable in terms of change in their behavior. For some of these middle-aged men it is to make only those changes which help them to maintain the appearance of youth. Like Carl Foster, these men alter their dress, weight, hair as they seek to correct the effects of age. Some, like Carl, go beyond cosmetic changes to adopt more youthful ways of thinking and behaving. For most of these men sexuality is not at issue. Yet the number of men who can detach their own vanity from their virility is very small. Most men associate physical appearance with sexual performance, not in their perception of women (although women with "good" figures are assumed to be better sex partners than women with "poor" figures), but in their perception of themselves. Thus, for most middle-aged men, physiological changes, whether cosmetic or not, represent potential threats to virility.

The effects of these threats to the middle-aged man's vanity/ virility are among the most dramatic and traumatic to be found in the files of mid-life crisis cases. Responses range all the way from avoidance of the threat—avoiding sex, avoiding relationships which may have a sexual dimension—to attacking the threat, affirming through behavior that there is no threat, verifying virility by sexual conquest, typically with younger women.

Common to all of these responses, despite their varied consequences, is the apparent inability and/or unwillingness of middle-aged men to acknowledge their crises and the consequent difficulty of working with women to a constructive resolution of the crises. In discussing the vanity/virility crisis of middle-aged men, it is clear that for most middle-aged couples there does not appear to be a climate in which men and women can deal openly and honestly with the inevitable changes in their lives. It is clear that any efforts at constructive resolution of mid-life crises (whatever the cause) must begin with creating a climate for communication. Wherever this climate is not present, the middle-aged male will not feel free to acknowledge his problems and any interaction toward resolution with a woman will be riddled with threats, accusations and recriminations. By contrast, where couples such as Paul and Beth, through whatever means, have managed to arrive at a mutual acknowledgment of the problems the middle-aged man faces and some understanding of the causes, the chances for constructive resolution are greatly improved. Many couples like Paul and Beth have been able to work together patiently and persistently toward solutions to the mid-life crisis, recognizing at all times the strength and value of what they once had, attempting less to restore the old than to discover new forms and new functions for their relationship.

This is not to say that these crises *can* always be resolved within the context of an existing relationship, or even to imply that they *should* be resolved. In a great many instances, the mid-life crisis of vanity/virility serves as a catalyst to disclose basic flaws in a relationship—flaws which have evolved over time and flaws which in themselves are the most serious threat to the relationship far beyond the threat the mid-life crisis presents. Individuals do grow, and as often as not they do not grow at the same pace in the same direction. Individuals change in terms of their own sexual needs, desires and preferred expressions. These changes often create deep, yet unspoken, unacknowledged chasms between men and women. The mid-life crisis coming as it does on the heels of these changes only serves to draw attention to the chasms which already exist. The frantic, frenetic attempts to return to something that has not been for some time (and perhaps never was) only serve to deepen and widen the chasm in the relationship. There are numerous cases where the mid-life crisis was a catalyst to separation and divorce and was reported by all involved to be a catalyst to a new and happier life alone, or with new partners. This is noted here only as a means of underscoring that oftentimes the mid-life crisis cannot be resolved within the framework of the existing relationship. Without fundamental alterations in the nature of that framework it may be necessary to leave the relationship. This pattern of separation as solution was seen first in responses to the goal-gap mid-life crisis, where many men reported that their crisis led them to see the need to leave their work and organization only to find their careers reawakened in new jobs with new companies. Similarly, for many men and women, husbands, wives and lovers, the mid-life crisis can heighten awareness of the need to leave a relationship which no longer is satisfying and no longer has the potential to satisfy. In these instances, separation may be at least part of the solution.

As difficult as it is to reach acknowledgment and resolution of the vanity/virility crisis for middle-aged men, there is much to be learned here that can be applied to the resolution of other crises with other causes.

5

The Empty Nest

THE "EMPTY NEST" has long been associated with mid-life crises of women, more specifically with menopausal changes. It has been assumed that coincident with menopause many women also experience depression associated with the loss of the mother role as children grow and leave home. Now evidence is emerging which suggests that men, too, in the roles as husbands and fathers, can experience the empty-nest syndrome much like that experienced by women. A brief review of what is known about the syndrome from the study of women will aid understanding of it as a cause of mid-life crisis for men.

The empty-nest syndrome refers to a specific pattern of depression typically noticed in women between the ages of forty and sixty who have been mothers. This depression is generally believed to be caused by the family changes which occur when there are no children left at home and the woman loses her role as mother. Loss of this family role brings consequent loss of many other social roles related to motherhood. There is a sorority of mothers with attendant motherly activities and functions which can often totally consume the time and consciousness of its members. For women like these, who have relied upon their role as mother as the primary source of their self-identity, the offspring departing the home for lives of their own represents the end of a role and, if it's the *only* role, the removal of identity.

Mourning over the loss of identity and unable to find a new role, a new source of identity, these women often undergo very severe depression. A woman who has evaluated her womanhood exclusively in terms of her performance of these roles leaves herself vulnerable to the feeling that her life has lost purpose and meaning when the wife and mother roles are no longer relevant. Some specific studies have revealed interesting aspects of this post-parental pattern in middle-aged women. As might be expected, housewives have been shown to have a higher rate of depression than working women following their children's exit from the nest. Housewives do not have ready substitutes to supplant this loss. The working women, on the other hand, have other roles to be active in and to maintain their identity. It has also been observed that women who seem to be overprotective of or overinvolved with their children (the stage mother, whatever the child's area of activity) are more likely to be depressed in the post-parental period than women who do not have intense relationships with their children. Perhaps most interesting are the several studies which indicate that depression in the middle-aged woman is caused more by a lack of important significant personal and societal roles, and consequent loss of self-esteem, than it is due to the hormonal changes associated with menopause. This perspective is supported by research which indicates that in other cultures where the status of post-parental women rises rather than falls, middle-aged women do not experience predictable post-parental depression.

All of this evidence verifies one perspective of the male mid-life crisis which is being presented in these pages. The depression which women experience as a result of the empty nest is in direct relationship to the extent that they invest themselves and find their identity solely in their roles as mothers. It is no doubt because the empty nest has so long been associated with the menopausal woman that it has not been given proper attention as a potential cause of the male mid-life crisis. Such neglect is another manifestation of the chauvinism seen so often in discussions of the personal concerns of middle-aged men. The conventional thinking, among men at least, seems to be if women experience something it can have no relevance to men. Yet it is obvious that there are men who are as involved in their roles of husband and father as women are in the roles of wife and mother. It stands to reason that these men will be as prone to the depression which accompanies the empty nest as will women. Dean Narbor is one such man.

Dean and his wife, Betty, together with their children, Dean Junior and Elizabeth, epitomize the all-American family. Dean is a well-respected attorney in a mid-size, Midwestern town. Betty is active in civic and social groups. Dean Junior and Elizabeth are bright, attractive young adults, the kind of children every parent wishes their child would become: all-American kids. Beyond their excellent academic records, Dean Junior has been active in athletics since his grade school days and Elizabeth is an accomplished public speaker, winning awards throughout the state. Dean Senior is "Father of the Year" material. During the four years that Dean Junior was in high school, Senior (as he's often called within and outside the family) did not miss a single athletic contest. Whether it was a practice game, at home or away, he was at the sidelines whenever and wherever Junior took the field. Elizabeth, two years younger, received the same attention for her public speaking activities as Dean Junior did with his athletic endeavors. Senior traveled to every speech, every debate tournament, regardless of how near or how far. Oftentimes he drove the family station wagon loaded with Elizabeth and her friends who were to speak in some far corner of the state, leaving Friday afternoon and not returning until late Saturday night or early Sunday morning. During the two years that the kids were in high school together, Senior did little more than travel from one child's activity to another, managing to squeeze in business here and there, but clearly making his children, and all that was important to them, most important to him.

Dean Senior's attentions were well rewarded—not only with the performance of his children but with the genuine affection and admiration they had for him and appreciation for the sacrifices he made to give attention to them. Both Dean Junior and Elizabeth sought their father's advice on every issue from what classes to take, what reports to write, to whom they should date, and what to do on those dates. Theirs was the closest of all families, but that closeness is clearly past tense. Things began to change for the Narbors a little over a year ago. When Dean Junior graduated from high school, he enrolled in the local community college, continuing to live at home, continuing to enjoy his father's attentions and affections. He was, as always, ever active in athletics. He graduated from the community college at the same time Elizabeth graduated from high school and they decided to go away together to school at the State University. Senior supported this move, happy to see his children staying together, and particularly happy that they were enrolling in his own alma mater, even though it would be some distance from home. This was to be the children's last decision that was supported by their father. Betty Narbor gives a vivid picture of the chain of events that began that September when Dean Junior and Elizabeth left home.

"I'm afraid Senior had never really done anything to prepare himself for the time when the children would no longer be at home with us. I think that it came as a shock to him. One day they were here, bustling about the house as usual with their friends constantly in and out, so much activity, so much life, so much togetherness. The next day they were gone. I remember how that first week he came home every day for lunch, something he rarely did, just to be the first to get the mail, to see if the kids had written to tell what was going on, to see when they were coming home, when they wanted us down there. I know he called them a lot from the office a lot of times he didn't tell me about. The kids told me he called but they were seldom in. Both Elizabeth and Dean Junior got right into things and like any normal college kids they didn't hang around their room waiting for their father to call them. They were out meeting people and doing things. A lot of the things they were doing they did without Senior's approval. First of all there was the football deal with Dean Junior. He wasn't going to play at the University even though my husband wanted him to. Dean Junior said he'd had enough of athletics and was ready to do some other things. Then Elizabeth went through sorority rush even though my husband didn't want her to do that so soon. He felt she was giving up academics for an active social life. She felt she had been involved in academics long enough and wanted to have some sort of social life. I can understand that. I think that when your children go off to college it's time for them to begin to break away and start lives of their own, but Senior didn't feel that way at all. He still wanted to be as much a part of their lives as he was when they were here living at home and going to school down the block.

"I remember how he agonized waiting for them to invite us to come to school. They have a parents' weekend at the University that comes in the middle of October, after about six weeks of school. Senior felt certain that the children would want us there for parents' weekend, but they didn't invite us and of course all that time they didn't come home, not once—they were having too good a time. Finally, about two weeks after parents' weekend—this would have been about November, maybe two months, a little bit longer after they had gone down there, it was Homecoming. Of course we didn't need an invitation to go to Homecoming from the kids because after all, the University is *our* alma mater, so we had a big weekend full of plans, all around the children. Well, when we got there we found that they had a weekend full of plans, too, and none of it included us. Senior was so upset. He didn't like the children's friends, he felt that they had fallen in with a bad crowd. He was bothered by the fact they didn't want to do things with us and with their friends, the way we had always done when they were here at home. He was disturbed that Dean Junior was studying sociology instead of pre-law. He was bothered about how much time Elizabeth was spending with the sorority. Most of all I think that he just couldn't face the fact that his children were growing up and growing away.

"That was the most miserable Homecoming we ever had been

to. When we got home Senior went into this terrible depression and he's really been in it ever since. He seems always tired and listless. He never wants to go anywhere or do anything. I think he's drinking too much. I know he's not sleeping well and I wouldn't be surprised if it isn't beginning to affect his work, although there's no way I could know about that. Things between Dean and the children just get worse and worse. Lately they've been taking to not communicating with him at all, but just come right to me whenever they need money or want to tell us something, because every encounter with him just seems to lead to fighting, which only depresses him all the more. I keep telling him that if he doesn't let them grow up they will just go farther and farther away. What he always tells me in response is, 'They've already gone. I've lost them. How much farther away could they get?' I certainly think Dean is suffering from the empty nest. He's a father who has lost his flock and now that they are gone he feels like he's lost a part of himself.''

Dean's case is far from unique. A recent industrial survey of men in management positions questioned them about their major personal worries, workplace worries, and national worries. In the results, over one-third of the men said that their children were the principal personal worry. This high response may be partially explained by and blamed on the success of these men. It is possible that there is a relationship between success at work and the degree of a man's concern about his children. Most men can not boast of the record of attendance at their children's activities that Dean Senior reported. Fathers, whatever their walk of life or level of achievement, typically miss things like recitals, games, performances, forgoing these for the demands of work. Many men harbor feelings of guilt over their absence at these growing-up times, realizing too late that they can never be recaptured. They may feel that they have been less successful as a parent than they have been as a worker. This can lead to wondering at critical times in parenting if they have been as influential over their children as they wanted to be. ''Maybe if I'd been around more when they were growing up.''

Many middle-aged men express frustration in their attempts to pass on traditional work, family and personal values. Other men fear that what their children have learned in the home environment will be threatened and undermined by what they experience outside the home and long to protect them from those external forces as long as possible. As one man expressed it, "You do the best you can, but there is always the worry that something you have no control over is going to affect their lives." Or still another, "The standards of living and behavior are so different, sex, drugs and all, it's difficult for me to understand and accept them and even more difficult for me to help my children understand and accept them." Then there are those men who clearly and simply relish the affection and attention of loving children. The difficulty men have in developing close personal relationships is evident throughout the mid-life crisis literature. Unwilling and/or unable to seek these relationships at work or with friends, many men find them with their children. A man's children can serve as an outlet for the intimacy and caring that is blocked in his other relationships. With his children, his attention and affection is returned, measure for measure, no strings attached.

Whether a man's involvement with his children is a means to structure his time and activity (Dean Senior), a reflection of his concern for his influence over them, or a safe avenue for his own needs for caring relationships, it is evident that many middle-aged men find their identity in their role as father. It is tempting to draw this analogy with what is known about the empty-nest syndrome for women by applying it to middle-aged men. That is, once it has been established that many men may be as much identified by their roles as fathers as may women by their roles as mothers, it might follow that the reaction of these men to the empty nest will be (as it is for women) a depression syndrome. Here the comparison breaks down. It is clear from the research studies which substantiate personal case reports that the predominant response to the empty nest for middle-aged women is depression. It is equally clear that this depressive response is only one of many responses likely to be elicited from middle-aged men who are similarly struck by the empty-nest syndrome. The range of possible responses among middle-aged men stretches from depression at one extreme to freedom at the other. There can be a redirection in response to the relief felt following the removal of familial responsibilities which includes more active, aggressive postures toward the nest itself. There are two reasons why middle-aged men may respond to the empty nest with behaviors that are markedly different from the depression syndrome seen in the behavior of women. First, there may be a difference in causal effects. Not all men in crisis are responding to the loss of the father role; many are responding to the loss of the *husband* role. The female empty-nest syndrome is primarily a response to the loss of the mother's role. In the middle-aged man, however, it is often the loss of his role as a husband which brings about the behavior changes associated with the empty nest. This is increasingly true as women more and more often, and earlier and earlier, turn some of their attention and energy away from home and spouse and seek their identity in the world of work. Thus, in order to understand the middle-aged man's response to the empty nest it must first be determined whether he seems more affected by the loss of his role as husband or by the loss of his role as father, his reactions to each of these losses may be quite different.

The second major difference in the empty-nest syndrome for middle-aged men as opposed to women is that the male response may be at once more focused and more aggressive. Seldom do women act upon the cause, acting upon their children or other children as a release for the aggression they feel. More often women withdraw into themselves, hence the depressive syndrome. Responses of the middle-aged man are often quite different. In case after case, the empty nest manifests itself in behaviors directed against what is perceived by the man to be the source of his problem, be it children or working wives. These two dynamics, the alternative causes of the middle-aged man's empty-nest crisis, and the possibility of directed aggression, differentiate that response from responses in women.

The reactions of middle-aged men to the empty-nest crisis are as varied as are the family circumstances of the men. Nonetheless, in reviewing many, many empty-nest cases certain patterns do emerge. For both the loss of the father and the loss of the husband roles the most common response seems to be acceptance and subsequent depression. In those instances where the father role is at issue, middle-aged men are also likely to do one of the following: attempt to hold on to the father role; act against young people, rejecting them and their behaviors; seek those who will allow them to behave as a father. Where the loss of the husband role is at issue, in addition to the acceptance/depression, the middle-aged man may also engage in role reversal or act against women in roles other than wives. It should be understood that, as with the other forms of male mid-life crisis, the consequences of the empty-nest crisis are not inevitably negative. Many men report that rather than a sense of loss, they experienced great relief when their roles and responsibilities as husbands/fathers diminished. These men responded by viewing the loss of role as an opportunity to invest their newfound time and energy, to invest themselves in new interests and activities. The cases in the remainder of this chapter illustrate these many and varied responses to the empty nest crisis and, in doing so, enhance understanding of the causes of these crises and the potential consequences for middle-aged men and their families.

There is little doubt that most middle-aged men who invest their identity in the husband or father role, only to have this role taken from them and their identity threatened, passively accept the loss and the resultant diminished sense of self. This is the real source of the empty-nest syndrome depression—the diminished sense of self. Dean Senior is such a man who accepted his role loss as one might accept the death of a friend. He virtually went into mourning. For most of these middle-aged men, so identified as they are with being fathers or husbands, there is no fighting to forestall the loss or striking out against the source. There is instead a quiet, passive, acceptance of a lesser self. As Dean Senior wrote, "It's funny, I always knew that when they grew up they wouldn't be the same and things between us wouldn't be the same. But I never thought that when Junior and Liz grew up *I* would be so different. Now they've grown up and gone away and they took the best part of me with them.''

Of course not all middle-aged men accept the loss of the father role as passively as did Dean Senior. Just as some middle-aged men go to great lengths to put off aging, some go to great lengths to put off the loss of their influence as a parent. To keep the father role against all odds, some men refuse to let their children leave the nest, keeping them ''home'' by whatever means available to them.

Like Dean Narbor, Neil Sanders and his son, Steve, were very close throughout his son's growing years. That closeness remained even after graduation from college, as Steve got a job through his father in their hometown, married the daughter of Neil's partner and began a family of his own. Neil continued to monitor, nay, *manage* Steve's career, advising him which business clubs to join, what car to buy, how his wife ought to dress. He periodically gave Steve large sums of money as ''loans'' but the only real payment required was that Steve listen to his dad's advice. Finally the advice became too overbearing for Steve and he felt as though he had to leave town and leave his father to escape. This he did when he was twenty-five. He and his wife moved to the West Coast. It was the first major decision in his life that Steve had undertaken without seeking the advice of his dad. The move and what it meant devastated his father. As Neil describes what happened to him, ''When Steve moved out I was shattered. I guess I shouldn't say 'moved out,' but that's what it seemed like. He had been living out of the home for four or five years, what with college and then getting married and all, but he was still so close by I felt like he really hadn't moved out. We did all of those things together that fathers and sons do, fishing and hunting and going to the ballgames. Why lots of times I would stop by their house after work before I came home, just to check in and see how he was doing. I made sure that if he and Sherry needed anything or wanted anything I was right there to help them out with money or whatever. Then for him to take that job out on the West Coast without even telling me about it—it was a slap in the face.

"My first reaction was anger and Steve and I had a big argument—the first real argument we have ever had in our relationship. I said some things I probably shouldn't have about what he *owed* me, but at the time I felt them. Then I'm not too proud to admit this—in fact, I'm pretty ashamed—on the sly I did what I could to get the company in California to back off with their offer. I wanted them to tell Steve not to come. I made some calls, very subtle, but I made some calls and suggested that Steve would probably be taking over my business within a couple of years. But Steve told them that wasn't true and he was still going to move. Right after he moved I arranged my business so I could go out there. I guess I visited them every month for the first six months they were out there and I kept trying to get him to come back, to see that he had made a mistake. We would meet for dinner at a restaurant and get into terrible arguments. We never got through a meal without one of us leaving in disgust. Then I got sick. I had a heart attack and Steve came home. I know I could have recovered faster but it seemed to me (I only realize this looking back now) that as long as I wasn't well I could have Steve, my boy, right here with me where he belonged. As soon as I got well he'd go back to California and I'd lose him, so it's not as though I stayed sick, I just didn't get well. Then finally I guess Steve saw through the whole thing. He said he couldn't stay any longer, that he had a family, a career, a life of his own and he wasn't going to let me control that any longer. So he went back to California. For a year and a half we didn't talk to each other. Gradually, over time, I came to see what had happened to me, how wrong it was, how foolish I was to try to deny Steve the things I had so much enjoyed, raising my own family in my own way. Now we've reestablished contact and I think they're coming to visit us during the holidays. I think it's going to be all right. I think we're going to make it. We're not going to be the same kind of family, the relationship between Steve and myself will never be the same again, but it will be better than no relationship at all.''

Fathers like Neil seem to have as difficult a time keeping themselves out of the careers and marriages of their offspring as do mothers, although mothers' interventions get more attention. One curious piece of evidence in many of the cases of empty-nest crisis reported is the number of middle-aged men who see a role for themselves in managing the careers of their children, sons and daughters, much in the way that they might manage their own business. Middle-aged men often try to direct the marriages of their children either for better or worse. These marriage management efforts range from having husbands transferred out of the state (and in some instances, out of the country), to offering attractive cash settlements to wives to leave their sons. In some of the more subtle efforts middle-aged men exerted continual pressure for changes in the life-styles of their married children, some even making passes at their daughters-in-law as a way of convincing their sons that the wives were really no good for them. As an explanation for these behaviors, however bizarre they may seem on the surface, it must be remembered that for these men the key factor in their identity for many years has been the influence they hold over their children. They have expressed themselves by influencing what their children do, who they do it with, how they do it and for how long. To enjoy such a role for eighteen to twenty years, to delight in the respect and admiration that one reads in his children's response to such direction, then to have this role removed as the child leaves home for college or begins a family of his own is truly a traumatic experience for men who have so invested themselves in their identity as fathers. It is unfortunate but perhaps understandable that these men go to great lengths to attempt to retain some measure of influence over their children's attitudes, beliefs and behaviors. Overt attempts at continued influence are a primary and surprisingly persistent response to the mid-life crisis caused by the empty nest. Most children successfully thwart these attempts at influence by their middle-aged fathers, either by moving away and escaping or by confronting and openly rejecting their fathers' direction. For many middle-aged men who have invested themselves singularly in their father roles, this rejection results in direct actions against the source of their role and identity crises.

Wayne Zeist, forty-seven, had been a sales manager for a pharmaceutical supply firm. For fifteen years he had been one of the most successful sales managers in the company with a reputation as an excellent motivator. Year after year he took predominantly young, untrained employees right out of school and transformed them into skilled salespeople. Those who had been trained by Wayne continually referred to his excellent rapport with young people as the major factor in his success, and Wayne seemed to relish this relationship. About a year ago things began to fall apart in Wayne's territory. One of the young people closest to him at the time, Jerry Johns, tells what he saw happening. "It was almost an overnight thing. It seemed to happen so fast. One month Wayne was fun-loving as ever, joking around with all the new trainees, kidding them good-naturedly about their dress and their sex habits, the way he always did. That was one of the best things about Wayne. He really seemed to understand that young people were living differently and needed to live differently than a lot of other people in the company, and he could support that. Then one month things were just different. I remember a monthly sales meeting. We used to meet on the first Monday of every month with all the sales personnel. It was a time for us to meet as a group and deal with some issues which concerned the group as a whole, a time for us to compare performance and talk about direction—that sort of thing. Usually Wayne was at his best at these meetings. They were run efficiently and effectively and he always managed to give us some good solid instruction and training, along with taking care of business matters. I remember on this particular Monday Wayne got up there and started in on everything from politics to pants styles. He just went around the room and found something to dislike about everybody who was there. He used that as a takeoff point for saying the younger generation was going to hell, didn't understand what hard work was and had no appreciation for loyalty, tradition and no values that were worth a damn. I mean it was the sort of thing you would have expected to hear in the sixties and it was so unlike Wayne no one could believe it. He really got on to people about long hair and unprofessional dress and their sex habits outside the office. It was pretty bad. When we got out of there a lot of us talked over what had happened and the only thing we could figure was that maybe there was something wrong, going on with Wayne elsewhere, you know, maybe family or something. We felt sure it was a one-time thing and he'd probably get over it.

"But he didn't get over it. During that month Wayne visited all of the territories and it was more of the same one on one. The younger the salesman the harder Wayne was on them. He told two of the guys that if they didn't cut their hair he'd 'fire their ass.' He told our best saleswoman, who's only twenty-three, that the only reason she got so many orders was because she gave away a screw with every sale. As you can imagine, business went to hell in a hurry. In three months we lost accounts, sales went down dramatically, turnover went way up and after six months they let Wayne go. I understand why they let Wayne go. They had to. What I don't understand is why he started to attack all of us. What happened there? What went on? We didn't do anything. Nothing was different for us, but something sure was different for Wayne."

What was different for Wayne during that time was his relationship with his son, Bob. Ever since Bob had gone away to school he and his father had been growing apart and the physical changes in Bob did not help to ease the distance. He let his hair grow, was seldom seen in anything except jeans and a T-shirt, wore shoes only when absolutely necessary and in general adopted the laid-back life-style that seemed to be prevalent in his school. Bob was experimenting with drugs and sex, and his political views were changing rapidly as well. Each of these

experiments and changes was the occasion for a major argument
with his dad. Each argument only served to drive them farther
and farther apart but the crisis did not come until Bob dropped
out of school. At this point Wayne's wife, Louise, offers the
best recollection of what occurred.

"Things had been changing between Wayne and Bobby all
along, ever since Bobby went away to school. I didn't much
care for the way Bobby looked and acted either, but I thought it
was just one of those phases he went through and I remembered
that when Wayne and I were in college we were pretty wild
ourselves so I was willing to give Bobby time—but not Wayne.
Every little change in Bobby just seemed to make Wayne angrier and angrier. After we would see Bobby or speak with him
on the telephone Wayne would be irate for days, bumping
around the house, mumbling about kids these days and taking
every opportunity he had to put down young people. He always
was able to pull himself back together and find some saving
grace in the young people he worked with, but gradually even
they couldn't do anything right.

"Things really got terrible when Bobby left school. He took
the money set aside for his tuition and expenses and went off to
Europe. When Bobby did that his dad went a little crazy. Bobby
didn't even tell us—we learned from his roommate. We finally
got a postcard saying 'I figure at least here I can get away from
Dad.' That did it for Wayne. He became absolutely livid, not
just at Bobby but at all young people. Anyone who looked
young, dressed young, acted young, became an enemy and
Wayne tried to get back at every one of them for what Bobby
did to him. I heard the stories that they tell about how he was at
work with the young people there and I can believe it. Just from
the things he said around the house, I can believe it. It seemed
as if every young person, everyone with long hair on TV or in
the papers was the enemy and Wayne was on the attack. He
still is on the attack. He's got a new job now, one where he
doesn't have much to do with people, and I guess he's doing
okay, but he's just so bitter about Bobby. He doesn't even like

to think about it and he won't talk about it but I know just how bitter he is. I know how little it takes to get him started again, even though it's been almost a year now. Just the other day we were driving downtown and some young girl changed lanes in front of the car very quickly. I thought Wayne was going to have a heart attack. He got so angry and started yelling obscenities out the window at her, not because of what she had done but because she was young. God it's not her fault that she's young. It's not her fault that Bobby left. It's not her fault that Wayne can't get Bobby or any other young person to live the way he wants them to, but he took it out on her right there, yelling at her through the car window. I thought he was going to have a heart attack."

In Wayne's case his company was able to see the detrimental effects his behavior toward young people had on their performance and moved to do something about it. There are many other more subtle cases of middle-aged empty-nest fathers acting against young people, imposing their fatherhood on those who cannot escape it. Most of these efforts fall on young co-workers who, unlike their own real children, are bound to them through employment. Many middle-aged men set rigid dress codes at work: no pants suits for women; coat and tie for men; women must wear bras; men cannot have hair that grows beyond the shirt collar line; and on and on and on. Many of these rules represent attempts in some measure by the middle-aged man to exert parental control. More often than not these are not company policies, these are personal policies. As one middle-aged manager expressed it, "I long ago learned that I can't tell my kids how to dress, or talk or act and I can't fire them, either, but I can tell these young punks who work for me how to dress and talk and act and if they don't do it you can bet your ass I'll fire them."

Actions against young people, whether overt or more subtle, are a response to the empty-nest crisis frequently seen in middle-aged men. Even where there is no apparent action, many middle-aged men harbor a simmering anger toward young people that boils over at the slightest provocation. And middle-aged men find ample provocation today in the way young people look, dress, work and behave. As one wife commented, "It's such an embarrassment to go out. Martin acts as though every young person we see is involved in some conspiracy with our kids to hurt him, reject him. At restaurants, at the movies, he's always so angry saying things just loud enough so others can hear. Like, 'I wouldn't let my daughter out of the house dressed like that!' The young people will turn to look and that just goads Martin on. It's gotten so bad that we just don't go anywhere where there's likely to be young people, we try to avoid them. It's really better that way."

Many middle-aged men find, like Martin, that the easiest response to the empty nest is simply to avoid young people. This seems to be the preferred response of those who are angry but not actively aggressive, disappointed but not deeply depressed by being rejected by their children. There is a minority of middle-aged men left with empty nests who neither withdraw nor fight against the odds to maintain influence over their children. These men simply seek out those who will continue to let them behave as fathers. There is a powerful positive side to this response. Numerous youth groups from the Rainbows to the Boy Scouts have benefited from the avid interest and leadership of men who continue their involvement long after their children have ceased participating. There are hundreds of middle-aged men who give their time and energy to youth groups in exchange for being allowed once again to be a father figure. Not all such involvements of middle-aged men with younger people are so wholesome and healthful. Some of these men seek out father-daughter relationships with younger women that raise eyebrows and can bring ruin to other relationships. Dr. Leo Landy is described by his wife, Vivian, as such a "daddy figure."

Vivian Landy writes of her husband, "My husband is fifty-four years old. We have been married thirty-four years and have six sons. After medical school he began here with a group of three doctors which has now grown to nine physicians and two anesthetists. There are about eight or nine nurses and clerical workers in the office. The last two years my life has been a real nightmare, but actually I know this has been going on for four years. Four years ago our last son left home. Leo had never had any hobbies, took no interest in the home, never really wanted to socialize, always claimed he worked too hard for that. All he had was his practice and those boys and when the last one left home he started drinking pretty heavily. He began to pull away from me and the boys, even saying that he hated them and his work and that he had all along. Two years after that I learned that he was having an affair with a girl in his office, twenty-two years old. I overheard him tell her on the telephone that he loved her. From the information I gathered it had been going on for about four years when I found out about it. I became a private eye, collecting every possible bit of information and trying to prove to myself he was only lying when he told me he was through with her. He says he still loves me but my life has been nothing but frustration and anger, hate, anxiety and a multitude of mixed feelings.

"I know I am not the only person this has happened to. He refuses to get help of any kind and I believe now there is no other solution. I have to divorce him. I have filed for divorce three times. I pray to God this time I have the courage to go through with it. Tomorrow his thirty days are up. What bothers me most of all is that he would take up with this girl, this little tramp. Our eldest son has been over to see them and tells me Leo has been paying for an apartment for her for four years and spends most of his nights with her. Larry says it's just sickening to see them. Leo dresses this girl in these baby doll things and has her trot around, treats her like a little girl and she calls him, can you believe this, 'Daddy Leo.' It's really sick. On top of that she has a two-year-old son that I'm almost certain is Leo's, although he has never admitted it. I don't know who else's it could be. I don't know why he would treat her the way he does. It's like once his real family got to the point that they could take care of themselves he just decided to drop them and start all over again. Well I'm going to start all over too. This time I'm really going to drop him.''

Leo has considerably less to say about his relationship with Vivian and the girl but he does offer this. ''It probably does sound odd to other people but I just don't care. She is very young and she has a young child. It's no one's business whether it's mine or not. I do still love Viv but she and the boys don't need me any longer and Sally needs me. Sure, maybe I am a father figure to her, but so what. She needs me and I need her and I just think that I'm pretty lucky in middle age to be able to start over again.''

Leo's case and others like his suggest that at least a part of the attraction of young girls may be that they offer a chance to continue the father role that such men have lost, a chance once again to be influential in the lives of a young person, as they once were in the lives of their own children. The young women involved are often financially dependent upon the middle-aged man and may find it easier to relate to a more mature man (who is perhaps less sexually demanding) than to men their own age. In return they give the attention and ego support that the man once had from his own children. There can be little doubt that for some very small number of these men there is some psychosexual dynamic at work. A surprising number of men choose as mistresses girls who approximate in age their own daughters. It would be naïve to suggest that this happens by mere coincidence. Without detailed information about each of these cases it cannot be said categorically that middle-aged men who respond in this manner to the mid-life crisis brought about by the empty nest do so out of some deep-seated psychological desire to have sex with their daughters. In a few isolated cases middle-aged men have been sexually involved with their daughters. Such relationships are clearly an aberration, far from the mainstream of responses of middle-aged men to the loss of the father role. To give these behaviors greater attention is to engage in sensationalism that diverts attention from the real issues related to the empty nest. There are now in our society, perhaps more than ever before, tangible political, philosophical and personal differences between people of different generations. Today's young adults are not exposed to the same world as were their parents when they matured, nor do they experience the world in the same way. Growing up does mean, in so many ways, growing apart. As children grow up and depart the father's role as provider, protector, shaper of attitudes and beliefs diminishes and often disappears. Many middle-aged men cannot deal with this role loss because the role of father is all that they have known—all that has been important to them. The empty nest leaves behind an empty man; one may seek out others to father, one may strike out against young people or avoid them entirely, one may go to great lengths to maintain his role, or one may simply dwell in the depression that accompanies the loss of self.

The middle-aged man often finds his nest emptying not only of children but of his spouse as well. The normal changes in the structure of the family that occur during a man's middle years do more than alter his role as a father. Increasingly these changes alter or threaten his role as a husband. As an outgrowth both of the women's liberation movement and conditions in the economy, more and more women late in life are returning to school and to work. As they do so these women are subjected to new influences on their attitudes and behaviors, influences which may complement or which more often than not contradict those of their husband. The pattern is a familiar one, usually out of a desire to keep busy or "to have a little money of my own." When the children are able to care for themselves, the wife goes back to school or work. In the school or work environment she finds a role for herself which is very different from the one she has known as a wife. Here she encounters new people and attitudes that have not been formed in the context of her relationship with her husband, and which are not framed by the marital contract. These include attitudes about politics, religion, money, child-rearing, topics of conversation in any office or school environment, which present the wife with an opportunity to examine her own attitudes and beliefs away from the influence of her husband. She is also exposed to new behaviors, behaviors which are not dependent on her role as a marriage partner but which revolve instead around her own learning or her performance as an employee.

As she becomes exposed to new attitudes and behaviors through school or the workplace, a wife may become less dependent upon her husband as a source of ideas and activities and more dependent on roles she has created for herself. Many middle-aged men are able to accept these changes in their spouse with little or no problem, many men welcome the opportunity for growth in a relationship between two independent, free-thinking adults. Other men are neither so supportive nor accepting. For those men the change in their partner's role and consequent change in her behavior and attitude signals a loss of an important role of their own—the role of husband, man of the house, "provider." To the extent that these roles dominate a man's sense of identity, changes in the role and behavior of his wife will bring about very real changes in his own role and behavior in mid-life, another version of the empty-nest male mid-life crisis.

Two cases are characteristic of the responses seen in men whose mid-life crisis is brought about by the loss of their role as a husband. The first describes a role reversal between husband and wife and the consequent changes in the man's behavior. The second case, the more typical of the two, describes one middle-aged man's attempts to act against these changes in his life. The first story is told from the wife's perspective, Evelyn Roppen.

"Mike, my husband, is a mailman. Actually he's a postal supervisor but it's easier to describe his job as a mailman. He's been with the postal service for going on twenty-two years now, ever since he got out of school. It's secure, steady work, the pay is reasonably good and they have excellent benefits. He's provided us with a very comfortable life for all these years. It's not the kind of work you get rich at but it's the kind of work he really enjoys and I'm glad he has it. I'm in real estate. I have been for five years. I first got involved when Julie, our youngest daughter, got into high school. With both the kids in high school and pretty much able to take care of themselves, I found I had a lot of extra time on my hands so I thought it would be a great idea if I got into something part-time just to keep me busy in the afternoons. Mike agreed. At the time he thought it was a good idea, too. I took these classes at night at the community college and then I got a job with one of the real estate firms in town.

"At first I think Mike thought it was kind of neat and a lot of fun that I would have a job of my own, one that didn't take too much time and that might even bring in some extra money. Although it was a long time before I brought in much extra money and even then the first couple of years it was just a few hundred dollars here and there, nothing very big and certainly nothing very predictable. The extra money did mean that we could do some things that maybe we couldn't have afforded to do on Mike's salary alone, but it was nothing we really could depend on. Then three years ago a big change came. Two big new plants were built here in town and our company got the contract for relocating all of their people from the east. That meant that overnight there was a whole lot of money to be made in real estate. It was one of those things, I keep telling Mike, where I just happened to be in the right place at the right time, and it worked out right. As it was, in the space of about six months I made more money in commissions than Mike made all year. I think that was when things really began to change between us.

"At first it was very gradual. I started buying food and clothes out of my own money instead of out of our joint account. Then, because I felt like I should have a new car since I was showing so many clients around, I bought a new car and paid cash out of my own account. I think that was really hard for Mike to accept. We had never in all our lives paid cash for anything quite that big and the fact that I could do it all with my money, I guess that was quite an affront to his pride, to his manhood. But the money was there and it didn't make any sense to pay all that interest when I could pay cash for it, so I did. Over the space of a year or two we got more dependent on my salary than we did on Mike's. One of the things that I know really hurt him was that if the girls wanted something big like dresses for a dance, or especially when they wanted a car of their own, they came to me instead of going to their father because they knew I had the money.

"Gradually our relationship went through this change where Mike just became more and more passive and I became more and more active—more of the things he used to do I started doing, like paying the bills. I thought we should get involved in some investments because of our tax position and all, and so I made all the trips to the bank, selected the investments for us to make. I guess the impression that people would have gotten looking at us was that Mike was living off me instead of me living off him. Even around the house we changed roles. He just had more time than I had to do things like cook and vacuum and do the clothes, and he began doing those things after he would get home from work. He'd make dinner and have it ready for me when I got home after work. I wouldn't want too many people to know this but we really did just kinda switch our roles. I shouldn't tell this but even in bed, sexually, I became more active, he became more passive and now he wants me on the top all the time. I do all the work and he just lies there.

"Sometimes I worry about Mike and what's going through his mind because it seems that with my success at work, all the money and everything, he's become sort of a househusband. He's lost interest in most of the things he used to be interested in. I don't know what I can do about it, though. I've found this new life, this new role, this new me, and I'm not going to give it up and go back to being a housewife. I wouldn't want to be like that again. Funny, I wouldn't want to be the way Mike is now."

Mike is reluctant to talk about the change in his behavior as a result of Evelyn's new role outside the home. He does acknowledge that Evelyn's income is greater than his own and the demands of her job different from the demands of his own, "I've got more time to do some of the things that need to be done around the house than Evelyn does so I might as well do them. Anyway, she makes a lot more money using her time than I make using mine, so this is one of the best ways I can make myself useful. I am still the man of the house. There's no doubt about that, but nowadays being man of the house doesn't mean quite the same thing it always used to. Anybody will tell you that. There are probably a lot of guys who would like to be in my shoes. Hell, I don't have to work at all if I don't want to. Evelyn can take care of me.''

As women change, relationships between middle-aged men and women will change. While perhaps comparatively few middle-aged couples totally reverse roles as have Evelyn and Mike, most have seen role shifts. Such shifts are likely to continue as women increasingly seek and find opportunities outside the home, beyond their wifely roles. As the middle-aged husband of one successful career woman commented, ''The truth of the matter is at age thirty-seven her career opportunities are much better than mine, though I'm only forty-two. I can see that we'll be inviting *her* boss to dinner, going to *her* office parties, moving because *she's* being transferred. It's different all right and I don't like it much, but hell, I can't do much about it, either. I might even *like* watching soap operas.''

Not all men can accept a change in their role that comes as a result of new attitudes and behaviors on the part of their wives as easily as some have, nor as passively. Many middle-aged men see the entire women's movement as a threat to their role and identity, and when this threat is brought home and becomes personified in the behavior of their own spouse, their response is outspoken and at times outrageous. Al Crester is adamant in his feelings about the proper role of husband and wife in middle age. ''I don't want Shirley working, that's for sure, but I guess I can't stop her from working. It seems to me that if a man can't provide his wife with everything she needs by the time he's middle-aged, well then he's just not much of a man. These women who are going back to work, that's just their way of saying they can't get everything they need from their husband, and I don't want Shirley saying that about me. I know that's an old-fashioned idea. People call me a male chauvinist pig, maybe I am, but as a husband I think it's my role to be the provider and Shirley, her role as a wife is to make things easy at home so I can give my attention to being a good provider. Now if she wants to go back to school or something, well I can understand that, we've all got a need to learn new things. But I draw the line at her out there working. There's no need for it, no sense in it, and if I have anything to say about it, I won't have it. A woman's place is in the kitchen—'keep 'em barefoot and pregnant.' There's a lot of good advice in those old sayings; all this women's lib nonsense and everything—that may be fine for younger girls who are just getting a start and all, girls who don't have a family, but women Shirley's age, well, they've just got no business getting back into work.

"Oh she keeps bringing it up every now and then, and I can count on her saying something about finding a job almost every week, but I keep putting it down and I'm going to keep putting it down just as long as I can. There's a couple of guys on our block, their wives work, simple do-nothing jobs, I don't know why they have them around the office in those places where they do work. I don't know how those guys handle it. I'd feel like a pimp or something taking money from my wife. Maybe they just don't have as much pride as I do, but the way I see it that's their problem not mine. As for me, that little gal of mine's not going to work, no sir, not ever."

Not surprisingly, middle-aged men with attitudes toward women and their roles as wives, such as the attitudes held by Al, find it difficult to deal with women in the workplace. Al is no exception to this general observation. As his manager tells it, "Actually I'm quite proud of the record our division has in hiring and promoting women. It's clear to me that some of our best employees, our most committed, our hardest-working employees are women thirty-five years and older who are returning to the work force. But it would be naïve of me to try to believe that this attitude is held across the division. We certainly have our share of chauvinists in management and Al is probably one of the biggest. We just haven't been successful in placing a woman in his operations. He won't hire one voluntarily and when we force one upon him he makes things so difficult for her that she immediately requests a transfer out. On the other hand, he runs a good operation and I don't feel like I can justify firing him just because he can't get along with the women. You may have heard the 'dumb ass broad' story. Well it seems like someone fouled up an order in his division when we did have a couple of women working there, and this mistake cost time and money in Al's operation. When he found out about it he just bellowed out, 'Where is that dumb ass broad?' You could hear it all over the floor. Ever since then it's become a joke, and whenever Al and women are mentioned the dumb ass broad phrase crops up. Unfortunately, Al doesn't mean it as a joke. He really thinks that women who work actually are dumb ass broads. Try as I might to talk with him, counsel with him, and tell him that times are changing, I just haven't been able to get through. I know it has something to do with Shirley, Al's wife, wanting to go back to work and Al resisting that. What it comes down to is that Al just doesn't know how to relate to women in anything but a wife role. We will try to work around it but if it begins to get in the way of his operation, we will have to take some stronger action.''

Al's manager has hit upon one of the major issues in explaining middle-aged men and their response to the empty nest where the husband's role is concerned. Unlike their younger male counterparts, middle-aged men have not had the experience of growing up, going through school and their early career years with women as equals and co-workers. For most middle-aged men the only roles they know for women are the roles of mother, sister, wife and sex object. That sort of middle-aged man has clear ideas about how to behave toward the woman who is a mother and how to behave toward the woman who is a sister, how to behave toward the woman who is a wife and how to behave toward the woman who is a sex object, but he has no clear ideas of how to behave toward the female co-worker. Add to this a basic resistance in many middle-aged men to women as co-workers, which stems from an implied threat to their own security as husbands and providers, and there are all sorts of behavioral dynamics at play in a very difficult situation. In the absence of any other suitable behaviors many men fall back on responding to women solely as sex objects. This is their way of reinforcing the notion that any woman who chooses not to be a wife and mother, and therefore not to relate to the middle-aged man as husband or father, must necessarily be a sex object. Susan Hunter is, at thirty-nine, treasurer and controller of the food products division of a large corporation. Susan writes, "Interestingly enough I have the hardest time dealing with men who are around my own age in the company. The younger ones seem to understand that I'm interested in a career just like they are, and are willing to treat me the way they would a man who holds a similar position. For the most part that opinion is shared by the older men, although some of them tend to treat me like my father might. It's the middle-aged men, the men my own age, who seem to be at a loss as to how to deal with me in my position in the organization. I'm not a wife or a mother, so since they can't relate to me in those ways many of them fall back on sex. Maybe they think the way I got where I am in the company was by fucking my way here. I can tell you that is not the truth. Anyway they keep coming at me with one line after another. It's really pretty disgusting. After a while you get so used to it you get kind of jaded. What is saddest of all is it seems to me that middle-aged men just don't know how to relate to middle-aged women in any other way than as wife or sex object, and with women taking on so many other roles today, I think it's going to be plenty tough for middle-aged men."

This treatment of working women only as sex objects seems to be most prevalent in those men whose response to the empty-nest mid-life crisis is to put their wives and all other women in their place. As one middle-aged husband described it,

"The best place for women is in bed, the best position for women is on their back." Crude as it is, his comment captured the feelings of many middle-aged men—that they have been betrayed by a wife who has forgone her role as a supportive spouse to seek an identity of her own. It is out of this sense of betrayal that middle-aged men strive to strike back at wives and at women, striking where they believe women are most vulnerable, sex. These middle-aged men are truly caught between the values, attitudes, beliefs and behaviors toward women that they learned and have found to be effective for so long, and a very different set of values, attitudes, beliefs and behaviors women of today have toward themselves and toward men. There is little wonder that more incidents of divorce were reported among those men who experienced mid-life crisis as a result of the empty nest than for any other single cause.

Despite the general upheaval and havoc in middle-aged men's lives caused by the empty nest, some men respond positively. Rather than strike out at young people and wives, or seeking substitutes or any of the other characteristic responses, some middle-aged men welcome the change in family structure with its attendant change in roles and respond to the crises these changes occasion creatively and constructively.

More often than not these middle-aged men see the loss of the role as husband or father as freeing them from responsibilities, freeing them to find new roles and a new identity.

Tom Hiller, a forty-nine-year-old father of four, writes, "At first when the last one was packed off to school, all I noticed was how much more time I had, no more taxi services to this or to that, no more 'We've got to go, Tom, it's our daughter' attendance at events that weren't that good when I first saw them four kids ago and didn't get any better by the time the last kid rolled around. I just had all this time. It was scary. I had so much time and nothing to fill it with. That's how the crisis came about for me, realizing that I wasn't a father any longer, not a father in the sense that I had been one, and not knowing what I was going to do with all that fathering time. I don't know exactly when my sense changed from one of fear to one of freedom. One of the things I remember, and it's just a small thing, was being able to walk around the house in just my jockey shorts, or nude even if I wanted to, not having to worry that one of the kids was going to come bursting in with their friends and there I'd be hanging out for everybody to see. Of course that meant Peg and I could make love anytime we wanted to, anyplace we wanted to in the house—middle of the day, middle of the night, middle of the kitchen—and we did. To tell the truth we haven't had so much fun since before we had kids. Don't get me wrong. I love them dearly and I think of them often. It's not out of sight out of mind, but they're grown and gone now and they can take care of themselves. They don't need me in the same way they used to and because they don't need me I don't need them in the same way I used to. I've finally gotten a hold on that. Now I don't have to worry about what to do with all that time. There's more time than ever for Peg and me to do things we've always wanted to do. More time and more money—I didn't realize just how expensive those kids were until they were gone. Now there's more time than ever for me and my friends—more time and money for me to be *me* now that I don't have to be so much of a father anymore."

There are even those men who graciously and eagerly accept the change in their role as a husband that comes about as a result of changes in their wife. Horace Grillman: "To tell the truth as I look back on it, it's a good thing that Beverly changed when she did. It's a good thing she got out of that wife-mother sort of thing because about three years ago the spice had pretty much gone out of our life and I was beginning to cast an eye around and look for some variety to put the spice back. Bev must have sensed it, too, for I remember it was toward the end of one summer she just announced that in September she was going back to college. Well you could have knocked me over. She had never done anything like that. First of all, to make a decision like that on her own without talking to me about it was just unheard of. Then when I found out that she had already made all the arrangements—where she got the money I still don't know—but she made all the arrangements and she was ready to go. It was an announcement. It wasn't a question. She had decided and she was going to do it.

"That really set me back on my heels and I wasn't sure at first I was too happy about it, but I can tell you now it was the best thing that ever happened to our relationship. She is studying things that they hadn't even discovered when I was in school. She's meeting new, interesting people, carving out an identity of her own. She's no longer just an extension of me. That bothered me at first and gave me a feeling I was losing her, but now it's okay. It's better than okay. It's terrific. I did lose the old Beverly but the thing of it is that I was tired of the old Beverly anyway and now I have a new Beverly and she has opened up a new me. She challenges me, she argues with me, she pushes me, we're exploring whole new dimensions of our relationship, things that I never knew existed between us. It's fantastic—no, I'm not the husband I used to be—I'm a partner now and being a partner is better than being a husband any day."

Tom and Horace are not alone in their positive, constructive, creative responses to the empty-nest crisis of their middle years. Many middle-aged men reported new dimensions and new directions in their lives as a result of the empty-nest crisis. Some, like Tom, found new interests with the new time on their hands. Others, like Horace, discovered new relationships with their own wives. One man told the story, "I've been having an affair ever since my wife went back to work—the affair is with her. We meet once a week for a long lunch hour, go off to a hotel and screw our heads off, then it's back to work and home that night. I know it sounds kind of weird and strange, but it's exciting as hell. It's something I never would have thought of doing with her when she was just a wife, but she's so strong now, so independent, that's made her more attractive and the affair is fantastic."

The crisis presented by the empty nest is no less real for these men, its attendant changes no less traumatic than the crisis experienced by those who choose other responses. Why then the difference? Given two middle-aged men equally invested in their roles as husband(s)/father(s), what is to explain why one is frustrated and forlorn by the empty nest and the other is freed? The data suggests that the odds are three to one that the middle-aged man who identifies singularly with the husband/father role and experiences loss of that role will respond with one of the following:

Depression
Attempt to sustain role
Act against the other (young people or women)
Seek those who will respond to the role
Role reversal (husband/wife)

The normal events which occur in families—children growing and leaving home, a wife awakened to her own needs—signal a shift away from the middle-aged man as the focal point of family activity. The shift serves as an alert, signaling the man to changes in his role as a husband and a father. For the men who do not derive their identity primarily from these roles, they respond to the alert with a heightened sense of awareness but with no sense of alarm. They continue to find a sense of self-value and self-worth in other sources, in other activities. For those men whose identity centers on the role of husband or the role of father, the alert sounded by this change is indeed an alarming one. Many respond out of a sense of panic, trying desperately to forestall change, to continue to be the center of activity for the family, influencing children and spouse, directing their lives. Others, realizing that they cannot forestall this change, that it will happen inevitably, strike out against those forces which they see at the heart of the change, young people and women. Still others attempt to start over, to renew their role as husband or father with a new woman, a new family, seeking out for the most part young, dependent females who allow them to behave as a father. A very few are able to see in these changes an opportunity to discover new aspects of themselves or to discover new aspects of their relationship with a woman. For these few men the crisis brought about by the empty nest is enlivening, exciting, enriching. Perhaps the distinguishing characteristic of middle-aged men who so respond to the empty nest is that they are optimistic by nature, seeing an opportunity. More than likely the real reason for differing responses to the empty nest lies in the established framework of the man's relationship with his wife and children. Where that framework promotes and encourages exploration of self (for all concerned) there is in every crisis an invitation to invention. That invitation, by its very nature, frees the middle-aged man to see the empty nest as opportunity. Once again, resolution of the crisis must lie in the relationship which spawns it. (See Chapter 8.) For the others, for the majority of men who see in the empty nest not opportunity but oppression, oppression of their role as father, oppression of their role as husband, oppression of who they are and how they relate to the world, the empty nest is just that—empty, and so are the years which remain for them after middle age.

6

Meeting Mortality

IN 1915, Sigmund Freud wrote about death, "We were prepared to maintain that death was the necessary outcome of life . . . in reality, however, we were accustomed to behave as if it were otherwise. We displayed an unmistakable tendency to shelve death, to eliminate it from life. We tried to hush it up . . . that is, our own death of course . . . no one believes in his own death . . . in the unconscious everyone is convinced of his own immortality." For fifty years Freud's views on death and man's denial of death shaped the thinking of modern psychiatry, but few outside that field gave much attention to his views. Today Freud's analysis is felt by many to be an accurate expression of the situation most men encounter in middle age and an important cause of the crisis of mid-life. One observer of modern man has noted, "In mid-life, the reality of one's own personal death forces itself upon our attention and can no longer so readily be shelved."

Among the most common experiences to middle-aged men is the confrontation with their own mortality, the realization of the inevitability of their own death. This confrontation occurs in a variety of ways, direct and indirect, real and imagined. In his middle years the average man is witness to the incapacitation or death of his parents, terminal illnesses which strike friends and work colleagues, and often a decline in his own health. Forced

by these events to face the reality of death firsthand, the middle-aged man cannot help but contemplate the ultimate reality
of his own death. These events emphasize that immortality is
only a dream, and strive as one might it can never be obtained.
The meeting with mortality in mid-life need not be so direct.
The same message can be read in simpler, more subtle sources
which are commonplace in a man's middle years—a physical
required for employment or insurance purposes, changes in his
sleeping habits, or merely reading the obituary column of the
daily paper and finding how many more names he recognizes as
friends and associates, contemporaries. Whatever the source,
explicit or implicit, physical or psychological, the message remains much the same. Men are not and cannot be immortal, and
from the time of this realization onward, a man measures his life
less in terms of how long he has lived and more in terms of what
little time there is left to live.

For most middle-aged men this realization comes as other
realizations come, gradually. They adapt to the death of others,
parents and friends, and ultimately accept that mortality is a
natural conclusion of the maturation process and they, too, will
die. For these men there is no need to mourn prematurely or
pursue the false promise of immortality any longer. But many
men neither adapt to the death of others nor accept their own
mortality so readily. For these men their meeting with mortality,
their confrontation with the limits to their own life, constitutes
a crisis and brings about dramatic changes in their behavior.
Concern over health and mortality is important to a great number of middle-aged men. In one recent survey of male managers,
nearly one-fourth said that their own health is their biggest personal worry. Overall, more managers rated health as one of the
top three personal concerns. Other data, not limited to managers, reveals concern over the limits to life as the fourth major
cause of the male mid-life crisis. It seems reasonable to estimate
that between 15 to 25 percent of the male mid-life crisis cases
can be attributed to men "confronting mortality."

It cannot be said with a similar degree of certainty what specific effect these crises will have on the men involved. As is the case with other causes of the mid-life crisis, meeting mortality can have a number of possible effects upon a man's behavior. Three patterns of responses emerge from interviews and cases. These patterns are very closely tied to what is known today about the grief process. Concern over death seems to be on the minds of many today—not just middle-aged men. Popular books about death and dying enjoy record sales. College and even high school courses on death are offered on campuses across the country. There is unparalleled scientific interest in "life after death" and legal and ethical interest in the right to die. Professionals, churches and community groups offer counseling on every aspect of death from how to die to how to grieve for one who is dead. Given all this popular attention to death it is perhaps surprising that a much greater number of middle-aged men are not affected by meeting mortality. One of the many learnings to emerge from this attention to death and dying is a better understanding of the grief process. It is known that the typical response to the death of a loved one follows six stages:

Shock
Anger
Denial
Depression
Fantasy
Acceptance

It is possible to see the same stages in the responses of middle-aged men who are thrown into crisis by their meetings with mortality. In large measure their responses can be seen as grieving for themselves, with different men fixing on different stages in the grief process as appropriate to them.

The most frequent response middle-aged men display upon coming to grips with their own mortality is shock, followed by anger, then denial. The most obvious behavior changes are evident in the ways middle-aged men seek to deny their own mortality. Typically this denial-directed behavior takes the form of a heightened concern for their own health. For some men this means efforts toward fitness as they seek, through improved physical conditioning, to postpone the inevitable. This is not to suggest that every middle-aged man who is concerned about his physical fitness is trying to deny death, nor that all middle-aged men evidence their concern for their health through conditioning and exercise; some seek to postpone the inevitable by avoiding exercise and exertion. In either case the intent is the same —to deny that they are mortal and will, like all men, die.

Many middle-aged men are so shaken by their meeting with mortality that they pass through the grief process stages of shock, anger and denial and settle on depression as their response to the crisis. Most often this depression leads to self-depreciating behaviors such as drinking and drug abuse and a preoccupation with self-pity. These cases of crisis are not dramatic in their effects, there may be few visible behavior changes, but they are no less devastating for the man mourning his own mortality.

Brought face to face with their own death, some middle-aged men engage in those flights of fantasy in which they ask, "What if?" "What if I had done this?" "What if I had gone there?" "What if I had met her earlier?" More importantly, many middle-aged men ask, "What if I do it now?" and *they do it*. Faced with what they see as very little time left they fantasize and act out their fantasies. In these case files are some of the most dramatic behavior changes associated with the male mid-life crisis as men attempt to have the time of their life in the little time left in their life.

Ultimately all men must accept their own mortality. After all, the event does tend to force itself upon one. Some men accept their own mortality as natural and inevitable. Some accept their mortality and proceed to act upon it, prematurely putting into order the affairs of their life, preparing, in some instances in alarming detail, to "pass away." For many middle-aged men the avenue to acceptance of mortality is through religion.

Spurred by the realization of mortality, many men strive for and achieve a self-reported state of inner peace and harmony, a oneness with their God and His place for them in the world. In some cases this religious rebirth can lead the middle-aged man to disavow any responsibility for his own behavior, leaving his direction and destiny to the church, to faith, or to God. For these men acceptance of their own mortality can lead to a passivity that in itself creates problems, but these men clearly are a minority of those who through religion try to accept their own mortality.

All of the above are potential responses to the male mid-life crisis which is caused by a meeting with mortality. It is known that the men most likely to experience such a crisis are those who see in the events of mid-life threats to their own health and longevity. It is known that the responses available to a man parallel the stages of the grief process as he grieves for his own mortality with shock-anger-denial, depression, fantasy or acceptance. It is not known why one man chooses one response and another man an alternative response. The cases in this chapter reveal specific examples of the reactions of middle-aged men in this crisis. They may also reveal *why* men respond as they do.

At forty-six, Tom Donaldson had his first heart attack. Tom, overweight and overworked, had been told by his doctor for the five years preceding that it was only a matter of time before he had one. Tom's chances of avoiding heart trouble were not improved by chain-smoking and hard drinking; the former was a nervous response to his stressful managerial job and the latter was a tension release that grew to a minor dependence. The heart attack, neither major nor minor, hospitalized Tom for ten days; three days in intensive care, seven days in the hospital, with an additional seven days in bed at home. Try as he might, the doctors and the hospital regimen did little to slow Tom's pace. He actually ran his business from the intensive care unit, telling his key people to notify the hospital that they were members of the family and issuing orders through them to keep the company moving in the direction he had chosen for it. Symptomatic of Tom's behavior in the hospital was that in addition to conducting business he had his associates smuggle in pizza and cigarettes once he got out of intensive care. But the heart attack did scare Tom. There is little doubt of that. He vowed not to let it happen again. For six months following it he allowed himself only two cigarettes a night. He drank nothing but wine, he went home early from the office in the afternoon and did not come in on Sundays (Saturdays he came in as usual). Tom did not actually lose weight but he did stop gaining, and in six months' time he seemed more rested, less tense and generally in better health.

Pleased with his progress and pressured by business problems, Tom found it all too easy to slip back into his old habits. A year after his first attack, Tom Donaldson had a second, major heart attack that nearly took his life. At this point Tom picks up the story. "I honestly believe that if I hadn't had the second one when I did I wouldn't be here talking to you now. To tell you the truth I got to feeling pretty cocky six to nine months after the first attack. There I was in terrible shape and I'd gotten the warning with the heart attack, but I bounced back from it without any long-term effects, or so I thought. So it was a little too easy to fall back into smoking, drinking and working hard again and forget about some of the promises I had made to myself and to Gloria after that first attack. The second one— that's the one that did it, that one really rocked me back on my heels. I honestly thought for a while I wouldn't make it, wouldn't pull through. I think I may have even had some of those life after death experiences you read so much about these days. That's when I started changing my life.

"First of all, on the advice of my doctor, of course, I enrolled in one of those YMCA recuperation programs. In the city they have a program downtown for executives who have had heart attacks. They start you out with very slow, easy exercises and gradually move you up to the point where you are walking a mile and then running a mile and then more. I can remember at the very first I would break out in a cold sweat just changing into my workout shorts and shoes. It was that tough. But I was determined to stick to it. The doctors had told me, and I believed them, that number three would be a killer and I was going to make damned sure that there wasn't going to be any number three for me. Along with the exercise I knew I had to change my diet, cut out all the fats, all the cholesterol. I'm very, very careful about what I eat now, very little meat, maybe once, twice a week, but that's all. I take lots of vitamin pills nearly every day—a whole fistful of them for breakfast, the same at lunch and again at dinner. No smoking—absolutely none—not one cigarette, not one cigar. And only two glasses of wine on the weekends, that's it. Most of that diet stuff I worked out on my own. I read a lot and got lots of advice from doctors, but I had to come up with something I could believe in that would work for me so I pretty much wrote my own.

"The important thing is that I've stuck to it. I guess I have become kind of a fanatic about it. I don't exert myself unusually. I exercise regularly every day, thirty minutes of exercise in the morning and then I jog slowly, but I do jog two miles, then I have my pills for breakfast, watch my diet all day long, get into bed early, get lots of rest, and try to escape the tension and stress of my work whenever and however I can. That's really the hardest one, getting away from that tension and pressure. I know they call me a health nut and they call me a hypochondriac, but the point is I'm healthier than I ever have been, and they can call me anything they want as long as they don't call me dead. I feel better than I ever have and I'm not going to have number three—that's the point. I did meet my own mortality. I saw it right before my eyes and it did change my life, but it's all been for the better and I think anybody who knows me—you ask Gloria or the kids or the people at work—and they'll tell you I'm kind of a nut about health, especially about my diet and my exercise, but it's working. I'm still here, kicking and ticking like they say."

The comments of Tom's wife, Gloria, are particularly telling in this case. She wrote, "As funny as it may sound, I'm so thankful for that second heart attack Tom had. I feel like it gave him a second chance, a chance to live if only he would make the commitment to living, and he did. I'm so proud of the way he's stayed with his new diet and all. I honestly believe it has added years to his life. Sometimes it's a little frustrating cooking special things for him and getting up early so that his breakfast is there when he returns from his run and not doing some of the things I'd really like to do because he doesn't feel like he has the energy for it. Sometimes I think he is a hypochondriac and going too far, but then I remember all he has given me—his life —and I'll do whatever I can to see that he keeps it. He had a crisis and more than survived it. He has come back stronger, more alive than before."

Not all men are able physically or psychologically to reinvest themselves in the process of living as was Tom Donaldson. For some middle-aged men direct physical evidence of the natural limits to their life is devastating and they never return to full health. Like Tom, these men are shocked and angered by life's message to them, the message that they are mortal. But rather than protecting their health by becoming stronger, many middle-aged men attempt to protect their health and prolong their lives by avoiding becoming weaker. They escape exercise and exertion. The reaction of these middle-aged men to their meetings with mortality seems more psychological than physiological and in that regard, they are perhaps more disturbing.

Martin Harper is a forty-three-year-old accounting manager for a medium-sized manufacturing concern. When Martin went with Jamison Associates he was given job responsibilities far above anything he had experienced prior in his career. Not only would he be accounting manager but he would also have principal responsibility for one of the major production facilities of the company. This responsibility came about largely because the production facility was experiencing financial accounting and control problems, but also because Martin had expressed a desire to the owner to get involved with more parts of the business. He aimed to develop himself as a general manager. As further evidence of his commitment to what he saw as his future career, Martin enrolled in evening classes at the local college to take some advanced business training. Taking on all of this in a relatively brief period, Martin soon found himself overwhelmed with new duties, responsibilities, routines, new ideas and challenges. He openly acknowledged to himself and to all who showed concern, his wife, boss, friends, that he was indeed overwhelmed but it was temporary and he felt confident that he could handle it in time. Unfortunately for Martin, there was to be no time. The overload and stress got the better of him before he got the better of his stressful schedule.

Martin's heart attack came exactly six months after taking on his new job. Although the doctors classified it as a minor attack, he was nonetheless hospitalized for a brief period of time and at home for several weeks before he was given a clean bill of health and allowed to return to work. Martin was told that if he would follow a plan for a reasonable diet and moderate physical exercise, he could begin by returning to work half a day at a time. Martin's employer, Ernie Crane, was completely understanding of Martin's situation—he had conversations with the doctor himself and arranged to take on Martin's responsibilities as his own until such a time that Martin could return to work full time. Ernie felt that with a half-day schedule Martin would be able to run the production facility adequately, but might have to give up some of his headquarters responsibilities. This was agreed to by Martin and his employer.

Everyone was eagerly awaiting Martin's return to work. Certainly Ernie, who was himself beginning to feel the burdens of keeping up with his own work as well as Martin's. He looked forward to Martin's coming back as a way to get out from under the overload and to reestablish some order in Martin's division. Martin's wife, Marion, was anxious to have Martin out of the house, and felt that the demands of work would refocus his attentions, get him away from thinking so much about his health,

and put the situation into the proper perspective in his life.
Martin himself expressed a great desire to get back into action
so that he could feel that he was accomplishing something besides just staying alive. On Sunday afternoon before the Monday on which Martin was to return to work for the first of three
times a week, half-days, Marion decided to have a little barbe-
cue at home to celebrate Martin's return to health and return to
work. She invited just a few close friends from the neighborhood, Martin's boss and a couple of others from work. It was to
be more a picnic than a party, hamburgers in the backyard, beer
and wine, a quiet little time, as much as anything to thank
friends and family for the support they had given Martin, and
also to signal the formal end to his period of inaction. As Marion
later talked about the party, "I should have known that afternoon in our backyard that it wasn't all going to work out the
way we had thought it would. People were jovial and laughing,
having drinks and really enjoying themselves. At least everyone
but Martin was. He seemed so withdrawn all evening. It wasn't
just that he wasn't drinking. I think he just had one small glass
of wine the whole afternoon. No, it was more than that, almost
as though he knew that we shouldn't be celebrating what we
were supposed to be celebrating, almost as though he didn't
want to take part in anything which would symbolize the end of
his recuperation. I should have realized then that he was trying
to tell us that we were celebrating too early, that we were rush-
ing him. I should've, but I didn't. Martin's spirits eventually
dampened everyone's and the party broke up much earlier than
I had expected it would. I think everyone went away feeling as
if maybe Martin hadn't made it all the way back yet. That night
he seemed so restless and nervous and couldn't get to sleep. I
turned to him and tried to get him to make love to me. We
hadn't really had any sex in all that time since his attack, all
through his recuperation. I just didn't feel I could approach him
and demand from him and he didn't make any advances toward
me, so we didn't have any sex. But that night I thought I could
help him and I remember saying, 'Now that you're back on your

feet, don't you think we could get back on the track in bed?'
and he said to me, 'I really don't feel like it, Marion. It's too
early, maybe I'd better not risk it.' I felt so rejected, so hurt, I
said, 'Well you don't have to make love to me, maybe I can
help you. Maybe if you could come you could relax and get to
sleep.' I was thinking that if I could get him started back into
some sort of sexual activity, anything, we could return to what
was normal for us. But he shied away from even that and said
he was going to stay up and read for a little bit, so I just turned
over. I remember I cried myself to sleep that night knowing he
was out there reading those books. I haven't mentioned that he
bought all these books on how to recover from a heart attack
and what to do when you're coming back and all that sort of
thing and he was just compulsive about reading them. He was
always searching out new information and new articles and
bought every book he could find. That's how we ended that
night before he was supposed to go back to work—I went to
bed crying and he stayed up reading about recovery and recuperating."

As might be expected from the tone of Marion's remarks,
Martin did not make it to work the next day. He called his boss,
Ernie, and said, "I just don't feel like I can make it. I'm just not
ready yet. Give me a couple more days." Ernie agreed and they
decided that Wednesday Martin would come in to work.
Wednesday came and went and still Martin didn't show up.
Once again he called and begged off saying he just didn't feel
right, ". . . wasn't quite ready. Could he have until next Monday?" Ever more reluctantly Ernie agreed that Monday would
be okay and that Martin would then start coming in for a half-
day, three times a week. In the interim Ernie took the liberty of
calling Martin's doctor and talking to him about Martin's readiness to return to work. Ernie comments on his conversation
with the doctor: "As I expected he was reticent in discussing
Martin's physical condition with me, but after talking all around
the subject for a while I got the firm impression that physically
Martin was able to return to work, to begin to get back into

some kind of normal routine. The doctor even seemed surprised that he hadn't been coming to work. Apparently Martin hadn't been in touch with him.

"I didn't say anything about this to Martin at the time but I began to worry. If he was able to come to work and if everyone, doctor, Marion, all of us, felt like he needed to get back to work, why wasn't he coming to work? A full week after he was to return to work Martin did come in to the office. He came in late, stayed only briefly, making the rounds of the office, saying hello to everyone, thanking them for their cards and concern during his recuperation, then after about two hours, he complained of fatigue and went home. This pattern was to be repeated on the following Wednesday, the following Friday and the Monday, Wednesday and Friday following that. Each day he would come to the office late, spend some time talking with people about his illness, about what had happened to him, about the recuperative procedure, about how he was doing, and then ready himself to return home, complaining of fatigue. During this entire time he did little more than answer the mail. Even then it was only that mail which was of a personal, social nature, responding to business associates in much the same way that he had responded to people in the office, thanking them for their concern, expressing what had happened to him during his illness and what he was doing to recuperate. As far as I could see, he attended no business meetings, he neither read nor prepared business reports, he made no decisions."

Martin's secretary remembers the time very vividly. "Mr. Harper would come into the office during those days after he had been gone for so long and ask that I separate the mail into what just needed some response, and that which needed a decision. He only read the 'response needed' mail. I had saved all the business reports that he normally reviewed, but as far as I know he never touched them. When there were meetings that came up that he might normally attend, he asked that I notify someone else so that they might attend. To tell the truth, it was kind of spooky. He acted around the office as if he was still at the hospital, always speaking in hushed tones, never seeming to exert himself; he would get in one place, either in his office or someone else's, and just seemed to stay there for the longest time. I think that sort of rubbed off on the rest of us because we began to treat him as though he was still a patient. Everyone would come and ask me if it was okay to see Mr. Harper. That had never happened before; I felt more like a nurse than a secretary, and all this work was really piling up."

After a month of intermittent work behavior, Ernie called Martin into his office to discuss just what had been happening.

As Ernie recalled the conversation, "I asked Martin how he felt and right away that was a mistake. I got a retelling of the whole story—the heart attack, the time in the hospital, the recuperation—culminating in the fact that he just didn't feel right yet, he wasn't ready to return to the challenge of work, he didn't want to take any risks. I told him what my position was—that this coming and going and hospital-like behavior around the office was being more disruptive than it was helpful. I said that I felt until he was ready to come back full force that he ought to stay away from the office completely. At the same time I didn't want to threaten Martin, I didn't want to say to him, 'You get back to work now or else.' God knows I was afraid that if I did something like that I'd be the cause of another heart attack. We identified a couple of long-range projects that he could work on at his own speed, in his own time at home. They wouldn't demand a lot of office time. He designated somebody to take over his day-to-day responsibilities and I agreed that I would continue with him. I tried to reaffirm with him how important he was to the operation and how we didn't want to rush his return and that he should take his own time and that he should come back when he felt fully capable of coming back. We had that conversation three months ago and he hasn't come back full time yet. We keep in touch, and he reports that he is making some progress on the projects I gave him, and I guess he comes into the office once or twice a week for a couple of hours at a time, but to tell you the truth I don't think he's ever coming back to work. I think he's afraid to come back to work and I don't know what I'm going to do about it.''

Marion had a similar assessment of Martin's condition. ''The doctor has told me that Martin's health is good enough to allow him to return to work full time. It's good enough to allow him to return to a normal pattern of activity, moderate exercise, including sex, a cautious but normal diet and even a little alcohol now and then, but Martin will have none of it. Sometimes I believe he'd be happier back in intensive care. He's trying to live making the minimum possible exertion, taking no risks. He doesn't want to drive, he says, 'What would happen if I had a heart attack while I was driving? We'd have an accident and we'd both be killed.' So I drive, but my driving makes him nervous so usually we don't go anywhere. He watches everything he eats to the point where he's hanging over my shoulder in the kitchen as I prepare food, watching what goes into everything, afraid he's going to get too much oil or too much pepper or too much something, as though the slightest bite of the wrong thing is going to cause another heart attack. He never touches me, never. At first I joked with him about it. I told him once, 'I think you believe that hard-ons cause heart attacks,' but now it's no joking matter. We have no sex life. He's afraid of sex. He absolutely will not make a commitment to work. I am so thankful that Ernie has been as understanding as he has been throughout this whole thing because I don't know how we'd manage financially otherwise, but I know it just can't go on. I don't expect it to go on. Maybe Martin does. He distrusts the doctor because the doctor tells him he can go back to work. He won't go see a psychiatrist about it. He has completely withdrawn from life. I am trying as much as I know how to draw him back into life; the doctors have tried, Ernie has tried, but he is just so afraid and I don't know how to help him overcome that fear unless he will go for some help.''

Martin was approached several times for his side of the story by telephone and by mail. He provided the original data surrounding his heart attack and indicated a general interest in the subject, the male mid-life crisis, but to the many requests for an interview for some in-depth information from his perspective he replied, "I really don't want to go into it any further. I don't think reliving my heart attack would do me any good. It may even bring on another one."

Few events bring home more directly the realization of the limits to our own life than a major illness. The incidence of heart attacks and cancer, high blood pressure, ulcers, is already alarmingly high among middle-aged men. There is every evidence in the national health data to suggest that these rates are climbing ever higher. Most of the ailments which afflict middle-aged men seem to be of the death-rattle type, that is they are harbingers of things to come. Even though a middle-aged man may survive a heart attack or a cancer operation, the notion is firmly implanted in his mind that it is the beginning of the end.

Following the shock and anger over being stricken, over meeting mortality, most middle-aged men attempt to deny that it will happen to them. At a minimum they try to put off the inevitable, usually with a positive program for improving their health. These efforts may be as much a response to the fitness fanaticism which is sweeping the country as they are a response to individual health problems. The number of middle-aged men who jog, play tennis or racquetball, swim, are weight-conscious, or are trying to give up smoking cannot be explained entirely by the crisis of meeting mortality. (Vanity and virility may be the root of mid-life fitness concerns, see Chapter 4.) But neither can the fear of death be underestimated as a motivator of middle-aged men's efforts at improved health and fitness. Whatever the motivation, the middle-aged man who embarks on a positive program of physical improvement finds ample support for his efforts from his wife and family, business associates, and from a society which is increasingly concerned about good health. Given this supportive climate, it is not surprising that so many middle-aged men respond to the idea of mortality by investing themselves in improving their health. They are defying and denying death, if not its inevitability, at least its imminence.

Other middle-aged men choose to protect their "fragile" health by avoiding all that threatens health—work, sex, leisure, life itself. For these men the meeting with mortality in so foreboding a fashion as a serious physical ailment presents a fright so formidable that they literally withdraw from life for fear that life itself will bring death. These men feel the answer lies not in changing their life, but in avoiding life with all of its attendant risks and responsibilities, challenges and conflicts. Theirs is a condition far more psychological than physiological, but also far more debilitating. No longer in intensive care they nonetheless take intensive care with their lives. More often than not this is interpreted to be "take no responsibilities, take no risks, take no action, seek preventives through passivity, avoid projects, avoid passion, avoid, avoid, avoid." The long-term prognosis for these patients cannot be positive.

It is not known what causes some middle-aged men who meet mortality to respond in one way and others to act completely differently. It does not seem to be related to the severity or the immediacy of a man's meeting with mortality, nor is it connected to the man's health or life-style prior to his realization. There are of course other responses beyond shock-anger-denial to a middle-aged man's meeting with mortality. These two responses by no means account for all the behaviors which result from the crisis of mortality. Indeed, the response seen second only to the positive concern for health is depression.

In the grief process depression follows denial, depression over the loss of a loved one and all he or she meant. As a response to the crisis of meeting mortality in middle age depression is much the same, the man grieves for himself and all that he will be losing. In the depths of depression, many middle-aged men turn to drinking and to drugs, often under the pretense of relieving physical pain, but more often than not to find relief from the psychological pain of their depressed state. The dependence on alcohol and drugs provides further cause for self-pity and depression deepens.

When he was forty, Mike Cullen learned that the skin irritation on his face was cancerous. Skin cancer of course is gen-

erally regarded as among the most "curable" of all cancers, and
Mike was given every assurance that following surgery and
treatment he would be in excellent health. There would be some
disfigurement, that could not be helped; even with plastic surgery the scars would be visible, but Mike was told the important
thing was he would have his health. Apparently Mike did not
feel that would be true. One of his law partners describes Mike's
mid-life crisis as he saw it, "We were all so relieved to hear the
doctor report so optimistically about Mike's case. Compared to
a lot that could go wrong with you, skin cancer isn't so bad.
Who cares how you look as long as you're alive, and the cure
rate with skin cancer is practically guaranteed. Somehow Mike
never saw it that way. I remember him saying, 'Jerry, I've got
the feeling this thing is just the beginning, who knows where
else that cancer might be? No, sir, from now on it's just going
to be one thing after another eating away at me until there's
nothing left.' It was all pretty morbid hearing him talking like
that, and it seemed like nothing could cheer him—not his
friends here at work, not his wife, not the doctors—nothing.

"After the surgery Mike's attitude got worse, he was more
depressed than ever and spent all his time just sitting feeling
sorry for himself and that's when he started with the pills. I'm
not sure exactly what they were—uppers of some kind. He'd
take a couple of those 'medicines' as he called them and be on
top of the world for a couple of hours, then they'd wear off and
he'd be lower than ever. At some point he started drinking along
with the pills and that was the worst. As it turns out he had his
coffee carafe in his office filled with bourbon and he would sip
away at it all day long. Not long after that there were the malpractice suits and the disbarment. His wife is a checker at the
grocery, trying to bring in some money. Here in the partnership
we've agreed to pay for half of his rehabilitation expenses. He's
in a therapy program now and I guess he's doing better, but I
don't know—once you've been as down as Mike was I'm not
sure you can ever get up again. How can a guy get so down on
himself?"

How, indeed? Mike's depressive behavior may be extreme

but his depression is neither rare nor unusual. In meeting mortality many middle-aged men are plainly chagrined that such a fate should befall them. They begin to feel sorry for themselves, depressed by what they see ahead. Drinking, drugs and other escapes at once relieve the depression and provide further reason for self-pity, deepening the depression. It is a cycle which, once initiated, is very difficult to break as in his depression and self-pity, the middle-aged man isolates himself from those most able to help him—his friends and family.

In sharp contrast to those middle-aged men who become profoundly depressed upon meeting mortality, some men respond to the same message in flights of fancy. There is that stage in the grief process in which the aggrieved fantasizes, wonders "What if?" Confronting the real limits to his own life the middle-aged man may commit his remaining years to living out fantasies, answering for himself all of the "what if?" questions he dares to raise. Living his fantasies usually results in dramatic changes in his behavior and consequently in his relationships with others.

Leonard Wadden is forty-seven years old. For the past twenty-seven years he has lived in Porter, Connecticut, where he is the owner-manager of a small hardware store. Leonard and his wife, Claire, have two daughters who have married and moved away from Porter to raise families of their own. Leonard and Claire live a comfortable, orderly life which centers on home, business and community. Leonard, during the course of a routine physical, learned that he had a cancerous melanoma, on his back below the left shoulder. He received advice from the doctors that the melanoma should be removed at once, and surgery followed within the next week. After the surgery the doctors assured Leonard that the surgery was a success and they were reasonably sure that they had been able to remove all of the cancerous tissue, but the advice to him was somewhat standard in cases of this type. There would be a five-year period in which his health would be closely monitored for signs of remission before the doctors would be willing to give Leonard a clean bill of health. The days following the initial diagnosis were traumatic ones leading up to surgery and the remedial recovery. As Leonard's wife describes that time, "When you hear the word cancer your whole system goes into shock. It was all we could do to schedule the surgery, make arrangements for the business to be handled, and get Leonard into the hospital. There was little time to think of what would happen after the surgery. With cancer you are almost afraid to think of what comes after for fear that there may be no after." It is in this time after, the three-month period following surgery, that the meaning of Leonard's mid-life meeting with mortality became evident in his behavior.

For Leonard the post-operative period of recuperation was a time for reflection and, as he describes it, a time for counting up. In that time in the hospital he assessed how close he had come to dying, how close he had come to ending it all without ever doing many of the things he had always expected he would do, without ever living out any of his fantasies.

"While I was lying there in bed I made a list, nothing I was writing down, but I was making a list in my head of all the things that I had said to myself sometime I was going to do and had never done. Once they tell you you've got cancer you start thinking about that, about how, shit, if you don't do it now the chances are you may never get to do it. So I made that list, places I had always wanted to go, things I had wanted to do. Mostly they were catching up kinds of things, things I had to put aside when I got married or because of the business, kinds of things you think about in passing and say to yourself, 'Well maybe someday.' I'll tell you what was high on that list. I had never been to bed with anybody but my wife, and you know how all those times you think 'Well, maybe if I wasn't married or maybe some other time,' Well, I've been screwing my cock off ever since I got out of that hospital. Everytime I think 'well, maybe,' I don't stop at maybe, I just go right ahead. I've been drinking like a fish, that helps a lot, and when you're drunk you don't have to worry about how much longer you've got to be drinking. Hell, sometimes I go off and I might be gone for two or three days and nights at a time before I get back home. I've pretty much forgotten about the business. You don't need to work at it much, I make money even when I'm not giving it my full attention, and right now my full attention is going into living and living to the fullest. They tell you that, well, in five years they'll let you know how much longer you're going to live. I'm not going through that again. When I go out I'm going to go out knowing I've played the full time, that I got everything I wanted and then some. I know that it's hard on Claire, the drinking binges, the women, and being gone from the house, it's just something that I've got to do for me. I've got to live what life I've got left so I'm celebrating all the good things I've ever known and all the good things I thought I could know if only I'd taken the time and trouble. I'm living all of my dreams and loving every minute of it. The way I see it, when you're middle-aged and come that close to dying, you've got to take full advantage of every minute they give you and I'm doing it.''

It has been difficult for Leonard's wife. Her concern at the initial diagnosis of cancer turned to caring during Leonard's recuperation, both in the hospital and later at home, but the caring turned to chagrin at Leonard's behavior in the months following his recuperation. "At first, of course, I was worried sick, worried whether I'd ever have Leonard again. I was so worried that right after he was able to leave the house and go back to work I didn't feel bothered or concerned about his drinking and carousing. It was almost as though he was showing himself and me that he was alive and healthy and I was happy for it, but then his catching up turned into an orgy. He'd be gone two or three days at a time. I didn't know where he was or how to find him. Half the time I was scared he'd dropped dead somewhere of cancer. The other half of the time I hoped that he would drop dead. I didn't know how he could hurt me so. He would say that it was none of my business. He was just living what little life he had left to the fullest. I would try to call him at work and he wasn't there. He was out somewhere doing who knows what. It's just as though he's cut me out of his life, the same way they cut that cancer out of his back. He doesn't seem to care about us any longer. He only cares about himself, his satisfaction, his pleasures, his life, not *our* life. I've pretty much given up on him now. It's funny, I don't even care enough about him to get a divorce any longer. He's hurt me so bad. I don't think I care anymore if he drinks himself to death or dies in some cheap room with one of those girls. I thought that after they got the cancer and the doctor told him he could be reasonably assured of a long life without any more problems that, well, that everything would get back to normal, but I guess when you come that close to dying things can never be normal again. I know that my life with Leonard can never be normal, not as long as he continues to live out all that's so evil and dirty in life. Why can't he just enjoy being alive? Why does he have to rub my nose in it?''

Leonard's response to his bout with cancer is not at all an abnormal reaction among terminal or potentially terminal cases. Many times patients so diagnosed plunge headlong into life, pursuing all of its passions as if to prove that in the pursuit they live and will continue to live. There is in their frenetic behavior a desire to catch up with life, to capture feelings and experiences that they have fantasized and left aside. There also seems to be a desire to get ahead on life, to stockpile sensations and situations so that they may never again be caught short, may never again feel cheated by life. The men who, like Leonard, meet their own mortality in mid-life and choose to respond by living out their fantasies, their own sense of life, however they define it, are among the most dramatic and bizarre behavior changes that we see in the mid-life crisis. Drinking and prolific sexuality are only two of the many symptoms of this response. Irresponsible, unpredictable behavior is the norm as well as an apparent complete lack of concern for the feelings and interests of others. This entire response is characterized by a rampant restlessness as these men ask, ''What if?'' and go to every extreme to find the answer.

The natural cessation of the grief process comes with the aggrieved accepting the death of the other and having accepted it, moving forward with his or her own life. It seems that the natural resolution of a middle-aged man's crisis of mortality would be to arrive at a similar acceptance, acknowledging his own mortality and moving forward perhaps with a new sense of perspective. Unfortunately for many middle-aged men, the nature and form of their acceptance of mortality can present as many problems as does the realization that they are mortal. Two other manifestations of middle-aged men accepting mortality are mourning and religious rebirth.

Across the country from Leonard Wadden, outside Seattle, Washington, Dennis Tully and his wife, Doris, live a life very much like that of Leonard and Claire. At forty-five, Dennis owns and operates a franchised donut shop. Their eldest son is a lawyer and their daughter has just gotten married. The donut business requires a great deal of Dennis' time as owner-manager and also day baker. He is usually at the shop as early as four in the morning, preparing for the rush that starts each business day. He and Doris enjoy sailing and entertaining their neighborhood friends. They have little time for travel and now that their son and daughter have moved away they don't see much of their families. Like Leonard, Dennis was diagnosed as having a cancerous melanoma which would require surgical removal and a watchful period of recuperation. Here all similarities between these two middle-aged men ends. Having commonly met mortality, they chose to respond in very different ways.

Whereas Leonard's recuperative time was spent dreaming up all the pleasures in life which had eluded him, and planning to capture those pleasures and taste of them before life itself eluded him, Dennis spent his recuperative time thinking of the many things he had to settle in his life before it could end. As Dennis describes it, "As I lay there in bed I thought how totally unprepared I was for death, how irresponsible I had been in always living for the present, never thinking ahead, never thinking of what might happen to my wife, my family, if I died. My insurance picture was a mess. I had made no plans for anyone to take over the shop if something should happen to me. I hadn't attended to my personal relationships in such a way that I should have and I didn't have any religious peace and harmony, so I set about planning the things I would need to do. I had always thought I would have so much more time to take care of those things, the insurance, the business, personal relationships and all, I'd always thought there would be years and years when I was older and retired, when I'd have time to take care of all that. But the cancer taught me a lesson, that there wasn't time, at least no time like the present, and ever since then I've been quietly but effectively putting my affairs in order. There is really nothing more to be said about it. I have provided financially for my family, I have made arrangements for the business to be passed on, I think my friends know how I feel about them, I am making peace with my God and I am ready to die. This time it won't take me by surprise.''

Dennis' son has a somewhat different perspective on his father's behavior subsequent to the surgery. ''I'm sure that's just the way Dad thinks about it. That's just the way he would think about it. He says he was irresponsible but that the surgery taught him that he should be more responsible and what he has done since then is to simply put his affairs into order. I know he thinks of it that way. He called me from the hospital while he was recuperating and asked if I could come home right away, that it was serious. Well, of course I was ready to come home anyway because of the surgery and when he called I thought that things might not be as good as Mom told me over the phone. I rushed home and went straight to the hospital from the airport. When I got there, do you know what he wanted to talk about? He wanted to talk about his will. He wanted to talk about his insurance. He wanted to talk about legal arrangements for passing on the business. I tried to tell him there'd be plenty of time to talk about all that later on and we could put it all in order—that there would be plenty of time for that, but he kept saying to me, 'Don't you see, son, there isn't any time. I wasn't ready this time but next time I'm going to be ready to die.' Well, that sounds pretty morbid, someone getting ready to die and all, but as morbid as it sounds that's not half as morbid as it's been. For the last three months that man has been getting ready to die. He's bought a funeral plot, he's picked out his casket. He asked his best friend to write a eulogy for him. He's set up arrangements to pass the business on to this young baker kid he's got working for him. He spends all of his time working on dying—poring over insurance forms, revising his will, writing letters to old friends telling them how much he cared for them, how important they were to him. He's going through his own last rites. I think he'd honestly be happy if we could have his funeral now before he's gone just to see how well all of the things he's planned worked out. He has this absolutely morbid fascination with his own death and that's been so ever since his cancer thing. You talk to Mom about it, she'll tell you."

The mother, Doris, is confused and confounded by her husband's behavior. "It's very strange. I don't understand it at all. We were so happy to have him alive, to know that he would go on living, but he acts as though he is dead and dying. He always talks about 'after I'm gone, when I'm no longer here.' He's even tried to get me to meet some other men socially so that when he is gone I'll have some companionship. He is continually giving me these awful little tests, like 'Where are the insurance policies? Who is the man I call at the mortuary? How much money should I expect to get out of the business each year?' I don't care about any of that. He's alive now and I want us to get on with living but the only thing that has his attention, his energy, is dying. I can't understand that. It seems so morbid, so funeral-like. I can understand his accepting that he will die *sometime,* but why all this about dying *now?* It's beginning to get to me so much so that anytime he starts talking like that, all that death nonsense, I just stop listening. I just turn my head and stop listening. I refuse to pay any attention to that. I just wish Dennis would stop dying and start living."

There is in Dennis' behavior ample evidence of the sorts of

responses seen in middle-aged men who, having met mortality, accept it and decide to fully prepare themselves for a second, lasting meeting. These men, in accepting mortality, not only withdraw from life but retreat into death. Insurance policies, funeral plots and eulogies seem to be the only things which give meaning to their lives. For family and friends it is literally as though they are living with a dead man. There is no way to tell for certain, but it would seem that once these men give in psychologically to death, giving in physiologically must necessarily follow closely behind, and their second meeting with mortality gives reality to their death wish.

We have not mentioned here suicide as a response to meeting mortality. Clearly there are middle-aged men who for any number of reasons choose to meet mortality head-on and take their own lives. Yet information on suicides is very difficult to obtain. Serious questions exist as to how many suicides there are in this age group. There are those who suggest that single-car accident fatalities or hunting "accidents" might reasonably be counted as suicides. Even where the incidents of suicide can be verified, motives are impossible to obtain. Perhaps the most that can be said is that suicide is a *possible* response to meeting mortality, recognizing that it does occur, but realizing the difficulty of exploring how frequently or why.

Not all men who accept mortality in mid-life do so in such a morbid manner. There are many who prepare themselves for the inevitable by striving for an inner peace and harmony with one's place in the world. Most of the men who so respond to the crisis of mortality in mid-life turn to religion. Organized religion has experienced a resurgence of interest in this country in recent years as more and more families find themselves turning to the church. Membership is, if not on the rise, at least stabilizing, and church activities are increasingly visible in community and family life. It would be impossible to say how many of those men who find themselves in families returning to church are led to return by their experience of a mid-life crisis, a meeting with mortality. Nor is it the purpose here to give the testimonials of men who are "born again" as a result of the mid-life crisis. It is clear, however, that for a great and growing number of middle-aged men, they find in religion a response to the concerns brought about by their meetings with mortality.

Walter Robinson wrote, "If you had talked to me just before the heart attack I would have told you that I had achieved everything I thought life was cracked up to be, everything I ever wanted and yet, when the heart attack came, I suddenly discovered that that wasn't life at all. I realized that without an eternal purpose first and foremost in my life I could never live and with an eternal purpose I could never die. It seems to me that if a man devotes his entire life to the temporal, it is logical that when life is threatened he will feel that he has nothing. Everything that he has worked for is subject to decay, die, rust, and wear out. Man himself will be forgotten by others when he dies but I learned that if a man dedicates and devotes himself to the eternal he has something that lasts forever and can never be taken away from him. I don't walk with my head in the clouds. I've got a solid career in forestry, but my main purpose ever since I came so close to death is to help others find forgiveness for the past and a right relationship with God through Christ. That brings real life, life everlasting. There are many men who do not want to listen to me but they cannot deny God. He says 'He that has the Son has life. He that has not the Son has not life.' I choose life."

Carl McClellan wrote, "I came so close to dying, the doctors themselves say they don't know how I lived. I thought, 'What have I really accomplished of lasting value?' If I had gone ahead and died, what use would all of my life have been to me or anyone else? I knew in that moment the only way I could find eternal fulfillment was through the Word of God. I found Christ through me will also live on. God says, 'Don't lay up for yourselves treasures on earth where moth and rust destroy, but lay up for yourselves treasures in heaven.' Those treasures in heaven are the only life insurance I or any man ever needs. I know that what I do now for God counts forever. My relationship with Christ is what gives significance to the here and now. If he calls, I am ready for eternity.''

It is difficult to be critical of these religious responses to a middle-aged man's meeting with mortality. The threat to life can lead a man to seek life everlasting—the salvation that is only available through religion. However, religion can serve as much as a retreat from life as it does an acceptance of mortality and the promise of immortality. Religious rebirth may lead to a total reliance on religion and God's hand, to the exclusion of raising one's own hand. While there are very few cases of responses to the mid-life crisis which evidence this total rejection of individual responsibility in favor of divine intervention, it does happen. One wife wrote about her husband, ''It sounds terrible to say it, but I really think Stan has gone overboard on this God thing. I completely understand how the church has helped him to accept his disease and deal with death, but you'd think he was going to heaven tomorrow the way he's been acting! He's constantly spouting Scripture, prays at the drop of a hat, and whenever I so much as mention a problem with money or the house or kids he goes into his 'God is watching over us' thing and refuses to lift a finger to help. While he has accepted his time here on earth is getting short, and is busy preparing for the hereafter, me and the kids are going to hell here and now!''

As has been the case in examining the varied responses to other causes of the mid-life crisis there is no one response to meeting mortality that is any better than any other response(s) for the middle-aged man. There are only different responses, different effects for different men. The message of man's mortality seems inescapable in mid-life. The annual death rate from heart disease alone in the age group forty to sixty is nearly four out of every 1,000 men and increasing rapidly. There is scarcely a middle-aged man alive who has not had an intimate, personal experience with the threats to life either directly, through his own declining health, or indirectly, through the death of a parent or friend. These inescapable meetings with mortality come to most if not all men in mid-life, and they signal change and the need for a new perspective on life and living. Most middle-aged men take the message in stride as a sign of a new stage of life. Other men are thrown into turmoil by the message, threatened by what it portends. They are knocked off-balance, off-stride. For them the meeting with mortality brings about a crisis. There can also be little doubt that the responses of these men in crisis are not very functional in helping them to resolve that crisis. They alter the symptoms but fall far short of curing the cause. Real resolution can only come when the middle-aged man turns his attention away from responding to the threats he senses and toward discovering and dealing with *why* he is threatened. This is as true for the meeting with mortality as it is for any of the causes of the male mid-life crisis, including those that are concerned less with the loss of life and more with living, such as "In Search of Adventure."

7

In Search of Adventure

IN THE SUMMER OF 1978, three American men navigated the *Double Eagle II* to a landing in a small cornfield, twenty miles outside of Paris, France. They had completed the first trans-Atlantic crossing in a hot-air balloon in history. They succeeded in an adventure which had held the fascination and attention of balloonists and adventurers for over one hundred years. They succeeded where countless others had failed, where several had died.

As the *Double Eagle II* landed, Ben Mirado was in his garage in Frankfort, Indiana. Ben was building an airplane. He had never built an airplane before (had never built anything larger or more complicated than a doghouse), never flown a plane before. But when he was done he would learn to fly and embark on the great adventure of his life, a solo flight coast to coast.

These events are separated by space and scope; the one an international event celebrated and admired in every country in the world, the other a private, individual undertaking known to few, celebrated by none. Yet these events are not nearly so dissimilar as they may at first seem, for they are both the adventures of middle-aged men. The three American hot-air balloon adventurers were all middle-aged. Ben Mirado was in that same summer forty-nine. It is not possible to say that the balloonists attempted their heroic deed solely for the adventure involved.

They might have done so for fame, fortune, adventure, or any combination of such motives. In the instance of Ben Mirado it seems clear that neither fame nor fortune directed his efforts and indeed, probably it was adventure alone he sought. Adventure does have a powerful, almost hypnotic appeal for many middle-aged men. The lure of lost horizons, the thrill of threatening environments, the risks of rewards unknown, the true magic of mystery offer excitement that many middle-aged men find impossible to avoid. More than that they find it necessary to seek out adventure, necessary to pursue the excitement. This behavior seen in so many middle-aged men is viewed by some as evidence of what is felt to be a major issue late in adult life, the issue of changing and growing or continuing and stagnating.

One of the foundation theories of adult development has been Erik Erikson's life-cycle theory. The maturation process as envisioned by Erikson consists of a number of issues which arise for a man in the course of his life as he attempts to define himself in relation to others and to society. These issues appear in a patterned sequence, although the time and form of resolution is of course different from one man to another. Very briefly the issues are:

1. Trust vs. Mistrust
2. Autonomy vs. Shame and Doubt
3. Initiative vs. Guilt
4. Industry vs. Inferiority
5. Identity vs. Role Diffusion
6. Intimacy vs. Isolation
7. Generativity vs. Stagnation
8. Ego Integrity vs. Despair

This view of a man's development easily translates into an explanation of the mid-life crisis. In middle age events conspire to cause a man to consider the issue of generativity vs. stagnation. He asks of himself what will the second half of his life bring? Will he live out his remaining years in a straight-line continuation of the pattern he has established to date—doing the things he has always done, with the same people, the same results? Or will he change, grow, *generate* new experiences and encounters for himself? For those men who have seen themselves as vibrant, vital men, continually changing, continually creating new experiences, continually challenging themselves, the routines which they have established by their middle years may seem to be ruts. The stability they have striven for seems stagnating. For men who so value growth and change, the threat of life without newness is not a threat that can easily be avoided or denied. Panic sets in as it seems they must change now or never. Once the question occurs, the only response that seems available is to seek newness. Retreating into routine would only be a further reminder of those routines so the threat cannot be avoided—it must be met and overcome. For these men, more than any other middle-aged men who experience crisis, the change in personality and behavior that they undergo is valued less for its substance than for the fact that it is change. It might truly be said of these middle-aged men that they seek change for the sake of change alone. And where does the middle aged man find change? Where can he look for new experiences, new encounters?

The adventurous paths many middle-aged men embark on run the full range from the heroic to the humble, from the banal to the bizarre, but they share in common several dimensions. First, whatever the chosen adventure of the middle-aged adventurer it is certain to be a sharp and significant departure from his established routine. The cause of crisis may come upon these men gradually, but their response is rapid and resolute and leaves no question that they are indeed in search of adventure. Second, in these adventures there is always a substantial element of risk, very often physical risk, but there are frequently financial and psychological risks as well. Of course risk is relative. An adventurous act that may seem death-defying to one middle-aged man will be for another little more than "healthy exercise." What is important is that the middle-aged man himself views his behavior as risk-taking for him, regardless of how his behavior might be viewed by others. A third common dimension of these mid-life adventures is that once initiated there emerges a "chain of changes." Each adventure leads to another and the experiences escalate, each change riskier and more adventurous than the last.

Mention should be made of the sensationalism often associated with these cases. There are ample reports of dramatic and even dangerous changes in the lives of middle-aged men who seek adventure. But such sensational searches are not the norm. For every truly dangerous adventure sought by a middle-aged man there are a hundred other such men who also seek adventure on a much more mundane and limited scale. It is these men who buy the sports cars, the motorcycles, the speedboats. Those "normal" men who take on new, unfamiliar and unlikely projects and find small, often subtle ways of breaking the routines of a lifetime. These are hardly death-defying acts, but they do have the stuff of real drama and defiance on a scope that is inconsistent with the previous lives of these men, and represent their own, very personal way of striking out in search of adventure.

One very curious dimension of these crises of change is that they are typically met with a great deal of tolerance and understanding by the significant other people involved. The only other changes as a result of crisis that are similarly supported by the middle-aged man's wife, mistress and friends are those which result from the goal gap. Such people display great sympathy for the middle-aged man's need for change and adventure in his life. Beyond sympathy, in most instances they are willing to provide their active cooperation in his search for adventure. There are, of course, limits to such sympathy and support, but in almost every instance these limits seem to be broader, more tolerant and accepting than in the limits of support associated with other mid-life crises.

The cases of crisis reported here vary greatly in many respects, but they share in common the pattern of behavior that has come to be expected of middle-aged men in search of adventure: a sudden, significant change; a relative degree of risk; a "chain of changes"; and sympathy and support from significant other people (within limits). The first case below describes a frequent and familiar mid-life adventure. The remaining cases may be far less familiar, but perhaps surprisingly they are not a great deal less frequent.

Andrew Rails is forty-six years old. He's an accountant with one of the Northwestern public utility companies. Andrew (not Andy—he's quite firm about that) has been with them his entire career. For twenty-five years he has known no other work, no other company. Indeed, for much of those twenty-five years, Andrew has changed very little and he even looks much the same as he always looked. He is a small man, slight of build, with a full head of hair that shows graying only at the temples. Always impeccably dressed, Andrew usually wears a vested suit of gray or dark blue. Even at home he is likely to wear a tie. He is, by his own description, the picture of what one might imagine an accountant to be; absent only is the green eyeshade. "I guess you could say I lead a well-ordered life. I have a good job with a good company and I see to it that I do a good job for them. My work is far from what others would see as exciting, but I enjoy it. I value a sense of order and I'm proud of my ability to bring a sense of order to things, that's why I enjoy accounting. It's very disciplined work. My family life has been well ordered also. Roberta and I have been married for twenty-five years. We married right after I joined the firm. Our only son, Robert, is also an accountant. We are happily married and really always have been. Until just recently I had no hobbies to speak of. I've always collected stamps and feel I have a fine collection, but other than that, work has occupied most of my time. I often work at home on accounts. Roberta and I take in an occasional play or concert, but we do not have an active social life. We do belong to the local church and attend regularly. I guess you'd say that I am what an accountant is supposed to be, conservative in my life-style and politics, hardworking, thrifty, thorough and well ordered.

"At least that is the way I would have described myself up

until about a year and a half ago. Now, I'm not so sure that description fits any longer. I still have a good job and I still do a good job at it, but I don't think I could be described as the typical accountant any longer. It began oddly enough with a card I got on my forty-fifth birthday. I can't remember exactly what it said. It was from my son, Robert, and it suggested something like the most excitement I might get out of being middle-aged was blowing out the candles on my cake. In addition to the printed message on the card, Robert had written that he really found it difficult to buy a gift for someone who had no vices. He gave me a blue tie. I don't know why it struck me as it did just then. Certainly, I had been accused of leading a boring life long before that. I don't imagine there is a joke about how boring accountants are that I haven't heard. I know that lots of people probably think of me as a Caspar Milquetoast type, but frankly it had never bothered me before. I had what I wanted out of life and if that didn't seem interesting to others I thought that it was their problem, not mine. But Robert's message that year did upset me some. Maybe it had something to do with being told by my own son that I was boring. At any rate, I started thinking about just what was happening with my life. What I was doing. As I reviewed my stable job, good marriage, my orderly life, I have to confess that they seemed different to me. For the first time, that year when I turned forty-five, I saw that my routine was really sort of a rut. I remember trying hard to recall the last time I had been truly excited—the last time I had felt my adrenalin pump, my emotions surge, and I couldn't recall any last time.

"Of course I didn't come to this conclusion overnight. No, I thought about it for quite some time, probably a year, before I really decided to do anything about it. Even as I was deciding on the need for some change, it wasn't quite clear to me how I should change, what exactly would excite me. Finally I decided it would be a motorcycle. I don't know why I decided on a motorcycle instead of a sports car or something else. I do recall there for three or four months as I drove to work I noticed how many older men there were riding motorcycles. They seemed to be enjoying it so, weaving in and out of traffic, going much faster than the cars, their hair blowing, the wind in their faces. It just looked to me like riding a motorcycle would be exciting. So one Saturday morning I took my stamp collection and sold it. I got quite a bit of money for it, it was an excellent collection. That same morning I took the money and bought a motorcycle —not just a motorcycle, but the biggest, fastest motorcycle I could find—a 1000-cc. Harley-Davidson. It was big and it was heavy and at first even the sound of it was sort of frightening. It was so powerful there as I sat on it that I had some second thoughts. But they were very patient with me at the shop. The salesman was older than I was! He told me how a lot of people my age decided that a motorcycle was for them. As I rode away I felt that he was right—having a motorcycle is a pretty natural thing for a man my age to do. Of course I couldn't stop with just a motorcycle. I had to buy goggles and they explained how you needed different sets of clothing so I bought a jacket and some coveralls, sort of riding leathers that went on over what you were wearing, and I started home. Oh, the look on Roberta's face when I roared up the driveway on that machine! I have often thought how great it would be to have a picture of that look. Well, of course she wanted to know whose it was. When I told her it was mine I thought she was going to faint. All day long she kept asking why I got it. I really couldn't explain too clearly. I said things like 'needing a change' and 'wanting to put some excitement back in my life,' 'looking for a couple of thrills.' Whatever it was that I said she really seemed to understand and even began to see it as a good idea, even though she wouldn't get on it with me. Her only real concern was about the safety of having a bike like that, so she went out the following week and bought me a helmet—one of those gold-and-silver-flaked ones.

"At work they thought I had gone absolutely crazy. I took a lot of kidding about going through menopause and second adolescence, but it didn't bother me any. I love riding that bike. To get on it every morning, listening to it roar, weaving in and out of traffic, revving up that huge engine, feeling the wind blow hard on my face, it really is a thrill. You just can't imagine a feeling like that until you've done it yourself. I'm only sorry I waited forty-six years to do it. That motorcycle really opened my mind to a lot of good things I had been missing. First of all, a lot of people I never would have met if it had not been for bikes, people who weren't accountants. A lot of people who didn't know what an accountant was. Not Hell's Angels or any of those bandit bikers that you read so much about, just people from different walks of life who had in common with me an interest in bikes. I joined a group that goes on weekend rides to the mountains or the coast. I've had some great experiences on those trips, done some things I never would have imagined doing before.

"Some of my bike friends convinced me that I should put a little bit of my savings into this bike shop downtown, so I've done that. It's not a lot of money but I enjoy knowing that I'm supporting my hobby, and it's great fun to go down there as an owner and tinker around. I suppose there are those who would say that what I've done at my age is a pretty risky thing, riding a bike as much as I do and as fast as I do, and putting some money up in something as unpredictable as a motorcycle shop. It doesn't seem like all that big a risk to me. It's just a change. I should have done it a long time ago. I'm just glad I made it when I did, glad I didn't wait any longer. Sure, not everybody starts riding a motorcycle and buying motorcycle shops when they're forty-six years old, but then not everybody has led as boring a life up until the time they're forty-six years old as I did. I haven't gone as far out as a lot of people I know about have. I've just done some things to help me enjoy life a little more, that's not so risky, is it? I just want a little adventure and a little excitement. Where's the risk in that?"

Roberta, Andrew's wife, seems to feel that the change in Andrew is worth whatever risk has accompanied it. "It was very strange at first. Life had always been so orderly with Andrew, you know, a place for everything and everything in its place, really predictable, and then all of a sudden one day out of the blue he comes roaring up the driveway on this machine. I just didn't know what to think. Driving that thing the way he does, so fast, sometimes I still have visions of his being slaughtered out there on the highway, run into by a truck or something like that. I've even imagined him taking up with a bunch of motorcycle girls, you know, long hair and big breasts and little leather vests. Even now I don't know too many of his motorcycle friends, though he tells me they're nothing like that. I know he's part-owner now of a motorcycle shop or something. I never paid much attention to what he does with the money. We've always managed so well. He's been going on like this for I guess about a year and a half now, but I still think it's just a phase he's going through—something that captures his attention now, but sooner or later he'll forget about it and get back to his routine. I have to admit, though, that he's been more alive this last year than I can ever remember. He seems to enjoy life so much. He gets so much out of every day. I guess I should be thankful he hasn't run off like some middle-aged men we know have. I guess I should be thankful he hasn't taken up anything more dangerous than motorcycles and I really am. If he gets some adventure and excitement in his life out of riding motorcycles, well, he deserves some adventure and I'm happy for him as long as he doesn't get too reckless and get himself hurt."

As might be expected, a woman's tolerance for the adventures of a middle-aged man decreases as the risk he takes on increases. Most women are very supportive of their men adding a little zest to their life, a little manageable excitement—nothing too bizarre or burdensome—just a little change to keep things lively. However, as the risk increases, or as the frequency with which a man takes risks increases, the woman has her tolerance tested. This is particularly true where the middle-aged man embarks on a spiraling search for adventure, with each change more exciting, riskier than the last. There is the woman's natural and obvious concern for the physical safety of the middle-aged man. There is also concern over her role and their relationship together as he searches for ever greater adventures. What becomes of the safe, secure relationship that she has known as he becomes a new adventure-seeking man, continually looking for excitement? Must she become more exciting if she is to keep him? Must she become as adventurous as he?

Lois Kelpat has considered these questions in her attempt to live with her husband's adventures. "My husband is forty-seven. He is going through the crisis you hear so much about. I am forty and not crazy about it, either. I am sympathetic with his needs but I am finding it extremely difficult to condone what he believes to be the cure-all—that is to quit his job ($42,000 per year) of twenty-one years and buy a small ranch and raise cattle and break wild horses. He wants only a small ranch, because there wouldn't be enough money for a large ranch. This is not the first time he's had some radical ideas and I have, at great expense to my own mental health, tried to humor him. First there was learning to fly and piloting small planes. From the outset I was opposed to his flying, but eventually I gave in. That lasted for about two years. Then he took up skydiving; this at age forty-three. It wasn't enough that he had to be flying around in those dangerous things, he started jumping out of them as well. After skydiving, came hang-gliding. To tell you the truth I don't know which is the more dangerous, but I do know that I couldn't stop him from doing either one. He did hang-gliding for a year. Now he's tired of all of these and no longer does them and for the last year he's been on this ranch kick. What I'm saying is that I've tried all of our married life to give him the kind of freedom that I've never seen in any of the relationships of our married friends or relatives. I've protested these adventures of his, but I've never stopped him. But this time is different. This time it means a change for the rest of my life and all the possible insecurity that goes with it—a definite change in life-style that I do not care for at all. All that for a possible whim that he will probably tire of just as he did with all of the other ideas, and then where will we be with no job, no money, no nothing? In other words, this is the first time I have said 'no.' I am at my wit's end. Something like this has been going on for five years or more and it can't go on any longer. He has been a faithful man so far, but I am afraid that if I don't give in on this he may seek his pleasures elsewhere. In either case, whether I give in and we go off together on this adventure of his, or I don't give in and he goes off with someone else on this adventure, I am devastated. It looks like I'm faced with being either adventuresome or being alone. Neither one of them seems very attractive to me."

Gary, Lois' husband, understandably has a different view of the problem. "Here's the deal. At about forty I got tired of being a spectator in life. I'd been pretty active in college, played a lot of sports, went camping, hunting, hiking, took canoe trips, all that sort of stuff. When I started moving up on the job the games and adventure got set aside and I became a spectator, watching other people be adventuresome, seeing someone else have all the fun, get all the thrills. Looking back now I can't remember that there was any single event or day or anything that happened—It's more like I just made up my mind that I was going to put some excitement back in my life. I had always wanted to fly so that seemed like a natural place to start. Flying was a lot of fun and I got a real kick out of learning and then soloing for the first time. What a thrill that was. We leased a plane with some other people and could fly whenever we wanted and wherever we wanted. Lois may have complained about my flying but she sure didn't complain about the trips we got to take, even though she was a little nervous flying with me at the controls.

"Then after a while, well, there just wasn't much thrill to flying. It got to be kind of old hat. Even the promise of learning how to fly bigger, faster planes didn't seem as if it would be all that much more exciting, so I was looking around for some new thrills. I had flown for a couple of guys who were into skydiving and that looked like a lot of fun. I took some lessons and started skydiving. Now there is a thrill for you. There is just no way to explain the thrill you get when your feet leave that plane and it's just you out there in the air. I dove for maybe a year, year and a half, then this hang-gliding thing got real big and that looked like it might be quite a bit more fun, so I took that up. It was even a freer feeling than the skydiving was because you weren't dependent on a plane to get you up there to start with—you just go out to a cliff and jump off.

"I guess all of those things had an element of danger in them, but hell, I was never hurt doing any of them and it didn't hurt Lois for me to do them, either. They were expensive, but nothing we couldn't afford. I always have been kind of disappointed that she didn't do any of them with me. When I got to skydiving and hang-gliding she wouldn't even come watch. The thing with the ranch is a little bit different from all that. I have to admit that Lois' saying that these are all just fads that I go through kind of got to me. I stayed with flying a couple of years, with skydiving for a little over a year and a half, and hang-gliding for over a year. I did tire of them after a while—there just wasn't anything exciting about them anymore. I think I've discovered the reason for that is because those are just add-ons to what I normally do. Hell, every day of the week I'm working like all of the other slobs—eight to five, and when you just tack on what really excites you to what you're doing anyway, just fit it in as you can, there are bound to be limits to the thrills. It seems to me that what I need is not these weekend kinds of adventures but a life-style that would be a challenge. That's why I want the ranch. I want to go out there, Montana, Wyoming, someplace, and buy some land. I know there's all these wild horses out there (the government rounds them up now), hell, I could round them up and break those horses and sell them or raise some cattle. Now that would be a life-style with an adventure a day. Those guys that do that, hell, they're never bored, they never grow old. Every day brings a new thrill and that's what I want. I'm not going to leave Lois to do it if she says definitely no, but I'll tell you, she's not going to say no. She's said no at first all the other times but she didn't mean it in the end. She'll say no a little bit this time and she won't mean it, and I'll be able to convince her it's a life of adventure for the two of us. If she really decides that she doesn't want to go along, well, we'll cross that bridge when we come to it, but she's not going to decide that. There's no way she's going to keep me from what I want most in life and what I want most in life is an exciting life.''

The search for another adventure more exciting, more thrilling, longer lasting than the last is a never-ending search. For the middle-aged man who embarks on such a search there is a frantic, frenetic rush from one adventure to the next, never staying with anything long enough to see whether or not it will bore him, but always moving on to the next adventure, to the next greater risk. He tires of fast cars and buys fast boats, tires of fast boats and buys a fast plane, tires of planes and takes up skydiving, tires of skydiving and takes up hang-gliding, tires of hang-gliding and is on to another thrill. The challenge is valued as much for the *change* as it is for the challenge itself, as much for the difference as for the defiance. Defying routine is as much a factor as defying death. Most of these middle aged men need in some way or another the supportive framework of a woman to pursue excitement, the thrill of adventure. For some it is as simple as the notion that there cannot be heroes without heroines. For others it is the fact that the stability these women represent gives them the security to reach out, a firm foundation on which to rely as they spring into adventurous activities. For still others the woman is needed as a measuring stick, as a benchmark, something to remind themselves of how humdrum life once was and how heroic it now is. These middle-aged adventurers strike out for adventure but usually don't go far from home.

Some middle-aged men leave home in search of adventure, never to return again. For these men, wife, family, home, come to represent the very routines they are rebelling against. The middle-aged woman they have been married to for so long stands as a symbol of the stagnation they see all about their lives. To these men it seems that there can be no adventure, no excitement, no thrills, no growth without a complete break with the routine. They must escape the relationship which they see as the main fabric in the blanket which has fallen over their lives, a blanket which has wrapped them in a suffocating security. The stories of these adventurers are among the most unusual to be found in the annals of the male mid-life crisis. Take Bill House as an example.

"I suppose I did have a mid-life crisis if that is what you want to call it. What I really had was the feeling that unless I did something different real soon I was going to die right there in that job, in that house with that woman. It wasn't that life up there was all that bad, there were some years there, still are, when you could make pretty good money cutting hair, once men got sort of fancy and got concerned about how they looked— twelve to fifteen dollars for a shampoo and haircut. I worked in a nice shop there in town and did a good business, but hell, I'm over forty years old and all I've ever known is cutting hair. And that's all I've ever done—right out of high school, followed in my dad's footsteps, took up a chair in his shop, then moved into a bigger shop, then bought a piece of that shop that I was in last. Like I said, I made a good living at it. Linda and I, well, we didn't have any real problems, no money problems or anything like that, it was just a pretty routine life and that's what finally got to me, it was such a routine.

"Most of the people who came to the shop were businessmen, but every now and then we'd get somebody in who was a little out of the ordinary, somebody who had stories to tell. They'd been drilling in Arabia or working on the pipeline in Alaska. I remember a guy once who had gone searching for some lost treasure of gold in New Mexico somewhere. Another fellow had spent a year watching for the Loch Ness monster. Whenever those guys would come into the shop and start telling a story about where they'd been or what they'd done, I was fascinated by it. I couldn't get enough of it. I'd ask them questions, hang on their every word. Every time I heard one of those stories I thought, 'Someday maybe I'll do that,' but I never did. I never did do anything like that. I just got up every morning, went to the shop, cut hair and went home at night. That's all I ever did, more than twenty years of getting up, going to the shop, cutting hair. Finally I got up one morning and I didn't go to the shop. I didn't really plan it out or anything. There was just something about that day that said 'Do it *now* or you'll never do it!' So I did. I went to the bank and I took out exactly half of what we had in there. I figured I was only entitled to half. Linda needed something. I went to the airport and took a plane down here to Florida and I became a treasure hunter.

"I started out as a deckhand and the way I got on the deck was by offering to cut people's hair. They're always looking for people to be around boats and if you could do something else, as well as being around a boat, that's to your advantage. I was in reasonably good shape as I started out and that helped, too. I learned to dive and now I sign off on treasure-hunting boats and that's what we do. We go hunting for sunken treasures. I've found lots of stuff—cannons, jewelry, dishes—all kinds of stuff. You never know what you're going to find I've had some run-ins with sharks, have had things happen to my gear underwater. I've never had so many experiences in so little time. Hell, it's only been a year and a half. I feel like I've damn near caught up for all the living I missed out on. I miss Linda, sure I do, but I'm living too good now to go back. I know I can't go back into that rut I was in and Linda's part of that. Things are starting to happen in my life, things that are exciting. I wake up every morning and I can hardly wait to see what the day is going to bring. There's no more routine, there's no more rut, no more boredom. I try to take care of Linda, send her some money now and then, when I can, which is pretty often. It's not all that bad hunting treasure these days. We get these big fellows to bankroll us and pay our salaries and then they get a share of whatever we find. Of course finding it is not the most important part for me. The most important part is I'm out looking for it. I'm out doing something. I'm not just standing behind that chair listening to those guys who come in and tell their stories. Hell, now when I get my hair cut I know when I start telling my stories about hunting for treasures off the coast of Florida, about swimming like hell to get away from a shark, about having my tanks go out on me about a hundred feet down, when I tell my stories to some guy cutting my hair, standing in back of me, hanging on my every word, he's probably thinking like I used to think, 'Someday that'll be me.' Well I'll tell you, once you start thinking 'someday it'll be me,' you better get out there and do something about it because otherwise you just get older.''

For Bill House, Linda was another symbol of all that he disdained in his life, the security that was suffocating him, the routines which were once comfortable but now chafed, the business, once busy, now boring. Linda was but another part of a whole life which he threw over at age forty-two to create a new one. For Bill a more exciting, more adventurous life was worth any price—even his wife.

Other middle-aged men view their wives not as a part of the problem but rather as the problem itself. They see no chance of finding excitement and adventure so long as they stay in a relationship which has come to bore and burden them. For these middle-aged men excitement can only come if they can escape the family ties that bind.

Fred Morton is a former stockbroker turned guide and river-runner on the Snake River in Idaho. He speaks of why and how. ''There's just no way I can tell you how boring Marilyn was, and the kids too. I've got to throw them in there with her, just boring. That may sound cold but believe me, that's just how it was. She never wanted to do anything, to go anywhere, to meet anybody, to try new places or new people. The main thing in her whole life was security, security, security. I had to be stable so we could be secure. Well, it's pretty hard to be secure in the securities business but I worked my tail off for fifteen years doing just that, meeting her needs for stability and security, and being bored shitless in the process. She was bringing up the kids in the same way, they never had any new experiences either. In fact, they were afraid of anything new. Nothing used to make me so mad as the way my kids would react when there was something new going on. My God, you'd have thought you'd asked them to jump off a building to try to learn how to swim, ride a bike or roller-skate, not just the normal kids' fears—but really abnormal fears. I think she's making them sick with all that security-stability shit, and she was making me sick, too. Finally I realized that the only way I was going to have any adventure, any excitement in my life was to get away from Marilyn and get it for myself.

"I'd always wanted to run these rapids and now I do it for a living. Marilyn of course divorced me about three months after I came out here. It was pretty obvious to her that I wasn't going to be stable any longer and there went her security, so she divorced me and ended up marrying the lawyer who handled her part of the divorce. I could care less. Let him be bored! You just can't know what it's like to live with someone who never wants to grow, never wants to change, it's like a pool of water that never moves. It starts out being real clear and you can see through to the bottom and then it clouds over and the bugs start to land on it and the next thing you know, it's stagnant and you've got mosquitoes biting you. That's pretty much how it is with somebody who never wants to change, to grow, to do anything. That's the way I was with Marilyn, turning into a stagnant pool of water at forty-three. Now I'm running just as fast as that river's running, just as wild, and loving every minute of it. Oh I suppose it can't go on forever, a river sure doesn't, but I tell you while it's running, it's one hell of a lot of fun."

As they speed forward toward adventure, middle-aged men leave in their wake wives, families, friends and businesses to fend for themselves as best they might. Some men, like Bill House, experience a sense of loss but come to view that loss as a relatively small price to be paid for a life of excitement and adventure. Other men, like Fred Morton, feel neither loss nor regret, elated as they are over escaping relationships which were burdensome and boring, blocking them from a life of excitement and adventure. For every man who has so sought adventure there is a wife and family left baffled, resentful. Why? Where is he? What do we do now? One such wife, Jane Marley, was particularly articulate in raising these questions. Her husband, a hospital administrator, left her and their three adult-age children after twenty-six years of marriage, four days after his fiftieth birthday. She knows only that he is somewhere in South America living with a teenage boy.

"I don't know why he did it. I still don't know why. It's been two years now and I've read everything I could get my hands on and talked to everyone who would talk to me about this kind of thing, this kind of behavior on the part of middle-aged men. I do know that he needed change, he needed adventure. Obviously he did or he wouldn't have done this, but I don't know why he needed this. He worked so hard to build a family and a career, to provide some stability and security for our later years, and then to just pick up and throw all of that away. I've been so hurt and humiliated by it all. There's just no explanation that will help me get over that hurt. I suppose I'm at fault somehow. I must be for him to reject me so, but I don't know what I would have done differently. Maybe I should have tried to be more exciting, more alluring, but he didn't leave me for another woman so I don't see how that would work. Maybe his being with a boy proves he always was a homosexual, a latent homosexual. But maybe being with a boy is just another part of the adventure he's on. Maybe he'll come back. I haven't divorced him, you know. I have no way of knowing if he'll come back. He didn't take any money or anything with him. Really we're fairly well off financially and the children have helped a great deal. They don't understand it any better than I do, although I don't think they feel rejected in the way I feel rejected. What I want to know is why does life always have to be adventurous? Why does there always have to be some excitement? Couldn't he just enjoy life without being excited by it? Why did everything have to be a thrill? I just don't think you can live in a continual state of excitement, and I certainly don't think that's possible for a fifty-year-old man. I'd just like to know why. I'd like to know if it was me, if it was my fault, if there is anything I could have done or could do now that would have kept him from this adventure, this asinine, awful adventure.''

As is so often the case there is in most instances very little the wife/woman can do to keep the middle-aged man from seeking his adventure. Her options seem limited to either supporting the adventure, participating in it, or resisting it and running the risk of being rejected and left behind. A common ploy is for the middle-aged man to pressure his wife into joining him in his search for adventure. Reluctant to join him, but feeling at the same time guilty about standing in his way, the wife is often cornered into offering begrudging support. ''I don't want to, but you go ahead.'' In so doing she underscores the separation he may perceive in their lives, he alive and searching for more life, she a stay-at-home, stick-in-the-mud. This pattern was reported frequently in those instances where the middle-aged man was seeking excitement through a new social and sexual life-style. Margie Wallen describes her response. ''First Lee wanted to try marijuana. I don't know where he got it, probably from the kids. He kept pressuring me and finally I gave in. It was okay, even pleasant, but it wasn't so enjoyable that I wanted to do it again, after all, we're both forty-four. But Lee really liked it and began smoking instead of drinking at parties. Then he started in on the sex thing. I think he got the idea from those sex magazines. Anyway, he thought it would be exciting for us to 'swap' with another couple. I thought it was a disgusting idea and told him so, but that didn't stop him. He was forever pestering me about it, bringing it up when we were talking with friends, encouraging me to make passes at other men, always saying how we needed the excitement. Finally after he thoroughly embarrassed me one night with our closest friends, I told him if he needed some excitement like that so badly he could have it, but I wouldn't take any part in it. One night a week he gets to go out and do whatever he wants with whomever he wants, he doesn't even have to come home, and I don't ask any questions about what he's doing. It probably sounds strange to other people but it works for us. I don't really like it but at least I don't have to participate in some orgy just to excite him and he can't accuse me of standing in his way. Under the circumstances I just don't see what other choice I have. He needs the excitement and I need him, but I just can't do what he thinks is exciting so I have to let him do it on his own. I don't have any other choice. Do I?"

To join in the adventure, to resist it, or to stand on the side-lines as a "supportive" spectator—many women are not even presented with the option as was Margie. These women have come to symbolize in the context of their relationships with a middle-aged man all that he is rejecting, representing the routine, the security and the stability that he finds stifling. Here again the issue may be less what the woman can do, and more a matter of what the man feels he *must* do in spite of, or because of, the woman in his life. He *must* generate some newness. He *must* regain a sense of growth. To do these things he feels he *must* have an adventure. While an adventure necessarily means a break with routine, it need not be assumed that all such adventures are destructive to a man's established relationships. There are many middle-aged men seeking adventures on a far smaller scale which are every bit as rewarding as a treasure hunt or a skydive in bringing about that sense of growth and excitement that is so important to the middle-aged man. Moreover, these small-scale adventures do break routines but they do not break up relationships, they can be pursued by a middle-aged man within the context of his marriage and family. The motorcycle-riding accountant was one such man, the weekend warriors of amateur sports may be others. Scott Wright, in expressing his own search for adventure which came at age forty-seven, found the kind of adventure so many men successfully seek at middle age and he found it with his wife.

"I gradually came to realize that I, no, *we,* Helen and I, had developed quite a rut of a life for ourselves. I say gradually because it came about one summer when weekend after weekend we found ourselves with the same group of people in the neighborhood, partying and having a good time. Hell, we had a great time, that wasn't the point. But it was always the same people and the conversation seemed to always be the same. The women would go off in one part of the yard and the men in another and talk about the same things they always talked about, golf, lawns, baseball, the same things they had talked about last weekend and the weekend before that. My work week was just as predictable as the weekends were. I'd had the same job for quite a while, and frankly, it wasn't all that challenging. I had it pretty well down to where I probably could have done it just going in about two or three days a week. I felt the need to do something new, to bring back some spark, some thrill, some action. I realized that that need was probably true of most middle-aged men and I knew something about what can happen to them. I'd done my share of reading and I knew the damages of me changing and growing apart from Helen and I didn't want that to happen. So we discussed it openly, the two of us. I told her that there wasn't anything wrong with our friends but I was just a little tired of them. The funny thing was, she'd noticed the same thing. She was also tiring of them but wasn't going to say anything to me about it.

"I told her I wasn't finding much challenge at work either. Work was something Helen and I had never talked a great deal about, but we did then. I told her it just wasn't hard for me and wasn't really very exciting. I seldom encountered anything new there and it was pretty much just doing the same thing over and over again. I told her I was feeling the need to do something new, for me, for us. I remember our talking about whether this was just a phase I was going through, just a need for some temporary thrill, or if this was a real, lasting desire for change. Helen was worried that what I was actually trying to say was that I was bored with her, tired of her and our life together. It took a lot of reassurance from me to help her see that wasn't the case at all, that I wanted to find something *within* our relationship, not outside of it. I wanted an excitement I could share with her, not an excitement separate from her. She even offered to let me move out of the house for a couple of months to see if maybe it wasn't her. That is the kind of woman she is. I kept telling her no, that wasn't it, that what I wanted was for me to find some excitement. Sure, for me to have some adventures, but adventures that I could share with her. It couldn't be anything very expensive, we didn't have much money and still don't. It had to be something soon and it had to be something different.

"First of all, we joined a new church. I know this doesn't sound like much of a risk to a lot of folks, but it was to us. It was a younger church, with different people, no one from our neighborhood, none of our friends. We joined it because we thought that would be a good way to start meeting new people, then we decided that instead of me saving up all my vacation and sick leave days the way I had done in the past, we'd take them as they became available. We took long weekends and maybe a day off in the middle of the week or something. All of this time we still hadn't decided exactly what we were going to do for adventure. Then, through some people at church, we hit on it—backpacking. Now again, that's not the sort of thing that most people would think of as being real adventuresome or high risk, but it's got plenty of adventure and risk for Helen and me. After all, neither of us is as young as we used to be or in as good shape as we used to be. Through the people at church we got interested in backpacking, first with an adult group that went back into the woods and camped out. Now every chance we get we hop into our four-wheel drive, take the backpacks and camping gear, and go off into the remotest, roughest territory we can find. We've had plenty of adventures—run into wild animals, been lost, been rained on, snowed on, and we've swum in the nude and made love in the forest. We've been places where I don't think anyone else has set foot in a long, long time. And we've met lots of new people, made new friends, and not only do we enjoy the new friends more but now we enjoy the old friends more because we've got new things to talk about, new interests to share with them, and funny, now they seem a little more interesting. It's not like it saved our marriage or anything, our marriage was never in any trouble and I don't think I had a crisis of any kind, it's just that I needed to do something different, and well, this is just different enough.''

Both Scott and Helen find their backpacking just different enough, just enough of an adventurous departure from their routine to give Scott a sense of generating something new. He now has the excitement he felt he needed in his middle years. It may be, as it has been said, that adventure is where one finds it. If that is the case, then there is no doubt that many women involved with middle-aged men would have the hope that, like Scott, their men might seek adventure much closer to home. Even when a man looks for excitement closer to home there can be no guarantees that his adventures will not turn out adversely for him and his relationships. Whenever routines are broken, there is always the risk of ruin. Certainly the testimony of wives and families left behind as the middle-aged man strikes out in search of adventure speaks to the tragedy that excitement can bring to interpersonal relationships. Middle-aged men in search of adventure risk more than their relationships—they often risk their lives as well. Ben Mirado, whose story began this chapter, died when the plane he built crashed during a test flight. The adventure which was to bring excitement to his life brought an end to his life.

Wherever there are adventures there are and will continue to be middle-aged men who seek them. They are certain that in adventure they will find the thrill, the excitement, the lust for life that will return to them the excitement, the growth, the creativity, the challenge in everyday living that they never knew or only knew as younger men. In this day when a man is routinely exposed to much that seems moderately risky, he may feel that in order to be truly thrilled he must extend himself beyond mere difference and toward defiance. It may seem to him that only the most radical of departures from the routine constitutes a true adventure—a challenge to life and limb, the risk of financial ruin. Time and time again middle-aged men in their search for excitement extend themselves beyond their physical and psychological limits. For these men their response to the threat to growth which comes in mid-life brings on its heels a consequent crisis—the crisis of coping with an adventurous life which is beyond the capacity of the adventurer to live it.

8

What to Do if He Is You

"I HAVE TO SAY that I am pretty critical of this talk about male menopause, the mid-life crisis, or whatever you want to call it. No, it's even stronger than that, I'm more than critical, I'm downright cynical about it. Don't get me wrong, it's not that I don't believe it goes on, hell, I know it goes on, I'm one of the victims—one of the 30 percent of middle-aged men who has a crisis. The thing of it is I don't see where all of those statistics and all of the writing and talk about it is getting us, the middle-aged men who are having all of these crises. What's in it for me?" Elmer Henry, forty-seven, is talking about the male mid-life crisis, his own and that of others. He wonders what, if anything, can be done about it.

"I've been in the middle of the mid-life crisis for probably as long as two years now. At least I've gotten to the point where I can acknowledge that. Hell, for a year there I didn't know what was going on. I'm not proud of it, you understand, but I am willing to admit I'm having a mid-life crisis. After what I've been through with the family and work, a man would be crazy if he didn't have a crisis of some kind. The point's not that I had a crisis, the point is that I am *having* a crisis, and I want to know what to do about it. I have these terrible fits of depression that last two or three and sometimes as long as six weeks at a time. I'm irritable and cranky. I jump at everything and everybody. I don't seem to find enjoyment in any of the things that I used to—my work, family, hobbies. I can't even seem to get interested in any of that long enough to find out if it still is enjoyable or not. I guess I've got all of the classic symptoms of the mid-life crisis case. Never mind how I got them, I don't think what caused it is all that important. That's all you ever read about though—what *causes* the crisis. You never see anything about *what to do about it,* and that is what I'm concerned about now. Now that I've got all these symptoms, now that I'm ready to admit that I'm having a mid-life crisis, what in the hell do I do about it? I don't enjoy being depressed, I don't enjoy being irritable, I don't enjoy much of anything about the way I've been for the last year. I'll do anything to get out of it if someone, somewhere will just tell me how. You can read all you want to about the mid-life crisis, you can talk all you want to about it, but I've yet to hear from anybody just what to do about it once you've got it. What do I do if all I see in all those stories is me?''

Elmer Henry is not alone in his lament. There are many middle-aged men who have come to the point of saying "I'll admit I'm having some problems and it could even be called a crisis, but tell me, what do I do *now?*'' In all that has been written and said about the male mid-life crisis in both the popular press and the academic press there has been relatively little attention given to what the middle-aged man in crisis is to do. How can a man resolve the turbulence and turmoil of his middle years? There is something to be learned from reading cases of other middle-aged men and the various causes of crisis. However, few of these cases provide insight for a man into what is to be done from his own practical standpoint. The middle-aged man who seeks advice on how to resolve the crisis in his life must look to one of three sources: those middle-aged men who never experience a crisis, those who experience a crisis and do not achieve a successful resolution, those who have a crisis and successfully resolve the crisis to create a better second half of life for themselves.

It is estimated that nearly two-thirds of all men between the ages of forty and sixty will never experience a mid-life crisis. Surely there is something in the events and experiences of these men's lives to suggest to those who do have a crisis how best they might deal with it. For example, a common characteristic of those middle-aged men who do not experience a crisis is that their identity is not threatened by the events of mid-life. This is not because these men have somehow isolated themselves from events which are common to most men in mid-life, these events occur to them as they do to others. The difference is that these men are not affected in the same way by these identity-threatening events because they have multiple sources of identity and are, therefore, less vulnerable to a loss of identity in mid-life. Research verifies that the men least likely to have a mid-life crisis are those who have a variety of ways of defining "self." This is excellent advice for those who have not yet experienced a crisis and would like to know how to prevent it: diversify your identity, find multiple ways to define *who* you are, several sources of self. What this suggests for those looking for a solution to the mid-life crisis is dubious, it offers a goal but not a means to that goal. Most middle-aged men in crisis find the advice to diversify comes too late, they see the merits in multiple sources of identity but see nothing in the reports of those who have not experienced a crisis to tell them how to get there.

Another potential source of advice on how to deal with the mid-life crisis are the cases of those men who have not achieved a successful resolution. The case files of the male mid-life crisis are replete with examples of men who have experienced a crisis and have been unable to resolve it. Many of their stories have been told in these pages. One way to find advice and counsel from these cases is to project how these men might have behaved differently, what they *should* have done to deal with their crisis. Obviously these cases of unsuccessful attempts to resolve mid-life crises are going to be of limited utility to those looking for answers, they vividly portray how crisis should *not* be handled, but leave one guessing, at best, as to how they *ought* to be handled.

The remaining source of advice is the best. There is much to

be learned from those middle-aged men who have constructively dealt with crisis in their lives. In every category of causes,
be it goal gap, vanity and virility, empty nest, meeting mortality
or in search of adventure, there are cases of men who found an
identity severely threatened by the events of their middle years.
What set these few men who were able to deal effectively with
their crises apart from the many others is that their response to
the threat and the consequent crisis was to change in such a way
that the crisis turned out to be a constructive force in their lives.
It led to a better, more productive second half of life. How can
the crisis of a man's middle years be constructive?

There is a pattern that was found in every case where resolution was successful, and it comes as close to prescribing a solution as anything currently available. The pattern of resolution
may be said to consist of five steps:

1. *Recognition*—Before any steps toward resolution can be
taken the middle-aged man must be able to recognize the
changes that are taking place in his life. He must come to see
himself as others see him. Given the limited introspective skills
of most men, this initial critical step is not as easy as it may at
first seem.

2. *Acknowledgment*—Having recognized what is going on in
his life, the next step toward resolution must be an acknowledgment of these changes for *what* they represent, a mid-life crisis,
and *why,* the causes of crisis. Without this open acknowledgment there will likely be little real commitment to taking further
action toward resolution.

3. *Consideration of the Consequences*—Before the middle-
aged man takes any *direct action* to resolve crisis he must carefully consider just what is at issue. What are the consequences
of his crisis for him and his relationships with others? Are these
consequences necessarily negative? What's good and what's
bad about what's going on with him?

4. *Choosing to Change*—Effective resolution of the mid-life
crisis inevitably requires change. The middle-aged man must
change his sense of self and his behavior if he is to creatively

and constructively respond to crisis. *Committing to change* is the first issue in this step toward resolution; *choosing a change* is the second issue. One without the other, commitment without change or change without commitment, will do little to reach resolution.

5. *Integration of the Change*—Resolution of the male mid-life crisis can only be realized when the man integrates his changed perspective and pattern of behavior into his personality. When the man fully accepts his new sense of self, and views as natural his new behaviors, it can truly be said that he has resolved his mid-life crisis.

Presenting a list of steps that should be taken by a middle-aged man to resolve his crisis is akin to advising someone that they ought to give up smoking—it's great advice but how does a person make it happen? It is one thing to present a list of steps to be taken by a middle-aged man to respond constructively to the crisis in his life. It is quite another thing to make a list come alive for middle-aged men so that they read the steps to be taken not "I *should* do" but rather "I *can* do." To move from "should do" to "can do" requires more than a simple listing. The middle-aged man will need to understand what each step means for him and how he can take it. He will need examples of how others have taken those steps and details of the difficulties they encountered that he might also expect. Thus armed, the middle-aged man who confronts crisis can respond creatively and constructively, creating from the crisis of his middle years a profile and a posture toward his own life that will prepare him for the years ahead. The intent of this chapter is to prepare middle-aged men to do just that.

Recognition. The limited introspective skills of men have been frequently mentioned throughout these many reports of the male mid-life crisis. As a rule, most men who have reached their middle years are neither accustomed to nor accomplished at looking inward and recognizing themselves as they are. Not only is there an absence of introspection in most middle-aged men, there is an actual aversion to introspection. This stems more from trained neglect than it does from any inborn disabilities. The average man of forty to sixty has never been encouraged to be introspective, nor rewarded on those occasions when he has looked inward. In truth he has probably found introspection to be viewed as a handicap in his career and personal life, generally put down as being "too sensitive to others" or "too self-absorbed to take action." It is accurate to say that men, particularly younger men, are increasingly coming to realize that the real handicap is the absence of introspection. This handicap prevents them not only from developing a fuller understanding of themselves but from acquiring a fuller understanding of others as well. For many middle-aged men this realization comes all too late. They remain unconvinced of the importance of introspection and unskilled in its arts. They have, in short, a hard time recognizing themselves.

For a man whose insight is inhibited, the changes which occur in mid-life, whatever their cause or consequence, may be particularly confounding and confusing. Readily apparent to others, the changes go unnoticed by him. More to the point, he isolates himself from the insight that others might provide him, reacting defensively when they notice and point out to him changes in his behavior. Richard Stenhand comments on the difficulty he had recognizing the changes in his life: "In retrospect it all seems so clear I wonder now how I could have been blind to it for so long. I know now of course that it wasn't just that I couldn't see, I didn't want to see. I can remember Phyllis, my wife, saying to me, 'How come you're so down, how come you're moping around?' Immediately I'd get on the defensive and say, 'I'm not down, I'm not moping around.' Or the boss would say, 'Gee, you've been pretty irritable around here lately, what's wrong?' Which would only irritate me more. 'Nothing's wrong, what the hell are you talking about?' My friends asked, 'How come you never have time for golf anymore? Aren't you interested?' I'd put them off with something like 'Of course I'm interested, I'm just busy, preoccupied.' I defended myself to my wife by blaming it on work, to my boss by blaming it on my wife, to my friends by blaming it on both of them. I was so caught up in defending myself against whatever they were saying that I really didn't listen to what they were saying. I really didn't want to.

"That went on for six, nine months, maybe more. It wasn't a constant thing but hardly a week went by that somebody didn't tell me how I had changed, how I was behaving differently. Every time I got more defensive. I just refused to listen to them, refused to believe them. Then it all blew up. I remember it really well. I spent the whole weekend walking around the block. Does that sound crazy? Oh, I'd come home and I'd sit down in my chair and read the paper a little bit, and then I'd get up and tell Phyllis I was going for a walk. I'd walk for an hour or an hour and a half, come back, sit down for a while, get up and go out for another walk. That went on four or five times and then finally Phyllis said, 'What are you doing?' That started a huge fight. I said, 'I'm going for a walk. Is that okay with you?' She said, 'Well I don't mind you going for a walk, you can do with your weekends what you want, but do you realize that's all you've been doing this weekend? Walk, sit, walk, sit.' I said, 'Well if I can do anything I want with my weekends, then how come I'm getting so goddamn much shit because I'm going for a walk? How come I can't seem to do anything right around here anymore without you jumping all over me?' Well, Phyllis started crying, getting really upset and saying things like 'Oh Rich, don't you see how strange you've been acting? Don't you see how much you've changed?' Then she dropped the bomb, the one that really got me thinking. She said, 'Rich, I'm afraid there's something terribly wrong with you. I'm so afraid you're really sick.' Well, I said, 'Sick shit,' and turned my back on her and walked out of the house.

"I had never ever done that before. I started thinking, Phyllis noticed it, people at work noticed it, friends noticed it, maybe I had been blind. Maybe there was something there that I just couldn't see. I decided to see a doctor to try to find out if I was right or if they were. I went to our GP on the pretense of getting a checkup (which I really did need), but in the course of that I told him some of what had been going on. I told him how people had seemed to be very critical of me lately, pointing out things that I was doing or saying that they saw as changes. I said to the doctor that I just couldn't see that I had changed at all but I was beginning to wonder. He gave me some really good advice that I'll be forever thankful for. He said, 'Rich, why don't you go back to those people and just listen to what they have to say. Don't get caught up in defending yourself or denying whatever they have to say, just listen. Try to really hear what they're telling you and decide for yourself whether it's true or not, and then you come back and let's have a talk about it.' So I did that, I talked with Phyllis and tried to really listen to what she had to say. It was hard but I bit my tongue and told myself that I wasn't going to respond at all. I was just going to listen. I did the same thing with my boss and the same with my friends. They were all right! I *was* changing. There were things going on with me that I didn't want to admit and therefore didn't see. But after talking with them with this new open attitude, I was able to hear them and through them to finally see myself. I recognized that my life was changing and I wasn't at all sure that I liked what I saw.''

Richard's reaction to the impressions of others who saw him changing is not at all unusual. Resistance and reluctance to recognize others' perceptions is the norm among middle-aged men. These men are simply not in the habit of seeking feedback from others, soliciting others' opinions or feelings about themselves. Because most men don't seek this information it is seldom welcome or openly accepted when it's forthcoming. The natural, initial reaction to someone, a wife, employer or friend, who says "You certainly have changed" is a defensive one. The man responds "Me, changed? Of course I haven't changed." In this defensive posture the perceptions of others are viewed with suspicion. Their descriptions are heard as judgments, their observations as evaluations, their comments as criticisms. When these descriptions, observations and comments concern the man's personality and behavior he is all the more resistant. Unskilled at looking inward, insensitive to the insight others might provide, blind to the mirror they hold for him, there is little wonder that for the average middle-aged man the first step in solving mid-life crisis, recognition of the changes in himself, is the most difficult. Not knowing, not seeing what is going on, he is scarcely motivated to do anything about it.

The key to recognition is receptivity. This means the man must be receptive not only to his inner reflections but receptive to the reflections of others as well. Most often others see the man much more clearly than he sees himself. They are witness to the symptoms (and often the victims of those same symptoms) which signal crisis long before they become apparent to him. The best avenue available for the middle-aged man to learn about himself is for him to listen to others, and to hear how they see and experience him. This does not mean that he needs to take the most casual observation from friends and co-workers to heart, overreacting to every response to his behavior. It means merely that the middle-aged man does need to look for the common message in others' responses and reactions to his own behavior. Where that message is uniform, where there is consistent comment about noticeable changes in his behavior, changes in his personality, or his outlook on the world, there is cause for the middle-aged man to recognize that the crisis may be upon him.

Acknowledgment. Middle-aged men often come to recognize through a variety of means that changes are occurring in their lives. It is a much rarer occurrence for a middle-aged man to acknowledge that these changes are of a significance and scope which could signal a mid-life crisis. The first requires a little more than opening one's mind to the reflections of self and others. The second moves a man toward admission, and with that admission come the questions of action: Will he take action? What action will he take? John Roth speaks of his difficult transition from recognizing to acknowledging. "Last year I was hospitalized for three weeks; officially as far as the company is concerned and the health insurance and all that, it was from exhaustion. I know that it was a breakdown, but that's just between you and me. What happened was that at the beginning of the year I'd been given some new job responsibilities, new in this instance meant less. I was taken out of a sensitive, important position and put in a simple, unimportant position and right away I began to notice changes in myself. Others noted change, too. The whole thing could probably be summarized as a general depression on my part and a lack of purpose.

"I was directionless and pretty down and out. I didn't try to hide it from anybody, far from it. When people pointed out to me that they thought I'd changed, I was more than happy to recognize that they were right. Hell, there wasn't any sense in hiding it. Everybody could see it. But what I was not prepared to do and I still am not really prepared to do, is acknowledge *why* I was changing. There was a week there at work when I'd be asked to do something in line with my new job, go to a meeting or file a report, or make a call, and I just couldn't do it. I really became catatonic. I'd sit there at my desk immobile, literally not able to get up and get to the door. It scared the hell out of me. I went to the doctor and he put me into the hospital, voluntarily of course, for three weeks of observation. They ran every imaginable test, conducted umpteen analyses, and concluded that I had had a breakdown. I knew why, and from what I told the doctors I am sure they got a pretty good idea of why, too, but it was nothing I would admit to others, especially the people at work, so I just filed for my hospital expenses as exhaustion, overwork. It would be the end of my career if I told the company that I had had a breakdown, if they knew what they did to me and my career caused that kind of crisis. The same is true of Helen, my wife. I wasn't going to let on to her just what had happened to me around work. I wasn't going to let on to my friends or anybody else. I'm more than willing to recognize what happened and how it changed me, but I just can't admit to others the reason why. I know I should do something about it. I know I should maybe get myself some professional help, counseling of some kind, that's what the doctors all tell me, but to do that seems to me like giving in, like admitting to myself and everyone else that I can't handle it. I'd have to acknowledge that I couldn't handle the change. I'd have to give in to it and I can't do that. I'm back at work but I'm not really working, not really functioning very well. I guess I won't act on it, not for now anyway. Maybe it will all just go away.''

For John Roth and for countless other middle-aged men acknowledging the scope and source of the changes in their lives is seen as resignation, rather than movement toward resolution. John speaks of admitting to the causes of his crisis as "giving in," "admitting I can't handle it." He is reluctant to acknowledge his crisis to himself, and he is outright fearful of acknowledging his crisis to others. This behavior is common to many middle-aged men. While some men in the privacy of their own minds can recognize that they are changing and perhaps even why, to come forward and openly acknowledge the cause of change so that they might act upon it is a step beyond what they feel they can bear. Yet without acknowledgment there can be no action, and without action there can be no effective resolution of the mid-life crisis. How can the middle-aged man overcome his resistance to acknowledging his crisis? How can he be helped to see that admitting to himself and others that he is in crisis is neither weakness nor withdrawal, but rather a further step toward taking action to resolve his crisis?

There is much that the middle-aged man and those involved with him can and should do to aid him. First the man can become acquainted with the phenomenon of mid-life crisis in general. By reading and observing he can come to understand that his case is not unique, he is not alone nor is his crisis necessarily a calamity. It will be particularly important that the middle-aged man reach the understanding that *he* controls the crisis and *he* can determine whether the consequences will be calamitous or constructive. Learning about the mid-lives of other men can both put the man at ease and point him in the direction of resolution. He will find it easier to acknowledge his own crisis knowing that others have had similar experiences.

Most middle-aged men find it helpful to get an objective assessment of their own situation. They come to the brink of acknowledging their crisis but would like a "second opinion" before they take what they perceive to be "the great leap." In seeking a second opinion middle-aged men are handicapped by their own reluctance to acknowledge crisis. For them talking freely and directly to a spouse or very close friend is not an acceptable option. The second opinion they seek must be relatively anonymous and as non-threatening as possible. Symptom checklists or questionnaires such as the one provided in Chapter 2 and in the Appendix can be a helpful means for the middle-aged man to get an external assessment of his situation. While not in any sense intended to be a definitive measure of the crisis experienced by a middle-aged man, such questionnaires can provide him with a low-risk source of objective information about the changes occurring in his life.

Far more effective than reading about the mid-life crisis or answering self-administered questionnaires is talking with other middle-aged men about the mid-life crisis. Sharing similar experiences with other middle-aged men, both about their life prior to crisis and in undergoing a crisis, is the best possible encouragement to a man to acknowledge his own crisis. From sharing with others he learns not only that his experience is not unique but, more importantly, that there are no significant personal or social costs associated with acknowledging what he is undergoing. Indeed, some middle-aged men have found it helpful to work within an organized group of other men who have similar experiences. These groups, usually organized by a counselor or minister, someone in one of the helping professions, provide a ready arena for acknowledgment and a supportive atmosphere for corrective action. Not all men can avail themselves of a group, nor would a group be appropriate for all men. After all, joining such a group is a greater acknowledgment of crisis than many men are prepared to make. But all men can have access to a conversational exchange with others who have had similar experiences.

With these aids to acknowledgment—learning about the mid-life crisis, a low-risk objective assessment, sharing with others —the middle-aged man can come to grips with acknowledging his crisis and its causes. In essence he must admit to himself and to others that he is experiencing a mid-life crisis and he must accept the reasons for that crisis. The real risk in this acknowledgment step is that once having acknowledged the crisis and its cause the man must do something about it. At this point he can no longer pretend that the crisis does not exist. He cannot ignore it in the hopes that it will go away. Having acknowledged his mid-life crisis he must either choose to live with it, or he must act upon the crisis, beginning with a careful and conscious consideration of the consequences.

Consideration of the Consequences. Reaction without reflection is almost always regrettable. This is as true of the mid-life crisis as it is of behavior in other arenas of a man's life. Before the middle-aged man takes action on his crisis he should reflect on just what response is most appropriate for him. In actuality, this type of reflection seldom occurs when it ought to, more often than not the response to the crisis is more *reflexive* than *reflective*. The two most often seen reflexive responses to the mid-life crisis are: (1) passive acceptance and (2) active affirmation. Neither of these reflex responses leads toward real resolution.

For many men it appears that the easiest response to the crisis which occurs in mid-life is passive acceptance. Faced with substantial and significant threats to their sense of self, the reflex response of many men is to continue—to change neither their identity nor their behavior. This response is readily available, made alone in the privacy of one's own thoughts. While not conquering the crisis, most men who choose this response feel they can adapt to whatever conditions the crisis brings about. Without changing his sense of self or his behavior, the middle-aged man in crisis must face the fact that he is likely to be subject to continual threats. This means that he is likely to continue to suffer the effects of crisis, whatever those may be— depression, erratic behavior, unstable relationships, or whatever. Associated with every cause of the mid-life crisis are many cases of men who consciously or unconsciously respond reflexively, and in so doing choose to live passively with the crisis and its effects. This passivity perhaps explains why so many middle-aged men appear to have lost the lust for life, lost the sense of vitality and vision, settling instead for a lessened sense of self. One could hardly call such a reflex response to the mid-life crisis a resolution. It is more appropriately a resignation.

The number of men who live passively, privately with their mid-life crisis cannot be known, for they suffer and survive in silence and often in solitude. Such is not the case with those middle-aged men whose reflex response to crisis is to strike out at the source of their identity in an attempt to affirm who they are. These men do not change their behavior so much as they intensify it, doing more and harder whatever they have been doing for the first half of their lives. The men who so respond in many instances escape the immediate threat, but because they have not materially altered the source of their identity they leave themselves vulnerable to future crises in later mid-life. Theirs, too, is a solitary consideration, even though the consequences are felt in every relationship in which they are involved. Some of these men do overcome the immediate crisis. They are able in their renewed efforts to generate sufficient new experiences and new information to reaffirm their identity as career man, ladies' man, husband or father. But theirs is a tenuous resolution because their identity remains rooted in a single source, and they will forever be vulnerable to one mid-life crisis or another. Their subsequent years become years of dedication to the continual demonstration of self, a continual search for more and greater proof that they are who they believe themselves to be. Yet this reflex response is low-risk, because this middle-aged man need not change his behavior. He can confront the crisis with what he considers to be his strengths, those behaviors which got him where he is. He need not consider a new identity for himself, nor new behaviors. He need only do more and harder those things which he has been doing. Moreover, the middle-aged man who reinvests himself in his identity this way has the sense that he is doing something about his own crisis, taking affirmative action. However, such action provides at best only moment-to-moment relief and does little toward real resolution.

The difference between reflexive response to the male mid-life crisis, and reflective response, is the difference between resignation or relief and real resolution. Following recognition and acknowledgment, the third step on the path to resolution must be a conscientious consideration of the consequences. The middle-aged man in crisis must disdain the reflex responses which are readily available and consider *change*. It is clear that those men who most effectively manage the mid-life crisis, who create out of its chaos a more constructive sense of self, are men who have been able to break away from a single sense of identity and have been able to get in touch with the many aspects of who they are as a man. In so doing, they not only reduce their vulnerability to threats to their identity, they also develop new meanings for their lives and they find new behaviors. Such changes in self and behavior are not reflex responses, and they are too high-risk for the ordinary middle-aged man to be pursued without careful reflection.

A man searching for new sources of identity cannot seek alone. He needs to draw upon others who know him well to help him identify alternative meanings in his life, alternative sources of self. Having lived so long thinking of himself in the context of a single definition, the middle-aged man is often blind to his other potentials of self. Relying on the intimacy and trust of close personal relationships, he can receive the guidance of others who know him well, others who can point to alternative sources of his identity, prod him to consider them, and support him throughout this difficult consideration step. This all-important consideration step may appear to be a Catch-22 for the middle-aged man seeking resolution to his crisis. It has been noted throughout these pages that one characteristic of the lives of most middle-aged men is the absence of close, caring relationships. Now it appears that the real hope of resolving the mid-life crisis lies in the context of such close, caring relationships. What is the man faced with this paradox to do? On the one hand a potential causal factor in his having a crisis is that he does not have close personal, intimate relationships with others. On the other hand he is told that in order to resolve his crisis he needs close personal relationships. Of course the middle-aged man may choose to buy such a relationship. He can pursue professional help, through a counselor, psychologist, psychiatrist. This help is readily available for a price, but such an alternative is abhorrent to most middle-aged men. Counseling is traditionally viewed by middle-aged men as a sign of weakness and an inability to solve one's own problems. He may look to his existing relationships with a spouse, work associates, close friends, doctor, to see if these can provide the suggestions and support he needs as he considers changing his identity and his behavior. Upon close examination many of these existing relationships will have the capacity to provide a context in which the man can resolve his mid-life crisis, but that capacity in most instances needs to be activated by the middle-aged man. The relationships are there and they can provide a helpful environment for the middle-aged man to consider who he is and how he wants to behave, but he must tap into that relationship, its intimacy and its caring, in a way that he probably has not done heretofore. Herein lies the second real risk in this reflective response—the man must reach out, expose himself, *he must trust*. Most middle-aged men do not have a history of good experience with trusting relationships. They are unaccustomed to developing trusting relationships and unaccustomed to participating in them. There are some guidelines that men can look to for assistance in developing trusting relationships, be those relationships with their wives, co-workers or close friends.

First there is the issue of who to look to for such a relationship. Where is the man most likely to find the person or persons who can help him most in a time of crisis? In general the middle-aged man who desires a trusting relationship in order to resolve his mid-life crisis should look first to someone who is committed to a relationship with him. He should look to someone with whom he need not test their level of caring and commitment, someone who has demonstrated that he/she has a high regard for him and who values the relationship with him. In addition to evidence of commitment, the middle-aged man should look to someone who by all indications will be competent to handle the sorts of issues the middle-aged man will bring to the relationship, someone who can deal with personal and intimate information without embarrassment, without sensationalism, without a lessening of regard. Beyond seeking a person who seems committed to the relationship and competent to handle the kinds of information that must be discussed, the middle-aged man seeking a trusting relationship should seek a person with whom he has had good experiences with disclosure. It should be a relationship in which there is a norm or generally accepted notion about revealing oneself. This requirement alone may eliminate many individuals. Many long and apparently close friendships exist only on a rather superficial level, and after a great number of years neither party has revealed much of great intimacy to the other. Or, if there were moments which were particularly revealing, it was a bad experience and consciously blotted out. In addition, a man should seek a relationship in which there are relatively few taboos or prohibitions about what may be discussed. Interestingly, this excludes many spouses as candidates for a relationship that is to provide a context for resolving the mid-life crisis. Most men find it difficult to discuss with their wives such things as their feelings for other women, or their real feelings and experiences in their careers. Indeed most marital relationships have as one of their foundations a strong understanding of just *where* and *what* the taboos are. Stability in a marital relationship often means merely that the couple has successfully avoided the taboo subjects.

In summary, the relationships which are most likely to provide a constructive climate for the middle-aged man to consider necessary identity and behavior changes will have these characteristics:

- The other person is committed to a relationship with the middle-aged man—he/she values the relationship.
- The other person is and will be competent to deal with the issues surrounding the mid-life crisis—not necessarily professionally knowledgeable and skilled, but certainly understanding and discreet.
- The other person has dealt effectively with disclosure in the past—he/she has revealed some of himself/herself to the middle-aged man.
- The other person places few taboos on the relationship, and may be approached about anything which concerns the middle-aged man.

If the middle-aged man reviews his existing relationships with his wife, work associates, friends, doctor, minister, using these prerequisites as a guide or checklist, he is certain to identify at least one relationship which promises to provide him with the trusting climate he needs to reveal and explore himself. Having identified such a relationship, the middle-aged man need not and indeed should not leap headfirst into the issue at hand. He will be more comfortable with "testing the water," using a rather cautious approach at first, a discussion of events of the past rather than the present, a discussion of ideas, opinions, rather than present problems and feelings. This "testing of the water" can begin to build into the relationship the degree of trust required to go further. Then, confident in the relationship and in his own abilities to use it, the middle-aged man can take up the issues which he hopes will lead him to resolve his crisis.

Checklists and caution can be of tremendous help in establishing a trust relationship, but even with these aids the middle-aged man may find this the most difficult step of all.

Don Epson, age forty-four, speaks about the difficulty he had in finding someone in whom he could confide about his particular mid-life crisis. "For me it was the whole sex-masculinity thing. I think that made it particularly difficult for me to find a relationship that I could really be open in. It wasn't easy to find someone I could talk to about the problems that I was having with the mid-life crisis. I first noticed the problems when I just didn't want sex as much as I usually did. Like I suppose everybody else, I tried to pretend that it wasn't true. I made a conscious effort to keep up my sexual activity with my wife so that she wouldn't notice that anything might be wrong. While I think I pretty well managed to hide it from her, I really couldn't hide it from myself. I just wasn't performing and it was really getting me down on myself, starting me to wonder about my masculinity. So like a lot of other guys, I started looking around. I figured that maybe it was my wife, Gail. She isn't as young as she used to be, doesn't look nearly as good, and our sex was getting to be pretty routine. I thought all I needed was to hook up with some sweet young thing who could really turn me on and that would solve all my problems. I tried that for a while, always looking for someone and something that would tell me that I was still a stud, you know, but even that didn't do it for me. I came this close to getting caught quite a few times, once in my own house. That scared me off, but also I realized that I couldn't just keep balling younger and younger girls for the rest of my life. If I was going to come to any real solution to the problem, something about me and my life was going to have to change, but what? And how to find out what? Who do you go to to talk about a problem like that? Where can a guy turn?

"Obviously I couldn't go to my wife and tell her that because I couldn't get it up with her I was worried, so I was chasing girls I could get it up with, and now I was giving them up and wanted her help. I can tell you what kind of help she would have given me—a swift kick in the nuts is the help she would have given me. You always read about going to a professional counselor or a minister or a doctor. I guess there's nothing really wrong with that nowadays but I've always felt they just made the problem worse instead of better and screwed you up even more. Besides,

I didn't think I was all that sick. I just had these worries, you know? There was this one older fellow at work, Ken. He's not all that much older—in his early fifties—and he and I always have been pretty close. We didn't see each other all that much but when we did get together we really hit it off. Not just a good time, but good talk, too. I felt our relationship was important to both of us and from time to time he had revealed some pretty intimate stuff to me. One time when he was thinking about moving out on his wife we talked about that, and another time when he was having real serious problems with his kids. Anyway, I thought I could talk to him about my problems and he wouldn't put me off or put me down. He would really listen to me, understand, try to help me figure some ways to go.

"I didn't just jump into it, you understand. I didn't go up to him and say 'Hey, Ken, I need some help. I can't get it up, what should I do?' I sort of tested him out to see if I really had made a good choice in him as a person to confide in, you know. I sort of talked around about things that happened to me a while back, or about things I would like to do in the future, just to get his reactions, to begin to get some sense to how he would respond when I really got down to telling him what the problem was. The best thing is when I did get around to telling him about my problems he understood completely. Something close to that had happened to him a few years back. He could feel along with what I was going through, and he really helped me to see how I could do something about it. We talked a lot about what it was to be a man nowadays and what was manly and I began to get a sense that if I was going to come to any long-range solution I was going to have to change some of my ideas about myself, change some of my behavior. I got some mighty good advice from Ken then. He said that I couldn't just change like that overnight. That would probably start more problems than it would solve. He said it would probably give Gail and me some real problems and that whatever changes I made I better consider her. That was great advice. It worked for me and I would give the same advice to any other man. The whole thing was, in

talking with Ken I was really able to open up. In being honest
with him I was forced to be honest with myself. I don't think I
could have done it alone. I don't think without someone to talk
to I would have been as honest with myself, and I know, too, if
I hadn't been hurting so bad I never would have been able to
risk trusting Ken the way I did. But I had no choice. It was
either risk that or, well, I don't know what. I just know that I
had to risk it and I'm glad I did. I'm glad for the changes, too.''

The irony of the male mid-life crisis lies in the fact that crisis
is caused by changes and yet it can only be resolved by changing. The crisis comes about because changes are forced upon a
man in mid-life, changes which for many men threaten their
sense of who they are and how they are in the world. The initial
reflex response is, like Don, to pretend that these changes have
not occurred, or ignore them in the hopes that they are just a
phase and will quickly pass away. Another reflex response is for
the middle-aged man to seek information which tells him that he
has not changed, he is in mid-life as he was in his younger years
and he can prove it. These reflex responses are only short-term
resolutions. Long-term resolutions create a constructive response to the crisis of middle life, and that comes about only
after reflection, careful consideration of change, a redefinition
of self. Here the middle-aged man must exercise great caution.
To leap boldly into change without due consideration of what or
how to change is to continue and further the chaos that crisis
has caused. Careful consideration in the context of a caring
relationship begins the change process. Having carefully considered *what* changes to make the man must give the same care
and consideration to *how* these changes are made, or run the
risk of losing the progress he has made toward real resolution of
his mid-life crisis.

Choosing to Change. Change is not a choice that is easily
made by middle-aged men or by anyone for that matter. There
is the tendency to see in change only the most negative consequences, the direst effects. There are reasons why change is so
resisted, and those reasons have primarily to do with *how*

change comes about more than with what is changed. This impacts upon the middle-aged man who faces change as a path to resolution in two ways: (1) he must feel that he can choose to change—not that he is forced to change; (2) he must select a change and then change in a way that involves others rather than imposes on them.

The first of these effects is relatively clear-cut. The middle-aged man will be more committed to those changes he freely chooses to make than to those forced upon him. Then, in choosing what and how to change, the middle-aged man needs to be ever mindful of others—for the sake of his own welfare, if not theirs!

What typically happens to people involved with a middle-aged man who is changing is that they assess the effect of those changes on themselves and their relationship before responding to him. At the same time he is dependent on their response to follow through with his change. For example, if a middle-aged man decides in response to his own mid-life crisis to change in such a way that that change is viewed by others who relate to him as destructive, they in all probability will try to persuade or force him not to change at all. There are many such examples of men who decide that in order to resolve their own crisis they must leave their jobs. The family may view such a change as destroying their way of life and resist it at every turn. In the face of such resistance many men give in, turning their backs on a job change and consequently resigning themselves to further career-related crises. Even where the man's intended change is not clearly destructive but only threatening to existing relationships (as anything unknown is), his efforts will be met with resistance. Still other changes envisioned by the middle-aged man may be seen by others as having no effect on their relationships with him, for example, changes in the way he dresses or his hobbies or interests. The typical response to these changes is one of passive tolerance, neither resisting nor supporting whatever it is the man attempts to change. Very often this absence of a response can be as deflating and defeating for the middle-aged man as can open resistance. Finally, there may be those changes on the part of middle-aged men which are viewed by others as truly enhancing and bettering their relationships with him. They recognize that the changes relieve his depression, reduce his irritability, and perhaps may truly resolve the crisis in his life. When the middle-aged man's changes are viewed by others as enhancing both him and his relationships, the others can become truly supportive, helping the man to change, encouraging him and rewarding him.

From the standpoint of the middle-aged man who is making a conscious attempt to make those changes in his life which will lead to resolution of his mid-life crisis, it is only this latter response which is truly helpful. If he encounters resistance on the part of others to his changes he faces an uphill struggle that he may never win. If he encounters passive tolerance on the part of others to his changes he may find it difficult to remain committed to a path of change. Where his changes are perceived by others as truly bettering their relationships with him he will find support, encouragement and reward. Clearly it is these changes which will be the easiest for him to make, and therefore these which are most likely to lead to resolution of his mid-life crisis.

The key in this step, Choosing to Change, seems to be to make those changes which will be viewed both by the man and by others as truly contributing to his relationships rather than conflicting with his relationships. There are ways in which the man may pursue his own change in behavior that will increase the odds that his changes are viewed by others as positive. The more a man seeks out the opinions, feelings and involvement of others in deciding the changes he needs in his life the more likely it is that he and the others will ultimately see these changes as positive and something to be supported and encouraged. It is also clear that the more information that other people have about the changes the man is undergoing the more likely they are to support these same changes. Finally, in those relationships where a man has in the past successfully changed, he is likely to find the greatest support for changes in mid-life. This means that as a man is about to change he must:

1. Involve other people with whom he has valued relationships;
2. He must inform those same people of the changes in his life, and
3. In order to build a feeling of confidence about his abilities to change without damaging the relationship, it may be necessary for him to begin with small, almost superficial things, to build his confidence and the confidence of those to whom he relates.

While this may sound like a complex process of change, in practice it's really quite simple. Don Epson talks about the change process he embarked on after his conversations with Ken Marter.

"It was clear to me, and Ken agreed, that there was no way that I was going to be able to change who I was, no way I was going to be able to make being such a stud less important in my life without involving Gail. At the same time I just knew there was *no* way I could tell her exactly to what lengths I had gone to try to maintain my thing about sex. She certainly wouldn't have appreciated my chasing after women and I really didn't think it was necessary that she know all about that in order for her to be able to help me. I began just telling her some of the things I had been going through, some doubts I had about my sex drive, how I wanted to be less dependent on being so 'macho' as a source of identity, how I wanted her to help me find other things that could be important to me in the second half of my life. I talked a little bit about some of the sex problems, about how I have as much desire for it and how I had doubts about my ability, but I was very clear with her that it had nothing to do with her. I told her I knew for certain that it was not because of her that I had this happen to me. I didn't want her feeling that it was her fault. Well, after I gave her all that about what had been going on, I asked for her advice. I asked for her input, for her to tell me what she saw and what she noticed, how she thought I might resolve the problem. She had some really fantastic ideas. She did say that she thought maybe she had been partially to blame, maybe she had emphasized our sex life too much or my looks and maybe she had, without meaning to, led me to believe that what she loved most in me was my ability as a lover. We decided together to change things. We started with some pretty simple things, you know, new hobbies, doing some things together that didn't always end up in bed or weren't so social like. We are still working on those small things but the change is coming. I feel so much more comfortable now with sex and everything. I don't feel like I have to perform anymore. Gail has been really understanding. I couldn't ask for more from her. I think the crisis is pretty much gone. I haven't really settled on what you might call a new identity, a new me, but I have moved pretty far from the old me. I know my looks and body are going to change but I don't think that's going to bother me anymore. I've just kind of outgrown that really, with a lot of help from my good friend, Ken, and my wife, Gail. It's really true, without them I couldn't have done it, I couldn't have done it by myself. They're as important to me now as they were then because I get all sorts of rewards from them for changing. Ken always asks me, 'How's it going?' Gail always goes out of her way to say something loving that has nothing to do with looks or sex. I need those little pats on the back to keep me going. I feel plenty good about the changes I've made but when they show me that they do, too, it sure helps."

As was the case with Recognition and Consideration of the Consequences, others seem to hold the key to the middle-aged man's successful "choice of change." But again that key can only be used at the invitation of the man, who through his involvement of others improves his own commitment to change and his own choice of a change. Successful completion of the final step toward resolution, "Integration of the Change," also depends upon the middle-aged man's relationships with others.

Integration of the Change. A middle-aged man can be said to have resolved his mid-life crisis successfully only when he has fully integrated his new, broader sense of self and his new behaviors into the ongoing pattern of his life. But few men are altruistic enough to engage in behaviors for which they experience no reward. This is as true of their work behavior as it is of their personal behavior. If a man is to effectively resolve the crisis by changing his behavior he must receive some reward for that change, however small or inconsequential the reward may seem. This reward ideally must come in the context of his relationship with significant others and it must come repeatedly. Simply put, this means that people who are important to the middle-aged man must recognize he has changed and reward him through their behavior toward him. This is the single most important role that others can play in a middle-aged man's attempts to resolve his crisis, yet it is the role most often overlooked by wives, friends, employers, who seem all too willing to focus on what is wrong with the man, rather than rewarding what is right. Just as Gail rewarded Don for evidence of his attempts at a new sense of self and new behaviors, it is incumbent on those who value changes in middle-aged men to show by word and deed that those changes are indeed recognized and appreciated. The man who is truly committed to these changes will seek these rewards and be drawn to those who provide them. Oftentimes the wife, who has so pointedly argued for her husband's change, finds herself left for a mistress who did not forget to reward the changes once they were made. Where the man's commitment to change is shaky, he will have little incentive to continue the difficult task of seeking a new self if no rewards are in sight. Regardless of how successfully he has negotiated the first steps on the path to resolution, in such a circumstance the middle-aged man finds it very easy to return to a former identity and behavior, becoming, once again, crisis prone.

Elmer Henry's query "What do I do if he's me?" is echoed by literally thousands of men, men who may find themselves less involved in a "crisis" than they are deeply concerned about what's happening to them. They have neither the patience nor the perseverance to delve deeply into models and theories of how to resolve the crisis brought about by changes in their lives. They seek instead simple, effective solutions. There are of course no simple solutions but there are effective ones, and there are clear steps that can be taken by the man who finds himself in crisis. They have been taken by others and they have led to real resolution. They can be taken by any middle-aged man who is in crisis if he will:

1. *Recognize* the changes that are taking place in his life.
2. *Acknowledge* the changes for what they are and why— threats to his identity.
3. *Consider the Consequences*—what's good and what's bad about what's going on. How should he respond?
4. *Choosing to Change*—increase his commitment to change and improve his choice of a change by involving others.
5. *Integrating the Change*—find ways to get rewarded for his new self and his new behaviors.

The one issue that has not been covered in this plan is the question that occurs to most middle-aged men who start out on it, "How long does it take?" It is a question which cannot be answered. For some, resolution seems to happen overnight, for others it takes months, still others require years, and some never get there. How long it takes seems to depend on three key elements: (1) the nature of the crisis and its effects, (2) the man's own pursuit of a resolution, and (3) the man's relationships with others and the help they provide. It seems appropriate here to turn attention to these "others" who are so important to the middle-aged man. Chapter 9 deals with "What do Do if He Is Him."

9

What to Do if He Is Him

WOMEN OFTEN APPEAR to be far more concerned than men about the male mid-life crisis and what to do about it. This is evident not only in their questions about causes but in their search for solutions as well. Women seem more willing than men to be open about their concerns and to seek advice on what to do. It should come as no great surprise that women find it easier to speak up about the male mid-life crisis than do men. After all, it's not their crisis. It's *his* crisis and anyone finds it much easier to talk about the problems of someone else than about their own problems. Beyond this point it seems that women are much more inclined to deal openly with their emotional and psychological concerns than are men. This is clearly evident in their desire to deal with the problems of identity in mid-life. Perhaps the major reason women express so much interest in the male mid-life crisis is that they are the ones who must deal with the changes and the consequences of the middle-aged men. It is wives and mistresses who are most often confronted with the changing middle-aged man and all the implications of his changing for their relationships with him. Given these circumstances it should come as no surprise that the most plaintive and consistent cries for help and guidance in dealing with the male mid-life crisis come from women; women who are married to middle-aged men, women who have middle-aged men for lovers, women who in their business contacts must deal with middle-aged men. What then are these women to do? How can they aid the man in resolving his mid-life crisis?

The importance of a helping relationship to the middle-aged man trying to resolve his mid-life crisis cannot be overstated. Without someone close to him, who cares about him, the middle-aged man will find it very difficult to navigate the path to resolution. Most men will look to their existing relationships for the help they need, they will turn to their wife (or mistress) for reassurance, redirection and reward. The ready availability of these relationships is attractive, but this availability alone does not insure the middle-aged man that there is any help to be found in his existing relationships. Nor is it enough for the woman to simply "be there." There are some specific behaviors, a definitive role that must be played by a woman if she is to truly help the middle-aged man resolve his mid-life crisis. The fact is that these behaviors can be helpful to the middle-aged man whether they come from a man or a woman, a friend or co-worker, a wife or mistress. Anyone who has a genuine concern for helping a middle-aged man through his crisis, whether male or female, can be helpful. The message here is couched primarily in terms of women quite simply because it is most often women who actively seek advice on how to help middle-aged men, and because it is most often women who are sought out by middle-aged men as helpers. The "helper" has three major responsibilities, each of which relates to the steps the man will be taking (see Chapter 8). She must:

- Help him to *see* himself.
- Help him to *understand* himself.
- Help him to *change* himself.

Helping Him to See Himself. Few people see a middle-aged man as perceptively as does the woman he lives with. Her day-to-day, intimate interaction with him gives her a vantage point from which she can note the changes in his behavior, both subtle and significant, which come with middle age. Where he is often blinded to the changes in himself, her vision is clear and consistent. Others may see the middle-aged man at work or at play, in bits and pieces, but she sees the whole picture. She holds the mirror which can reflect the changes in a man's outlook and behavior. She, more than any other, can help him to recognize and acknowledge the crisis in his life. And, speaking generally, she tries—most women are sincere in their efforts to help the middle-aged man see himself. But what is easily seen is not so easily made visible to another. Seeing him change is one thing —telling him so that he sees himself is quite another. Beyond sincerity, it requires skill.

Ross Edwards talks about the difficulty he had in "hearing" what others saw in his behavior and how that difficulty served to make his crisis worse. "A lot of people think I left Debra for Joyce just because Joyce is younger and better looking. Well, that's only partially true. I can't deny that had something to do with it. Joyce is still a girl and she has all the youthful beauty that a young person has, but Debra for her age is a mighty beautiful woman. We never had all that many sexual problems. What really forced me into leaving Debra was, more than anything else, Debra herself and the way she treated the problems I was having. Here I was going through this mid-life crisis thing (for me most of it was around work) and I guess I was pretty depressed and irritable and not a whole lot of fun to be around, but of course those changes were hard for me to see. I really didn't know what was going on. I guess Debra was trying to help but the way she went about it was no help at all. It only made it worse. She was so goddamn certain that she knew my problems and the answer to my problems. She acted like a judge of everything I did or said, like she was evaluating every part of me, coming across so goddamn superior. It seemed to me that she wanted to be in control of my life. She wanted to be calling the shots, and I wasn't sure that her motives had my best interests at heart. It didn't seem that she was concerned at all about me. What she was concerned about was that the changes going on might screw up *her* life.

"As I said, my natural reaction was to get pretty defensive about it and the more certain, the more superior she got, the more she tried to control my behavior in that crisis, the further away from her I got. It seemed to me that for me to do anything about what she was telling me I would have had to say, 'Okay Debra, you're in charge of my life. You know more than I do about what's going on with my life. You know best how I can solve these problems. I'll do whatever you say.' Well, shit, there's just no way I was going to do that. I don't think any man would. It was just easier to pull away from her and not even listen to what she had to say. Joyce, on the other hand, well, she was just fantastic about it. I never got the feeling that she was judging me or trying to control me. I never wondered what her motives were. She saw all the same things that Debra saw, but the way she talked about them it was just much easier for me to see. It's like she never judged or accused. She just described to me what she saw was happening, how she felt about it. She didn't act superior or know it all or anything like that. I felt that even though she had some bad things to say she respected me and trusted me. She didn't pretend to have the answers, either. She told me she was willing to help me experiment, to find the answers, to experiment with my feelings, to experiment with her own behavior to help me to solve some of the problems with my behavior. I got the feeling that she really wanted to work this out *with* me instead of telling me what to do and have me work it out by myself. I always got the feeling that she respected me and cared about my feelings. Well, with her coming on like that and all, it was just a whole lot easier for me to look at myself, to look at the changes I was going through and recognize what was happening to me for what it really was—a mid-life crisis. There is no way I ever could have admitted that the way Debra came at the problem. I really needed Joyce's caring and her way of communicating that caring to help me see myself. When it came to a choice between Debra and Joyce, I chose Joyce—I've never regretted it."

The first role and responsibility of a woman who wants to help a man resolve his mid-life crisis is to help him see himself as others see him. There is much to be learned about how this important helping role should and should not be performed in Ross' recounting of the responses of Debra and Joyce to his mid-life crisis. While both of these women saw and experienced the same changes in Ross' behavior, they chose different means to bring these changes to his attention. Debra's feedback cornered Ross into a defensive posture where he felt his only real option was to reject any information about his own behavior that came from her. Joyce communicated her perception of these same behaviors in a way which made it easy to accept her information as a valid reflection of the way he behaved with others. It seems from this that if the woman attempts to tell the man in crisis what she sees and experiences in his behavior in a way that he sees as evaluative and controlling, superior and certain, without caring, he is most likely to reject her impressions and her insight, however accurate they might be. On the other hand, if the woman reveals her reflections about the man to him in a way that is descriptive and spontaneous, displaying empathy and equality with him and an openness to experiment in search of solutions, then the chances are that he'll hear her reflections for what they are—an honest expression of how she sees him. He can then choose to act on her information or not based on the information itself rather than on his ego-centered emotional reaction to *how* she had told him what she sees.

The following can serve as a checklist for how a woman can help a middle-aged man to see himself.

1. Describe, don't evaluate: In order to be most helpful the information coming from the woman about the man's behavior must be descriptive rather than evaluative. By describing her reaction she will leave the man free to use the information or not to use it as he sees fit. If she can avoid evaluative, accusatory language she will reduce the need for him to respond defensively. Statements such as "You should . . ." or "Why don't you . . ." or "You'd be better off . . .", while symbolic of what the woman feels, are likely to be rejected out of hand. The mirror analogy is important to keep in mind here, a mirror does

not judge, it merely reflects, and so, too, should the woman who wants her observations to be heard.

2. Be specific, not general. The middle-aged man will be little helped by observations that he seems somehow "different" or "changed." Such generalized impressions leave the man with little to act on. Wherever possible, comments on his behavior should be as specific as possible rather than general. They should refer to concrete experiences. If the man is told that he is dominating or irritable it will probably not be as useful as to be told that, "Just now when we were deciding, you didn't seem to listen to what I was saying" or "You seem to react out of proportion to the problem."

3. Be timely, not random. The timing of communicating information to a middle-aged man about his changing behavior can be critical. Three considerations are involved here: (a) Is he *ready* to hear it? (b) Can he relate to it? and (c) Is it reliable? The woman's opinions and feelings will have the most effect on a man when he indicates his readiness to hear such information by asking for her views. These requests can be very direct, "Do you think I've changed lately?" or more subtle, "Things don't seem to be the same . . ." Where possible she should wait for those opportunities when he solicits her opinions and feelings, when he asks, however subtly, for her response to his behavior. The middle-aged man may find it easiest to relate to observations about his behaviors when those observations come immediately on the heels of the behavior in question. There is often a tendency to save up observations and feelings from one experience to another, waiting for some later point to unload them all at once. When this occurs the man has difficulty relating to the real point because he is overloaded and the information is so removed from the indident(s). Often his frustration is only increased if he is reminded of shortcomings in the past over which he has no control. The man can best relate to information about his behavior when it comes at the earliest opportunity after the behavior occurs; not "Last week when . . ." but rather "Just now when . . ."

The timeliness of giving a man feedback on his behavior is also dependent on the availability of other sources for him to check out the reliability of the information. This is not always possible, but where supporting observations are available from others, they add great weight and impact, making it easier for the man to see himself and more difficult for him to discount the information.

4. Try problem solving, not solution giving. Few things close a man's eyes and mind quicker than being told, "Here's what *you* ought to do." Too often that is the message which comes, explicitly or implicitly, with the observations of others. Reflections of the man's behavior must be given in a spirit of collaboration, not control. A special effort must be made to avoid approaching the man's behavior problems with a view toward teaching him what he should or ought to do, for these imply his inadequacy and are sure to be rejected. The helper must be as determined to question and experiment, engage in problem solving *with* the man, not *for* him, as he himself is.

5. Offer empathy, not sympathy. All of the above requirements may be met and yet the man will not be helped to see himself if he does not sense a genuine concern and respect on the part of the helper. It is important for the woman who seeks to be truly helpful that, as she gives the man feedback about his behavior, she take into account not only her own needs but his as well. If the information serves only her need to be heard or to make her point, and fails to consider his needs on the receiving end, it can be destructive to the relationship. An emphasis throughout the communication on equal trust and respect can overcome many shortcomings in skill. Caring and concern without condescension may be *the* key to helping the man to see himself as clearly as others see him.

6. Help him to understand himself. If the woman presents her reflections on the man's behavior in a conscientious, empathetic and effective manner she will be making a major contribution toward his resolution of the mid-life crisis. She must follow this important contribution by helping the man to help himself, ex-

ploring with him the causes of the changes in his life, the causes of his mid-life crisis. This can be a difficult point, for very often there are things about the woman's behavior which can cause or at least can contribute to the cause of the man's mid-life crisis. This can range from her behaving in ways which lead him to place all of his identity in a single source, a source which might be threatened by mid-life, or for her, through her own behavior, to become a threat to his identity. Moreover she may behave in ways which actually discourage him from even considering what the causes of his crisis are. The comments of the following three women illustrate these possibilities and underscore some of the difficulties a woman may face in helping a man in crisis to understand himself.

Susan Sutliff talks about her dependency on her husband, Keith, as a prohibiting factor in his understanding of his own mid-life crisis. "I have always been very dependent on Keith. From our first days in college that is what attracted me to him. He was someone who would organize my life, take care of me, provide for me. I guess in a lot of ways I was looking for a father figure and Keith was just that father figure. When he was around I never had to worry. I always felt safe. I never had insecurities about what I ought to do or how I ought to behave because Keith would tell me. He did everything for me, and that was so comforting. I felt so secure. I really was over-dependent, I see that now. Whenever Keith would show the slightest concern about his own abilities or talents or simply his own personal life I just couldn't handle it. It would upset me so to think that he might change and then what would happen to my security? I mean, if he so much as began to say, 'I've been worried about things at work lately,' I would get nervous and start to cry. Can you believe that? I would break down in tears if he showed the slightest concern about himself. I see now that I left no room for him to ask questions about himself, his own life, to consider what was going on with him because, if he did, if he showed any signs of doing that I just simply fell apart. I couldn't handle it. That's why his mid-life crisis went on for so long. My God, it must have been four or five years, but the reason was he could never really explore what was happening to him because I wouldn't let him. When you look at it, I wouldn't allow him to be human. Now that I understand that, I am stronger, and because I am stronger I can handle it when he has questions, fears, doubts. Now he can bring those up and we can talk about them and we can begin to understand what happened to him and now, after all this time, thank God, we are making some progress."

A major factor in all mid-life crises, from cause through consequences to resolution, is the unwillingness and inability of middle-aged men to be introspective. The comments of Susan Sutliff raise the question of whether or not, in some relationships, women promote this absence of introspection. Many women will not allow a man to question, to doubt, to be concerned about himself. So dependent on him are they for strength, stability, security, that the slightest sign of weakness or trouble sends them into flights of anxiety and sometimes anger. The middle-aged man involved with such a woman soon learns that he is expected to be macho, and to the extent that he suffers he must do so in silence. There can be no real consideration of the causes of a man's mid-life crisis under these circumstances because to do so requires behaviors which are beyond the established rules and roles for the man and woman. In such relationships there can be no communal effort to understand the causes of the mid-life crisis, because such an effort requires that there be mutual questioning and concern. The woman must communicate to her man that she is strong enough to help him help himself. In order to do this she must constructively allow him to express his doubts, his fears, his innermost concerns about himself and his life.

There are other ways in which a woman may be seen as contributing to the cause of a man's mid-life crisis. In addition to the expectations noted above, a woman may often behave in ways which support the singular identity which the man finds threatened in mid-life, making it difficult for him to find other modes of self-definition. Less frequently, but no less significant, is that the woman herself through her behavior becomes a threat to the middle-aged man's identity. Two examples illustrate these ways in which a woman needs to consider her own role as a contributing cause of a man's mid-life crisis.

Lisa Bullern writes about herself and Scott, her husband's mid-life crisis. "I have always taken a lot of pride in Scott's career accomplishments, maybe too much so. I've always tried to play an important role in his career, being the kind of wife he needed to progress in his job. I think together as a couple we've built a successful career for him. There are probably some people who would say I'm pushy but I think I've just been a good partner. I've tried always to let Scott know how proud I am of his career achievements, how important his career is to me and how I know how important it is to him. All the entertaining we do is related to his work, and I always try to see to it that not only Scott's bosses but the people who work with, and for him, too, have a good time at our parties. I know how hard Scott works and I've always tried to reward him for that hard work with special little things, you know, not just having the house quiet and orderly when he gets home after a hard day, but after he takes a business trip I always try to have some new clothes for him when he gets home. On those really special occasions when he signs a big deal, or when he gets a raise or promotion, well, I've got some special sexy things I do, things we don't do all the time, just for special. I guess Scott *could* have the feeling that the only thing I really care about is his career but I don't think that's so. He knows how much I love him and care for him and I'm just trying to help out however I can. I don't see anything wrong in that A man's career is important. It is important to him and it's important to his wife and she ought to do everything she can to reward that importance."

Scott does have some of the feelings that Lisa alludes to and sees her behavior as related to his crisis, "Sometimes I get the feeling from Lisa that I'm just a workhorse, that the only thing that really counts is that I am there at the end of the month with a paycheck and that periodically the paycheck gets bigger. I hate to think what would happen if I ever had some career reversals. The truth of the matter is things aren't going so good at work, but I'm afraid to tell Lisa about it. To hear her talk, the success of our marriage hinges on the success of my career. We're 'partners' in my career—that sort of thing. Well the career is not going downhill but it's not going uphill, either. Things have really leveled off for me and I'm concerned about it, more than concerned, I'm worried because I sense other things going on in my life that are probably related to this leveling off. You know, all the stuff you hear talk about, the mid-life crisis, depression, irritability, all that stuff. Hell, it's all happening to me. It's not that I think my career is all that important. I've done a good job and even if I never get another promotion or another raise I've done pretty well considering where I started. It's just that it's so goddamned important to Lisa. I can't begin to think of how it might be to try to tell her that this is just about as far as my career goes, that we're going to have to try to look for some other things to be partners in. I'm not sure she could take it—All I ever hear from her is career, career, career. Everything's related to that, who we entertain, when and how we screw, what we do, *everything* is career. I just can't go on with everything about me being my career. It's not working now and it's not going to work in the future. I've got to find some way to help Lisa see that, to help her help me get out of this crisis.''

Oftentimes a man's singular identity is initiated and supported by his wife. There is no one identity that seems more prone to this than any other. It is just as likely that a woman will encourage her husband in his identity as a career as it is likely that she will encourage him in his identity as a husband or father. It is just as likely that she will see him as virile and masculine as it is that she will see him as adventurous and creative. At issue here is not that the woman supports her husband in his sense of self, but rather that she supports one dimension of him to the exclusion of other dimensions of self. To the extent that she does this the woman becomes a contributing factor in the cause of his mid-life crisis. Her supporting of a singular identity makes him vulnerable to threats in mid-life, and makes it difficult for him to find an alternative identity. If she is to help him to help himself toward resolution she must be open to the manner in which she contributes to the cause of crisis.

For many women, their role in frustrating a man's attempts to help himself is neither so subtle as their contributing to the cause, nor preventing through their dependent expectations his consideration of the cause. The role of some women is much more direct—they *are* the cause. Jane Hicks writes, "There won't be many letters like this. There probably aren't many women who feel like I do, who are willing to admit it, but I have some thoughts about this mid-life crisis thing, mostly about my husband, Larry, and his mid-life crisis. I won't beat around the bush, Larry is a loser. He always has been. I suppose the fact that I'm a winner probably hasn't helped him any, but why should I feel guilty about the fact that I'm a success and he's a loser? Larry was my second husband. I was married very briefly once and put my first husband through school. He no sooner got his degree than he dumped me. I looked around quite a while before I got married again. I thought that what I wanted was a real husband who would care for me, provide for me, and really free me to do whatever I wanted to do in life. Larry seemed like that sort of man so we were married. I was thirty, Larry was forty-one. The truth of it is I quickly learned that Larry couldn't begin to be a husband to me. We weren't married very long at all before it was clear to me that he could never give me all the money I wanted, all the success I wanted. He couldn't even give me all the sex I wanted. He just wasn't the sort of man I wanted, but I stayed with him. Sometimes it seems as if it's easier to stay married than to get divorced, especially when you've been through that once. I went back to work, I became successful, I started seeing other men, at first on the sly and then not so on the sly. Larry knows about it, but what can he do? To tell you how weak he is, he won't even ask me for a divorce. I know he's having a crisis now, he's having a crisis because he knows he can't be what I want him to be, what I demand of him to be. He can't be as good or better than me, but does that mean I ought to lower myself, that I ought to slow down, back up, that I ought to get less of what I want out of life just so he can feel better about himself? I don't think so. I'm strong enough to get what I want for myself, and if that threatens Larry or if it threatens anybody else, well that's tough. I deserve to have all I can get and I can get more than Larry can ever get for me, so I guess you'd say that I have caused Larry's mid-life crisis. Maybe I have. I know I'm not going to do anything to help him get over it, not if it means me being less successful or me being less sexual or me being less me. I'm not going to put myself down just to raise him up.''

Clearly not all women are as outspoken as Jane is about their contributing role as a cause in the mid-life crisis. Most women may be unaware that their behavior is a threat to the middle-aged man in their life, and yet increasingly women are threatening men, threatening men with their sexually liberated attitudes and behaviors, threatening men with their career successes, threatening men with their independence of attitude and thought, threatening men with their demonstrated ability to do without men in many instances. The woman who has a sincere desire to help a middle-aged man resolve his crisis must be willing to consider at least the possibility that she *may* be the cause of that crisis. This means that she must be as open to his experience of her as he must be to her experience of him.

The difficulty in helping a man through his crisis increases for women as they come closer to the realization that they may be contributing to that crisis; by directly threatening the middle-aged man's source of identity; or by behaving in ways that reinforce that identity at a time when reinforcement is unrealistic; or by discouraging him from being introspective about his identity and his behavior. If the woman is truly going to be able to help him to help himself she has to be open to considering her own role in causing a mid-life crisis. What if the woman is not a factor in causing the man's crisis? If that is the case, if she has

neither caused nor contributed significantly to his crisis, her role
in helping him to understand himself can focus on the consequences the crisis has brought about for him. Most women are
comfortable with this dimension of the helping relationship.
They can readily identify with the consequences of identity
crises, having dealt with similar issues in their own lives. But
more important in this helping step, the woman should express
a genuine concern for what the man faces for *his* sake. Many
women want to help because they fear the consequences of the
crisis for themselves, not because they are fearful of the consequences for him. That bespeaks selfishness, hidden agendas,
and even a lack of real caring. Sensing this the man may once
again turn to his defensive, isolated posture, withdrawing from
the woman and her efforts to help him understand what is happening. If, on the other hand, he senses that her concern is
genuinely for him and not for herself, he is more likely to continue to move forward toward resolution, relying on her support
to come to grips with the issues that face him. What most men
seem to seek at this point is the sort of statement that one
woman made, ''I told him he needs to do what is right for
himself, even if it doesn't include me. He can't begin to make
me happy if he's not happy first.'' So often the message that a
man receives from his wife or mistress who ostensibly are seek
ing to help him is that *he* must deal with *his* crisis so that *they*
can be happy, not he must deal with his crisis so *he* can be
happy. That motivation will undermine his understanding of the
causes and consequences of his crisis, and thwart his progress
toward resolution.

Helped by a caring, concerned woman to consider why he is
in crisis and what it means for him, the middle-aged man should
emerge committed to changing his identity and his behavior.
The final, lasting contribution that a woman can make to a man's
resolution of his mid-life crisis is to help him change.

7. Help him to change himself. Change for any individual is
most lasting, has the best chance of becoming part of the individual's personality, when it is rewarded by a significant other

person. For most men this significant other will be a woman. Hence, women if they are to help their man resolve the mid-life crisis must encourage and support and reward the changes he has chosen to make.

In truth the first reaction of the woman is often to punish change. After all, changes in the man are as threatening to her as are changes in his life threatening to him. She may wonder where these changes will lead to. If he changes his sense of identity, will that change her relationship with him? She may often think that it is better to stay with something that is not quite so good, than to risk changing to something that may be very much worse. As a result she may actually punish him when he exhibits new, different behaviors. This punishment may range from the subtle to the severe and obvious. At times her resistance to his change may be in the form of directly open, acrid arguments, or withholding sexual relations, or perhaps most commonly, the cold, uncaring shoulder as she turns her back on her "new" man. In the face of this resistance the man may turn to another, or simply become so frustrated at resolving his crisis that he resigns himself to living with the consequences.

In order for a woman to get herself into a posture and a position where she can support and reward change she has to be committed to the need for change as a means for resolving the man's mid-life crisis. If she lacks confidence that the change will be helpful, if she questions the impact on their relationship, she is unlikely to be able to provide the support and reward necessary for him to develop a new sense of identity and a new repertoire of behaviors. Once she is as committed to the change as he is, she'll be free to provide the support he needs.

There is in any relationship between a man and a woman a constant flow of subtle rewards and punishments, a word of caring, an intimacy here, a neglect there, a touch or a stroke, a turning away, a favorite meal, an unasked-for favor. All of these are common day-to-day occurrences in the lives of men and women living together and all of them signal far more than they really are. One avenue available to the woman to actively support and reward changes in the behavior of her middle-aged man is to become much more conscious of when and how she rewards behavior. The unasked-for favors, the word of caring and intimacy, the special sexual touch can be subtly connected to evidences of those behaviors which the man is trying to change. This may mean something as simple as fixing his favorite meal after he has worked all day at a new hobby he's exploring as a vehicle for discovering new aspects of himself. It may mean being as appreciative and attentive to the time he spends with the children as she is when he brings home a bonus paycheck. It may mean being as alluring and as sexually aggressive when he stays home as she is when he returns home from a long-distance trip. All of these everyday exchanges between a man and a woman can be used as a way of communicating her support for fundamental changes he is trying to make in his life, changes in the way he sees himself and changes in the way he behaves with others. In the absence of rewards and visible signs of support, the chances are high that he will quickly lose the incentive for change and fall back into his established sense of identity and his established behaviors—the very identity and behaviors which led him into the crisis. A woman's own behavior can be the major contribution to a successful resolution of a man's mid-life crisis.

These important resolution behaviors are not limited to women. The same would hold true for any individual who seeks to help a middle-aged man in crisis, male or female, family or friends, employer or other. It is clear that the middle-aged man is usually ill-prepared to resolve his crisis alone, isolated from others. He needs the context of a caring relationship in order to effectively resolve his crisis, and within the context of that relationship, certain roles must be performed. The steps outlined here represent a reasonable plan for how individuals can act to help a man resolve his mid-life crisis. As is the case with any general plan, as men and women begin to act upon it in the context of their own relationships, problems will emerge. Events and experiences unaccounted for in a careful listing of what to do will begin to interfere with how it's done. Many questions will arise, as they have for the men and women who have already come to grips with the mid-life crisis. In the next chapter the questions most frequently asked about the male mid-life crisis and its resolution are answered.

10

What Crisis? Who? How? Why?: Questions and Answers

WHEREVER THE MALE MID-LIFE crisis is discussed it is the object of considerable questioning and commentary. Whether raised in casual dinner-party conversation, or as the topic of a television or radio talk show, or presented as a program for an audience of husbands and wives, the male mid-life crisis never fails to evoke questions. Most often people's curiosity about it is prodded by their own immediate experience with the phenomenon. Either they are middle-aged men or they are married to or living with a man in mid-life. The questions typically ask for advice. A man at a businessmen's luncheon in Texas, asks, "How can people maintain exciting lives after forty-five?" A woman before a television audience in Chicago asks, "My husband is going through a mid-life crisis and I want to help him develop some new interests. How?" A young housewife before a women's group in Kansas City asks, "My husband is only thirty-two. What can I do now to see to it that he won't have a mid-life crisis?" These questions dramatically underscore the significance of the mid-life crisis, how deeply it is felt and how widespread its impact on individual lives of men and women. Certainly individual men and women feel the importance of developing a better understanding of the male mid-life crisis. But the answers that might be given to individual questioners are of course limited to the situation in which the question is raised. What is true for the Texas businessman may not be true for the Chicago wife or the young woman in Kansas City. Individual responses to individual questions may have little meaning beyond those cases.

In all of these audiences and throughout all of the discussions, formal and informal, there are certain questions which reappear frequently. Their very frequency suggests that they are the ones uppermost in the minds of most men and women as they read and hear about the male mid-life crisis. It is these questions which in a large part motivated this book, and the answers to them may be found throughout its chapters. However, it seems that an appropriate summary for a book on so controversial a topic as the mid-life crisis would be to raise the ten most frequently asked questions about the male mid-life crisis and answer them directly, basing our answers on the data revealed through the research and the many case studies cited throughout this book. The answers to these questions provide an overview of current knowledge and thinking about the male mid-life crisis. The answers also direct the interested reader to those chapters which present the issue in greater depth. Here then are the ten questions.

Question 1: *Is there really a male mid-life crisis or is this just the latest fad in popular psychology?*

A woman in Dallas, Texas, captured the sentiments that are on the minds of most skeptics who hear and read of the male mid-life crisis when she wrote, "I follow these things pretty closely, the popular psychological and sociological literature, and I don't recall having seen much about the male mid-life crisis until just recently. I have to admit to being suspicious. Men have been middle-aged for quite some time now and yet we've never talked about a male mid-life crisis before. Now wherever I look I seem to see it cropping up. That causes me to wonder if it isn't something that's just been made up, something new for the men's and women's magazines to write about, or is it real? Do men really have mid-life crises?"

Certainly there is reason to view with some suspicion much of what is written and broadcast about the male mid-life crisis. In actuality, suspicion should be directed only to the more sensational reports of the mid-life crisis. There is solid, longitudinal data to suggest that many men in mid-life, ages forty to sixty, experience events which cause them to dramatically and significantly change their personality and behavior. This change in personality and behavior may be appropriately called a "crisis." Why we are just now beginning to talk about and acknowledge the male mid-life crisis is another issue entirely. (See Chapter 1.)

The root reasons for current attention to the crisis seem to be: one, heightened interest by the populace at large in issues of personal development and two, the increasing inclination of men to talk about their own personal development. There has been a twenty-year trend in this country of increasing interest in psychological phenomena. This interest is manifest in things as diverse as the growth of the self-help industry and the popularity of psychology courses on university campuses. Whatever its specific form, they all attest to the unprecedented interest we as a society have in who we are as individuals and how we are as individuals in the world. In large part current interest in the male mid-life crisis is but another extension, another area of this general interest in psychological issues. At the same time one must point to the trend over the last ten years of individuals to be increasingly self-disclosing in terms of their personal concerns and activities. Here, too, a general trend takes diverse forms. The women's liberation movement is perhaps the most pervasive example of this ethic of disclosure, but at the same time evidence of the trend can be seen in the increasing disclosures by self-proclaimed homosexuals, alcoholics, drug addicts. While these latter personal issues are a far cry from the mid-life crisis, they nonetheless contribute to a general climate in which people find it more acceptable to speak up about their own lifestyles and life issues. Both of these trends have provided ample examples for men and because of those examples more men are willing to acknowledge the issues of personal development in their lives and more men are willing to step forward and discuss those issues with others. As more research data, more investigations become available, more men are encouraged to look into their lives and find relevant referents in the experiences of others. Certainly there are some who will have a mid-life crisis in large part because they are led to believe by the current literature that it is something *to* have in mid-life. How many men "create" a crisis for the sake of having one? There is no way to know. What is known from sound empirical research and from careful case studies, and what is far more important, is that for many, many men the mid-life crisis is indeed real.

Question 2: *How many men have a mid-life crisis—all, some, a few?*

Of all the questions asked about the male mid-life crisis this one question is probably heard most often. In part the question is motivated by a genuine concern to learn the extent of the mid-life crisis but in many instances the question seems to be a thinly veiled way of asking, "Could my husband (lover) be hiding something from me? Is he going through the crisis? Will he go through the crisis without telling me about it?" Whatever the motivation the answer remains the same. The best estimates of the extent of dramatic personality and behavior changes among middle-aged men, that is, those estimates based on scientific investigations and study with attention to reasonable sampling methods and all of the rigor of scientific control, the best of these studies estimate that nearly 33 percent of middle-aged men experience a mid-life crisis. This means that roughly one-fourth to one-third of the men between the ages of forty and sixty undergo dramatic personality and behavior changes.

It should be clearly understood that a man of any age, younger or older, has the potential to change his personality and behavior. But it is during the middle years that there is a better than one in four chance that a man will experience events which cause him to change his personality and his behavior. The chances are much smaller that this will occur before forty or after sixty.

The male mid-life crisis obviously does not affect all men, but it does affect a considerable segment of men and there is every probability that in the future it will affect many more.

Question 3: *Why does the mid-life crisis affect some men and not others? Who is most likely to experience a mid-life crisis?*

There have been many interesting hypotheses about the mid-life crisis and its occurrence raised by trained observers and lay observers alike. An earlier chapter (Chapter 2) noted the scientific schools of thought which relate the mid-life crisis to career, to family, to vanity and virility, to mortality and to adventure. The position advanced here is that the mid-life crisis is caused by threats to a man's identity which occur in his middle years. The more a man centers his identity in one aspect of himself, whatever that aspect may be, career, family, virility, the more vulnerable he is to threats and therefore the more likely he is to experience a crisis. This hypothesis is borne out by the research data and it can be said that the man who is most likely to experience a crisis is the man who has limited sources of identity as he goes through his middle years. As would be expected, this theoretical perspective has not completely satisfied the specific questions men and women have about the mid-life crisis and who is likely to be affected. People have asked, "Is this limited identity more often seen in middle-class, middle-aged men, or in upper- or lower-class middle-aged men?" "Does where a man lives have anything to do with it? Are city men more likely to experience a crisis than rural men?" "What about education? Does that have anything to do with the mid-life crisis?" "Marriage? Do more married men have a crisis than single men?" "What about race?" The questions go on and on and on, as men and women seek a tangible way of identifying who will have a crisis. Of all of the possible demographic variables that might be associated with the incidence of the mid-life crisis, area of residence, occupation, race, religion, education, etcetera, the data suggests that none of these is positively associated with the male mid-life crisis. This simply means that the conditions which create a crisis are no more likely to be found in men living in the city than they are to be found in men living in the country; no more likely to be true of rich men than poor men, professional men than laborers. In fact there is no single physical attribute or social characteristic or any grouping of attributes and/or characteristics which can serve as predictors of the mid-life crisis— not religion, or race, or occupation, nothing. No man is necessarily excepted from the mid-life crisis by reason of education, income or geographical location but neither is a man necessarily included in the mid-life crisis by reason of these factors.

All of this reinforces the idea that what is at the core of the crisis is the man's identity and the events of mid-life which may threaten that identity. Those who are most prone to crisis are those whose identity is most vulnerable to these threats—those with the narrowest, most limited definitions of self. Such definitions are well distributed in the middle-aged male population.

Question 4: *What are the symptoms of the male mid-life crisis? Is it physical or psychological? Is it like menopause?*

A woman stood up before a television talk show audience in Chicago where the topic of discussion was the male mid-life crisis and asked, "Much of what you've described I can relate to with my husband, he could be having a mid-life crisis, but I'm not really sure. Are there some specific things I can look for? What are the symptoms of the crisis?"

Perhaps in time it will be possible to say, "Yes, there are symptoms of the male mid-life crisis, and here is a list." At present any discussion of universal symptoms must be more speculative than specific—at best it is possible to suggest some things that seem to be associated with the mid-life crisis, things that have been mentioned throughout the case studies. The actual physical symptoms of crisis which might be visible to someone observing a middle-aged man are probably few. Once beyond the rather overt change in looks which many middle-aged men undergo, the symptoms become much less predictable. Some things that might be noticed are the change in sleeping habits, the diminished sexual desire and performance (see Chapter 4). Any physical signs of unusual stress or tension such as headaches, backaches, high blood pressure, irritability can be a signal. One woman wrote that she knew that her husband was undergoing something serious when he would break into a rage at the slightest sign of having to wait. A stoplight, lines at a restaurant or a movie, would bring on physical fits of anger. There were other reports of restlessness, muscle spasms and cramping, change in appetite, and so on. It seems as though the physical symptoms of the mid-life crisis are highly individualistic and, to the extent that they show at all, will be different from one man to the next.

It has often been noted in these pages that middle-aged men are fairly expert at concealing their feelings and emotions from others. Given the pattern it should come as no surprise that the major symptoms of mid-life crisis are more likely to be psychological than they are physiological. Of these, depression is the most general. This depression usually manifests itself in withdrawal, absence of interest, excessive daydreaming, difficulty in relating to others. Another psychological symptom that may accompany or take the place of depression is the inability on the part of the middle-aged man to make decisions, to commit himself, and to engage in fantasies as an escape. These symptoms are not readily apparent to the observer of a middle-aged man despite the evidence that they appear in so many cases. True, a wife or lover, someone close to the man, may over time begin to see clear evidence of depression, indecisiveness and fantasy, but these are not nearly so evident as are the overt physical symptoms. In any case, whether considering physiological symptoms or the psychological ones, it should not be assumed that every instance of mid-life crisis is accompanied by these symptoms. Nor should it be assumed that whenever these symptoms are evident in a middle-aged man he is experiencing a crisis. All that is meant is that these behaviors and attitudes or feelings may be suggestive of a mid-life crisis.

Women frequently ask if the male mid-life crisis is at all akin to the menopause. Certainly some of those symptoms listed above seem to be similar to those associated with menopause; however, it must be said that the male mid-life crisis is in no way synonymous with menopause. While there are some behaviors and emotional responses that may be similar, menopause is clearly rooted in fundamental hormonal changes that occur for *all* women. The male mid-life crisis is, in the vast majority of instances, not associated with any hormonal change (see Chapter 4) and affects only *some* middle-aged men. Continued identification of the male mid-life crisis with the menopause is a disservice to men. This association often leads men to believe that the mid-life crisis is feminine and therefore weak. Given such a belief system it will be very difficult for men to recognize and acknowledge that they are experiencing crisis. They may further repress the symptoms of their own crises. The mid-life crisis should be appreciated for what it is, a real and unique phenomenon of men in mid-life, unrelated to the menopause that women experience.

Question 5: *What about affairs? Does the male mid-life crisis almost invariably mean that the man will have an affair?*

A woman caller to a radio show interview in St. Louis asked, "I think that all this stuff about the male mid-life crisis is just another excuse for men having affairs. Isn't it true that middle age is when most men have affairs anyway, and aren't you really saying that now what we're supposed to do is just turn the other cheek and understand their need for an affair? Isn't it true that the real cause of this so-called crisis is young women and a middle-aged man's desire to have sex with them?"

While perhaps extreme in her question this woman nevertheless gave voice to concerns that have been echoed by hundreds of women who are concerned about their middle-aged partners. Wherever information about the male mid-life crisis has been presented to women, their predominate concern has been for their husband's possible relationship with other women. Indeed many women feel that the major threat to their relationship with the man is not his middle years but rather the presence of other younger women and his response to them. Many middle-aged men do have affairs (not always with younger women, many of their affairs are with middle-aged women); however, not every middle-aged man who has an affair with a woman younger or older does so as a result of the mid-life crisis. Many such men do not even have a crisis. Moreover, not every middle-aged man who has a crisis has an affair. It would seem that whether or not a middle-aged man gets involved in an extramarital relationship may have little or nothing to do with whether or not he is having a mid-life crisis. For some men who do experience a mid-life crisis, an extramarital relationship may be seen as a means of coping with that crisis. There are many reasons for this, most often the man sees in another woman, younger or older, a chance to reaffirm his identity which is threatened by the events of his life. Often this affirmation is not present in his existing relationship with a woman such as his wife, and he feels a need to go outside that relationship to find affirmation. This can be true whatever the man's identity may be. The other woman may affirm his view of himself as a successful career man, an adventurer or whatever, although she is most often sought when he seeks affirmation of his virility and/or his youth/health. Extramarital relationships are also at issue in those instances where a man may be seeking to constructively resolve his crisis (see Chapter 8). Searching for rewards for his new identity, his new behavior, he looks outside his existing relationships.

Whatever the reason for these extramarital relationships, it must be understood that writing about the mid-life crisis is by no means intended to excuse this behavior, nor is it intended to suggest that any excuse is needed. The intent is to explain this behavior. Whether or not it *need* be excused, and whether or not it *is* excused, has to be left up to the man himself and the women he relates to. It is not middle age that makes a man seek out other women. It is not other women that make a middle-aged man seek them out. It is the meaning of middle age to the man, and the potential meaning of other women as he attempts to respond to middle age, which accounts for the role of the "other woman" in the male mid-life crisis.

Question 6: *How long does the mid-life crisis last? When does it stop?*

A woman from Fountain Valley, California, wrote, "My husband has been having a mid-life crisis for the last five or six years now. Is there no end to this? How long does it usually take for a man to get over one of these things? When will our life together get back to normal?"

The answer seems to be that for some men the crisis is so brief as to be almost momentary. It comes, they recognize it, take action on it, then it goes. For other men the crisis seems to settle into the pattern of their lives and they live all their middle years in a state of crisis, continually threatened, continually searching for some way to respond to the threats. Still other middle-aged men seem to move in and out of a crisis condition, reaching temporary resolution, only to have the crisis reemerge and to live it again. As the cause of crisis differs for each man and responses differ, so, too, will the duration of each man's crisis be different.

The mid-life crisis stops when the man alters his identity in such a way that he is no longer vulnerable to the threats to that identity which brought about the crisis in the first place. If there is no fundamental alteration in his identity, the man will remain ever vulnerable to those same threats, ever vulnerable to crisis. While the crisis may not always be with him, waxing and waning with the events of his middle years, at the same time the crisis is never very far from him. Having never resolved his crisis, he never totally escapes its effects. Although it is not evident in his day-to-day life, it continues with him below the surface to emerge again whenever events threaten his identity. So it is that for some the crisis does indeed stop, for others it knows no end but becomes a lifelong struggle, a recurrent condition, capable of erupting as the events of his middle and later years change. Such a prognosis offers little comfort to the man and woman living in crisis. There is not the surety of a one-year period, a five-year period, or a fixed duration of any length. The mid-life crisis is over only when and if the man acts on the causes of the crisis. This realization should underscore the importance to the middle-aged man and the woman trying to help him, of taking some direct action and making a conscious effort to resolve the crisis. Otherwise they may well have to resign themselves to his life remaining forever crisis prone.

Question 7: *How can the crisis be stopped? Is there a cure?*

Everyone who experiences the mid-life crisis, either directly or through another, wants to know what can be done about it. Many men and women have gone to great lengths to find a "cure." A man in Minneapolis has taken a year's leave of absence (without pay) from his work in hopes that he can resolve his career crisis. A woman in Tallahassee, Florida, has encouraged her husband to move out of the house for six months and get involved with other women as a means of meeting his crisis. Each case represents the search for a "cure."

The word "cure" is misleading here. The mid-life crisis is not a disease, there is no medicine or prescription that can bring its end. There is a definite plan of action which *can* lead to resolution (see Chapters 8 and 9). This plan of action must be initiated by the man himself upon recognition of the changes in his life and acknowledgment of those changes for the crisis they are. He should consider the consequences, choose to change his identity and his behavior to make himself less vulnerable to the threats to his identity, and, with the help of significant others, integrate these changes into the pattern of his life. Pursuing this plan can lead to resolution of the crisis, but it may not have the look or feel of a cure. For one thing, pursuing this course of action will itself bring changes, and these changes may be viewed by the man and those involved with him as every bit as traumatic as the crisis itself. The middle-aged man may face a situation in which the cure may induce symptoms very similar to the disease itself. He must be courageous enough and committed enough to the need and desirability of resolving his crisis to pursue this path and withstand any unwanted changes it brings.

Many men faced with such a choice shy away from the challenge, preferring instead to live with their crisis condition in the hopes that ultimately, given time and changing circumstances, it will go away. Perhaps for some of these men the crisis actually will go away, evaporate as the changing events which accompany advancing age change. In the interim these men will continue to suffer. They put a stop to the crisis only in the sense that they stop doing anything about it, stop attempting to respond to it, stop attempting to resolve it. They have not put a stop to the crisis in the sense that they have changed their lives in such a way that they will not be crisis prone. The importance of a helping relationship cannot be overstated. If a man is truly to resolve his mid-life crisis, he simply cannot go it alone. He needs the perspective of others and the support of others to deal with the identity issues of his life. The prescription reads "partnership" as he pursues resolution.

Question 8: *How can it be prevented?*

Young men and women reading and hearing of the mid-life crisis can readily identify older men, fathers, work associates, friends, whom they believe to be experiencing a crisis. While they have some concern for these men, their real concern is for advice and counsel on how they may prevent such a crisis from occurring to them. As one young housewife expressed it, "My husband is twenty-eight. He's just getting underway in his career and we're just beginning building our family. I read about the male mid-life crisis and I can see how it happens to some middle-aged men. What I want to know is what I can do for my husband and what he can do for himself to prevent it ever happening to him. How can he become one of those men who are not affected by middle age?"

Preventing the mid-life crisis must be viewed as a process of making the man immune to threats to his identity before his middle years. Absolute and lasting immunity is not possible. A man's identity will always be subject to threats regardless of what sources he relies on for self-definition. However, any man can see to it that the effects of threats to his identity do not necessarily destroy his sense of self. This can be done by broadening his sense of identity, by drawing from a variety of sources to develop his self-concept, his ideas of who he is and how he ought to relate to the world. The preventative course of action for the younger man is to begin to see himself in a variety of ways. He must see himself as more than *just* a worker, or more than *just* a husband, provider, or more than *just* a handsome, virile young man, or more than *just* a conqueror of new worlds and challenges. In short, he must develop in his younger years a value of himself as a whole person, a person with diverse talents, diverse interests, diverse meanings and methods. He must construct for himself a diverse, well-developed sense of identity.

For a young man to develop this broad self-identity he must be reliant, not only on himself but on others. He must be open to their perspectives, open to their views, of what they value in him. Using these multiple images and impressions he can create a picture of himself which extends beyond a single source for his identity, embracing all of *who* he is and all of *how* he is in the world. If he manages to do this as a young man, he will enter mid-life not rooted in a single identity but rather with multiple definitions of himself, and therefore not so vulnerable to threats. These multiple definitions will balance one another, and as he is threatened by the events of mid-life his sense of self will not be irrevocably diminished. Experiencing a threat or severe change in one area of self-definition, he can rely on other sources of identity, other sources which are not threatened and which can continue to serve as affirmation of who he is and what he values in the world. Once again, it is important to realize that no man can escape all threats to his identity in mid-life. Throughout the cases reported here it is evident that the kinds of events which raise identity issues in mid-life are commonplace occurrences. Changes in one's career path, changes in the structure of the family, changes in one's own body and physical ability, the loss of close friends and relatives—these things happen to *all* men and will continue to happen to all men during their middle years. The only preventative course is for the man to see to it that when these events do occur and threaten his identity he is not devastated by it but rather can balance that threat, the loss of an identity or damage to an identity, by emphasizing or reemphasizing alternative identities. If he does not have these alternative identities going into his middle years, he faces the very difficult problem of finding new identities and finding new behaviors at a time when his entire life may be in chaos. But if he has already built these alternative identities and behaviors, he has a real chance to truly prevent a mid-life crisis from occurring.

Question 9: *How can someone make a man see what's happening to him?*

The wife of a middle-aged man in Calgary, Canada, asks, "It's so clear to me what my husband is going through. He has all the symptoms I've read and heard about, he's depressed and irritable, he can't sleep and he seems to be confused sexually. I see it all, but I just can't seem to make *him* see what's happening to him. He refuses to acknowledge these symptoms. He gets defensive when I talk about them and he isn't open at all to what's going on. I've tried to point out to him how he's behaving. I've tried to give him literature about the male mid-life crisis to show him that other men feel the same thing but he just turns his back on all of it and on me. I'm afraid that if he doesn't do something soon he won't be able to do anything at all. How can I make him see what's happening to him?"

The role of a "significant other" is very important in the male mid-life crisis. The other, whether he/she be wife, lover, employer or friend, is often the best witness to changes in the middle-aged man and best positioned to help him help himself. This person must hold a mirror up to the middle-aged man, a mirror which reflects an accurate image of how he is behaving in the world so that he may see himself as others see him. As simple as this role and function may sound it is the most misunderstood in all of what is written and said about resolving the mid-life crisis. The temptation is for the "other" not to hold a mirror but rather to stand in judgment, not to describe behavior but rather to judge behavior. This judgmental, evaluative stance does little to really aid the middle-aged man in seeing himself.

Most often (see Chapter 9) such behavior drives the middle-aged man into a defensive posture and leads him to cutting himself off from the very people most able to help him. Yet it is easy to see why people do stand in judgment of middle-aged men. In most instances, those who are motivated to help a middle-aged man in crisis are so motivated because they do not like the behavior changes they see in him. They do not like the new person he has become and they want *him* to do something about it. It is natural that when they attempt to point out his behavior to him they do so prescriptively rather than descriptively. That is they talk in terms of goods and bads, likes and dislikes, shoulds and oughts, expressing *his* need to change because *he's* behaving in ways that *they* don't like. What is needed from the other is not to present him with their feelings of his need to change what they don't like, but rather with an accurate description of his behavior and its consequences for others. Not for them to say, for example, "It's so childish of you to be irritated by that," but rather, "When you're irritated I feel uncomfortable with you." Not to say, "It's so unlike you to be so indecisive," but to say, "When you seem to have difficulty making up your mind I don't know what you expect of me." It's a difficult posture to adopt, this posture of being a mirror, of reflecting what one sees and not what one senses, but it's absolutely critical if one is really to help a middle-aged man in crisis. Without it he'll feel judged and put-upon, feel as though he must change for others, not for himself. With an accurate, objective reflection of how he is behaving, he can make the choice for himself to change, or not to change and live with the consequences. The risk of course is that he may decide not to change. Fearful of that risk and unwilling to rely on the strength and security of the relationship, the other person tries to point the direction for him to change, the direction that they desire, that they think is best for him. Such behavior more often leads to the middle-aged man reacting *against* them rather than taking action on his own *with* them to resolve the crisis. The way, therefore, to make a man see what is happening to him is to accurately reflect how he is seen, not to tell him how he was, or tell him how he should be, but tell him how he is.

Question 10: *What happens when the man and the woman are both going through changes?*

In truth, this question is not asked all that frequently in conversations or presentations about the male mid-life crisis. It is included here because it is such a significant question. When it does occur, the question takes one of two forms. Older women often ask about what happens if the mid-life crisis for a man is coincidental with menopause for his wife. Younger women, those returning to school, to the work force, after experiencing some time as a housewife and homemaker, frequently ask, "What happens if while I am in the midst of these changes in my identity, my husband is going through a mid-life crisis?"

Both forms really raise the same issue. What happens if both a man and a woman find themselves in crisis in mid-life? When change is coincidental, there is a rare opportunity for the man and woman to share together an experience that is very individual, the experience of changing their sense of who they are and how they will behave in the world. When the changes are experienced only by one it is difficult for the other to empathize, to fully understand not only the events but the feelings and emotions associated with those events. When these individual changes can be identified as being, at heart, the same, there is an exceptional chance to live the experiences of another as that person is living them, and to help another deal with those experiences because you are living them as well. In fact, however, this kind of sharing, empathizing and helping seldom occurs. The male mid-life crisis most often leads a man to a period of self-absorption, a withdrawal from others as he gets caught up with the events of his own life and his response to them. The menopause of older women and the search for identity that many women undergo in their mid-thirties today can have similar effects as they pull away from others, particularly from men whom they feel cannot empathize with them and understand what they are experiencing.

The resulting scenario is one in which two people, a man and a woman, are experiencing the same thing but are so caught up in their individual experiences of that phenomenon—the search for identity and their response to threats to identity—that they not only cannot reach out to another, they cannot respond when another reaches out to them. As they withdraw from each other they become islands unto themselves, totally self-absorbed, totally self-centered. In that self-centeredness and self-absorption they become self-destructive, as each separates himself and herself from the one source that might be available to help resolve those issues. Between these two extremes (the couple who, as they change individually, share their changes and their experiences with one another, and the couple who, as they change, change away from one another without reference to the experiences of each other), there are of course a great variety of relationships between men and women in change. Most follow some pattern of approach-avoidance—the man approaches, the woman avoids; the woman approaches, the man avoids; both avoid, both approach. Back and forth it goes, both struggling within themselves, each too caught up in that struggle to engage in the other's struggle. In the end those relationships that were strong and stable before the change began survive, those which were neither strong nor stable, but harbored insecurities and glossed over weaknesses before the change began, probably will not survive.

These ten questions by no means exhaust all those that arise when discussions of the mid-life crisis occur, but they are the questions that are raised most frequently. They express the thoughts that seem to be on the minds of most men and women as they first begin to consider the male mid-life crisis and what it may mean for them. They are the questions for which the answers have some general applicability. Far more interesting and of greater concern to the men and women who are involved with the mid-life crisis are the questions which deal with individual cases, with why this man had a crisis, with what this woman can do about the crisis her man had. Hopefully in the pages of this volume men and women will find the kind of information and insight that they can look to to find guidance and solace in dealing with their own personal cases. If that task has been accomplished, then the primary objective of this book will have been achieved. However, beyond that, some attention must be given to what this phenomenon, this pervasive phenomenon which affects so many millions and millions of men and women, means for our times and our society. These pages close with such a comment.

A COMMENT ON CRISIS

The male mid-life crisis is a real and pervasive phenomenon. There can be no longer any doubt of that. The surge of recent interest in this phenomenon is testimony to the fact that at last public interest is catching up with what has been private reality for some time. Given the popularity of psychology and self-help issues at the present time, it can be anticipated that interest in the male mid-life crisis will continue and even increase. In large part this interest is a reflection of changing values and changing times in our society. Further, this change in values and value systems is probably an indication that the *incidence* of male mid-life crisis will increase as well. Just as commentary on the crisis is a current cultural trend, so, too, in many respects, the causes of the male mid-life crisis can be traced to contemporary cultural trends. Two developments in particular seem to be related to the increasing incidence of the male mid-life crisis. One of these is the increasing role demands on men in our society. The other is the prevalence of ego and self-absorption in what has been called the "Me Decade" of the seventies. With regard to the first of these forces in society today, the increasing role demands, it seems that, more than ever before, it is unclear to a man just what is expected of him if he is to be a man. The rise of women's liberation has caused him to question the macho ethic that has dominated man's thinking for so long. At the same time, deteriorating economic conditions severely pressure his role as a provider. As organizations demand more and more of his time and attention and the career ladder becomes more competitive at every level, investments in career are insecure. The mere fact of living long enough to be middle-aged seems to bring with it dangers to his health—cancer, heart disease, and so on. The result is that as he looks around for some definition of who he is as a man, or what it is to be a man in this day and age, the average middle-aged man is likely to be quite confused. There is no clear and simple message. At every turn his ship of self is under attack, and there is no clear sailing in sight in any direction.

In the face of such ambiguity the tendency is to fall back on something that has proven to be effective for him in the past, whatever that may be. Rather than reaching out and experimenting with new ways of defining himself, and new ways of behaving in the world, he roots his identity evermore in a single, traditional source. He seeks a small island of identity. Obviously this leaves him vulnerable to be threatened by the natural events of mid-life and he becomes crisis prone.

Another development of contemporary society which raises concern about the increasing incidence of the male mid-life crisis has to do with the "me-ism" of our present culture. There exists at present a popular ethic which argues a "me first" kind of thinking as an avenue to success in any walk of life, popularized by books and pseudo-psychological approaches to life events. This way of thinking leads to a kind of individualism which tends to isolate people from one another, turning them away from caring relationships, placing the burden for their development squarely upon themselves, often at the cost of other people and other relationships. The man or woman of today who seeks advice on how to develop is told, "Be strong, be an individual, be aggressive," but too often this translates "Be alone, be an islander."

The confluence of these two contemporary developments puts the middle-aged man in a difficult double bind. In effect, he throws himself into crisis and at the same time isolates himself from the solution. The cause of crisis itself, his difficulty in finding alternative sources of identity, is pursued in a way that isolates him from those very relationships which might help him solve the crisis. He *cannot* discover more of himself because he *will not* discover more of others. If these trends continue, if we find greater and greater uncertainty about the roles of men and for that part women of our society, and if accompanying this there is an increasing reluctance to look to interpersonal relationships as a means of resolving personal problems, then it can unfortunately be anticipated that the mid-life crisis will affect considerably more than 25 to 33 percent of the men between the ages of forty and sixty. Indeed, should these developments continue it might be anticipated that the mid-life crisis will become our next national epidemic.

What should be done is very clear. Whether or not it *will* be done is not at all clear. Men and women, all of us, need to encourage men as individuals to explore who they are as whole men. What is the full range and extent of their identity? What are the possibilities and potentials for their behavior? We must avoid circumscribing men to a particular identity, a specific definition of self, a particular repertoire of behaviors. We must encourage and reward experimentation with the full range of individual identity—the full repertoire of personal behaviors. That is what should be done, but whether it can be done is quite another issue. For the current plight of men is not a one-time incident, but rather the culmination of years of acculturation and socialization. Boys are taught at an early age not to be emotional, not to be introspective. In effect, we encourage them to cut themselves off from themselves. The process of growing into a man is often nothing more than the process of finding out what narrow sphere of activity one can succeed in, be it athletics, academics, or whatever, and then experiencing rewards for that. When we do this to our children we can hardly be surprised that as men they have unidimensional identities and are cut off from their own feelings and emotions. After all, that is just what they have been taught to do, taught by the example of their fathers, the encouragement of their mothers, and taught by their experiences with other people. The child who is taught not to cry grows to be a man who doesn't understand what is happening to him when he wants to cry. The adolescent who only receives attention for his athletic endeavors finds himself without anywhere to turn but the playing field when his identity and ego are threatened. The young man who is applauded by his company for his extra hours and efforts and encouraged to sacrifice his personal life for his corporate life is shattered when the corporation no longer needs him. Perhaps most pernicious of all is that even as our boys and young men assimilate these things, they are also, in the name of individualism and self-reliance, being exposed to philosophies of selfishness and isolation that are bound to leave them bankrupt when they attempt to solve their personal problems.

The ships we have taught our boys to build are unfit to sail the seas they face as men. Their ships are sinking. The little islands they scurry to only separate them from themselves. How much better it would be to teach our young men when they are boys and beyond that there is in every other person a part of who they themselves are. They can only come to know themselves as they invest themselves in relationships with those other people. To set for them an example wherein they see that their experience of themselves is limited only by their experience of others. If they choose to isolate themselves from personal relationships, to cut themselves off from others and others' perceptions of them, then they choose by that same process to limit themselves to a narrow identity, vulnerable to threats and ultimately to crisis. But if they choose to fully invest themselves in relationships with others, to draw from their experience with others a variety of perceptions of who they are as individuals and how they might behave in the world, then they open up to themselves the full range of potential identities and behaviors. A range of identities that is rich and rewarding, a range that really knows no limits, a range that forever provides them with an avenue for affirmation, a diverse sense of self from which they can withstand threats. Then only can they respond creatively and constructively to change and experience a full life from its beginning through the middle years to its end. A man in his middle years is not too old to discover this message.

He is not too old to reach out to others and find in those others a new self. His ship may be sinking but his salvation is in swimming to others, not in seeking the inviting little island. He is too old and it is too late to go back on his life, but the time is just right for changing, for embracing new relationships, new ideas, discovering a new self and building a better second half.

APPENDIX

The Mid-Life Identity and Events Survey

This is the survey originally used by the author in research for the article he wrote for an academic business journal. Its results inspired so much interest that, in deciding to expand the findings for this book, he went on to interview hundreds of respondents, as explained in the Preface.

Please rank the following descriptive statements according to their desirability for you at your present age. Using 100 total points, assign some quantity to the statement you *would most like to be able to make about yourself,* a lesser number to the statement you would next most like to be able to make, less to the next, and so on down to the statement that is least desirable to you. Our interest is in what you would *like,* not necessarily in what is. Remember, the sum of the values you assign should not exceed 100.

_____ I am successful. I have met my career goals.

_____ I am close to my wife and family.

_____ I am healthy and have a long life ahead.

_____ I am active in professional, civic and social affairs.

_____ I am growing and developing as a person.

_____ I have realized my full potential, my ideal self.

_____ I am virile, masculine, attractive to women.

Instructions: Following are questions about your career, family, health. Please respond as honestly as possible. Check only one response per question unless otherwise indicated.

I. 1. Which of the following statements best describes your feelings about your career progress?

    a. _____ I have been successful beyond my wildest dreams.

    b. _____ I am making steady progress toward my ultimate career goals.

    c. _____ I am stalled and don't seem to be progressing at present.

    d. _____ I have not reached the level I wanted to attain at this time.

    e. _____ I have not made any progress toward my career goals.

2. To date, which of the following has been *most responsible* for your career progress?

    a. _____ Personal performance

    b. _____ Forces outside your influence

3. What is the highest level you would like to achieve in your organization? _____

    a. How many levels are you removed from that position at this time? _____

    b. What is your estimate of the probability of your achieving that level?

    (1) Certain _____   (2) Very Probable _____

    (3) Probable _____   (4) Not Probable _____

    (5) Impossible _____

4. Is your current career

    a. _____ The one work/career you desire?

b. _____ Your work/career now but not the only work/career you desire in your life?

c. _____ The only work/career you can do whether or not it is desirable?

5. Within the last two years have you . . . (Check all appropriate responses.)

a. _____ Been terminated?

b. _____ Been promoted?

c. _____ Been demoted?

d. _____ Had your responsibilities reduced?

e. _____ Changed careers?

6. Is your immediate supervisor
a. Younger than you?_____ b. Older?_____ c. Same age?_____

II. 1. If you have children, which of the following best characterizes your relationship to them?
a. Very close_____ b. Close_____ c. Mutual tolerance_____ d. Distant_____ e. Hostile_____

2. Overall, have your children turned out

a. _____ Better than you expected?

b. _____ About as well as you expected?

c. _____ Worse than you expected?

3. Check the following events which have occurred in the last two years:

a. _____ Divorce

b. _____ Separation

c. _____ Death of spouse

d. _____ Children moving out

e. _____ Spouse going to work

f. _____ Spouse going to school

4. At the present time is your influence over your wife

    a. _____ More than it used to be?

    b. _____ The same as it used to be?

    c. _____ Less than it used to be?

5. At the present time is your influence over your children

    a. _____ More than it used to be?

    b. _____ The same as it used to be?

    c. _____ Less than it used to be?

6. How much support (both emotional and financial) are you giving to your parent(s) at this time?

    a. _____ A great deal

    b. _____ Some support

    c. _____ No support

    d. _____ Parents deceased

III. 1. How would you rate your general health and physical condition?

Excellent _____ Good _____ Fair _____ Poor _____ Very Poor _____

2. Have you suffered a major illness or injury in the last two years?

Yes _____ No _____

3. Do you suffer from minor recurrent ailments or pains?

Yes _____ No _____

4. Over the last two years have you experienced any of the following?

Death of a spouse   Yes_____ No_____

Death of a close family mem-
ber other than spouse   Yes_____ No_____

Death of a friend   Yes_____ No_____

5. Over the last two years have you experienced changes in any of the following? (Check all appropriate responses.)

_____ Hearing   _____ Stamina

_____ Vision   _____ Teeth

_____ Hair color   _____ Skin

_____ Body functions

6. Which of the following best describes your feelings about time and the way you've used it in your life? (Check only one.)

_____ There is so much that I've done in my lifetime.

_____ There is so much that I've yet to do in my lifetime.

_____ There is so much that I won't be able to do in my lifetime.

IV. 1. Has your involvement in any of the following *decreased* in the last two years? (Check all appropriate responses.)

a. _____ Recreation

b. _____ Social activities (clubs, movies, visiting, etcetera)

c. _____ Church activities

d. _____ Family get-togethers

e. _____ Working hours

2. Have major life events (graduation, marriage, fatherhood, death of parents, career peaks, etc.) occurred for you

a. _____ At the same relative time as everyone else?

b. _____ Earlier than others experience?

c. _____ Later than others experience?

3. Have you made plans (other than financial) for your retirement?

a. _____ Yes

b. _____ No

4. In your work and social life do you feel others

a. _____ Respect you more than they used to?

b. _____ Have the same respect for you they used to?

c. _____ Respect you less than they used to?

5. Is your contribution to work and social activities

a. _____ Valued more than it used to be?

b. _____ Valued the same as it used to be?

c. _____ Valued less than it used to be?

6. Compared to other times are you currently experiencing

a. _____ More change in your life?

b. _____ About the same amount of change?

c. _____ Less change in your life?

V. 1. Are the most exciting years in your life

a. _____ Past?

b. _____ Now?

c. _____ Yet to come?

2. As you look ahead do you think that you will change your outlook and behavior

a. _____ A great deal?

b. _____ Some?

  c. _____ Very little?

  d. _____ Not at all?

3. Have you acquired a major new knowledge, skill, or avocation in the last two years?

  a. _____ Yes b. _____ No

4. Would you say about your own self-awareness at this time that you

  a. _____ Know all there is to know about yourself?

  b. _____ Know a great deal?

  c. _____ Know very little?

  d. _____ Know almost nothing?

5. Have you experienced any of the following in the last two years? (Check all appropriate responses.)

  a. _____ Voluntary career change

  b. _____ Return to school

  c. _____ Moved, changed residence or living conditions

  d. _____ Change in recreation or social activities

6. In the last two years have you developed any *new* close, intimate friendships?

  a. _____ Yes (How many? _____)

  b. _____ No

VI. 1. Have your achievements and accomplishments to date been

  a. _____ Very meaningful?

  b. _____ Meaningful?

  c. _____ Somewhat meaningless?

  d. _____ Meaningless?

2. In thinking about your early dreams and aspirations, have you

a. _____ Fulfilled your dreams?

b. _____ Moved closer to fulfillment?

c. _____ Not fulfilled your dreams?

3. Do you feel that you've had to neglect, suppress, or sacrifice part of yourself to get where you are today?

a. _____ Yes, a great deal.

b. _____ Yes, some.

c. _____ No, not at all.

4. As you reflect on your accomplishments, have you attempted too little, not stretched yourself, not seized opportunities?

a. _____ Yes, very much so.

b. _____ Yes, somewhat.

c. _____ No.

5. Which one of the following words best describes how you feel about your life right now?

a. _____ Unfulfilled

b. _____ Self-satisfied

c. _____ Free

d. _____ Trapped

6. Which one of the following words best describes how you feel about the rest of your life?

a. _____ Hopeful

b. _____ Resigned

c. _____ Competent

d. _____ Inadequate

VII. 1. How satisfied are you with your sexual performance over the last two years?

a. _____ Very satisifed, better than it used to be.

b. _____ Satisfied, the same as it used to be.

c. _____ Unsatisfied, not as good as it used to be.

2. Below are pairs of words which can be used to describe people's feelings about their sex life. Please check the space between the two words which comes closest to your feelings. The further you mark a space in either direction means that your feelings about your sex life are more like that word. Remember, only *one* check per line.

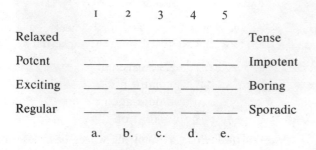

	1	2	3	4	5	
Relaxed	___	___	___	___	___	Tense
Potent	___	___	___	___	___	Impotent
Exciting	___	___	___	___	___	Boring
Regular	___	___	___	___	___	Sporadic
	a.	b.	c.	d.	e.	

3. Have you had sexual relations with women outside your marriage in the last two years?

a. _____ Yes (How often?_____)

b. _____ No

4. Would you say your concern about your virility, masculinity and attractiveness to women is

a. _____ More than it used to be?

b. _____ The same as it used to be?

c. _____ Less than it used to be?

5. In the last two years have you experienced any of the following sexual difficulties? (Check all appropriate responses.)

a. _____ Premature ejaculation

b. _____ Temporary impotence (inability to achieve or sustain erection)

c. _____ Reduced desire for sex

6. In the last two years have you experienced any of the following? (Check all appropriate responses.)

a. _____ Irritability

b. _____ Insomnia

c. _____ Depression

d. _____ Abrupt behavior changes

INTERPRETATION

The values assigned to the seven descriptive statements at the beginning of the questionnaire provide a general indication of what is important to a middle-aged man, where he invests his identity. The more points (out of 100) assigned to a particular statement the greater its importance as a descriptor of how the man would desire to identify himself, whether realistically or not. For example, the extreme case of a man who assigns all 100 points to a single identifying statement such as "I am successful. I have met my career goals," indicates a man who has totally invested himself in his career. For such a man career is the sole source of his identity. At the other extreme is the case of the man who distributes the 100 points evenly over the seven desired descriptors, with only minimal differential preference, 5 to 7 points. Such a distribution denotes a man who has multiple sources of identity, many ways of thinking about himself.

Research indicates that those middle-aged men who have limited sources of identity, only one or two ways of thinking about their lives, are the men most likely to experience a mid-life crisis. The limited identity of these men renders them vulnerable to the events of mid-life. The fact that a man is crisis prone or vulnerable does not necessarily mean that he will experience a crisis. A man may have a limited source of identity but experience no *threats* to that identity in the events of his middle years. It is only when a major identity is threatened by the events of mid-life that a man experiences a mid-life crisis. As an example, the middle-aged man who invests himself totally in his work and measures his life in terms of his career may be vulnerable, but as long as he experiences success in his career it is unlikely that he will have a mid-life crisis. The man who is likely to have a crisis is the man who invests his identity totally in his career and experiences threats to that career in his middle years.

Responses to the other part of "The Mid-Life Identity and Events Survey," the multiple-choice questions to be answered as honestly as possible, serve as an indicator of the extent to which a man's actual experiences in mid-life pose threats to his sources of identity. The method of combining and relating the two factors in the survey are too complex to detail here, but when the two values are so related, a statistical result is obtained that, at least in a general way, points very clearly to the severity, or the absence, of the threats in a man's mid-life experience, and the many various stages that can lie between a rewarding, full life and a mid-life crisis condition.

Scores on such a questionnaire should not be taken as definitive measures of the stability of a man's personality and behavior at present or in the near future. Nor should such scores be viewed as indicating *the* cause of personality and behavior changes. The survey is included here to give readers a point of reference which will allow them to place their own experience (or their experience with a middle-aged man) in the context of broader research on the phenomenon of the male mid-life crisis. Such instruments can be a useful tool in indicating potential problem areas and concerns that might be worthy of further examination and exchange.

About the Author

Michael E. (Mick) McGill was born in San Francisco, California, and grew up in and around Southern California. Upon receiving his Ph.D. from the University of Southern California he moved to Texas and began a ten-year career as a university professor and organizational consultant. In his research and practice he has been primarily concerned with issues of personal and organizational development. He has written two professional books and numerous articles, been consultant to a wide variety of organizations, and appeared on national television. This is his first book aimed at a popular audience. He lives in Dallas with his wife, Janet, and two sons, Jimmy and Adam.